PRAGMATICS AND

NATURAL LANGUAGE

UNDERSTANDING

Tutorial Essays in Cognitive Science

Donald A. Norman
Andrew Ortony

PRAGMATICS AND

NATURAL LANGUAGE

UNDERSTANDING

Georgia M. Green

University of Illinois

LAWRENCE ERLBAUM ASSOCIATES, PUBLISHERS
1989   Hillsdale, New Jersey   Hove and London

Lawrence Erlbaum Associates, Inc., Publishers
365 Broadway
Hillsdale, New Jersey 07642

Library of Congress Cataloging in Publication Data

Green, Georgia M.
Pragmatics and natural language understanding / Georgia M. Green.
    p.   cm.
"October 1987."
Bibliography: p.
Includes index.
ISBN 0-89859-853-2 ISBN 0-8058-0361-0 pbk.
1. Pragmatics.   2. Reference (Linguistics)   3. Semantics
(Philosophy)   4. Discourse analysis.   I. Title.
P99.4.P72G74   87-37956
401'.9--dc19   CIP

Printed in the United States of America
10 9 8 7 6 5 4 3 2

For my mother, MARJORIE FISHBEIN CLAVEY

CONTENTS

NOTATIONAL CONVENTIONS
USED IN THIS BOOK

Most of the conventions described below are standard in linguistic writing.

In the text proper:

ITALICS mark cited expressions
SINGLE QUOTES [' '] mark meanings of forms.
DOUBLE QUOTES [" "] represent discourse examples. Around brief
  expressions, they are used as scare quotes.
SMALL CAPS are used for emphasis and to mark the first use of technical
  terms.

In numbered examples:

ITALICS mark the use of a form being   demonstrated.
SLASHES [/] separate expressions that could be substituted as alternatives to illustrate the same point, though no claim is made that the
  alternatives are semantically or pragmatically equivalent. Thus, (i)
  abbreviates the two sentences in (ii).

  i. Philip/Her brother thought he would be caught.
  iia. Philip thought he would be caught.
  iib. Her brother thought he would be caught.

BRACKETS [{ }] are used for the same purpose, with longer
  expressions.
ASTERISK [*] precedes an expression that is ungrammatical; i.e. a
  correct grammar of the language will not describe it because no
  context could make it a natural thing for a native speaker to say.
EXCLAMATION POINT [!] marks an expression that is grammatical,
  but (likely to be) pragmatically bizarre.

ACKNOWLEDGMENTS

This book owes much to Sue Ann Kendall Crain, Steve Helmreich, Bill Ladusaw, Wendy Martin, Jerry Morgan, Tsuneko Nakazawa, Andrew Ortony, Craige Roberts, and Ladislav Zgusta for valuable comments on earlier versions, and to Jae Ohk Cho for discussions of honorific phenomena in Korean. Comments and questions from students who used preliminary versions of this book in pragmatics seminars at the University of Illinois in 1986 and 1987 led to clarifications in every chapter. The present form of the work owes a lot to the production staff of Lawrence Erlbaum Associates for their diligence, patience, and equanimity in working around my intolerance for alterations to my choice of relative pronouns, and to Robin Morgan, who dropped everything to prepare the author index.

1 What is Pragmatics and Why Do I Need to Know, Anyway?

0. INTRODUCTION

Writing is an act of faith, E.B. White said.[1] Speaking is no less so. Pragmatics is the study of the mechanisms that support this faith, a faith so strong that many can use the term *communicate* interchangeably with *speak* or *write,* never noticing that the term *communication* presupposes achievement of the intended effect of verbal action upon the addressee, whereas *speaking* and *writing* do not. Contrary to popular belief, communication is not accomplished by the exchange of symbolic expressions. Communication is, rather, the successful interpretation by an addressee of a speaker's[2] intent in performing a linguistic act. It is the purpose of this book to give an

---

[1] Quoting an anonymous writer (Strunk & White 1979, p. 84).

[2] I use *speaker* as shorthand for *speaker or writer* or the equally cumbersome *language-producer.* The principles I describe in this book apply generally to all modes of language production addressed to an audience with communicative intent. Quite likely they are trivially extendable to other cases, such as recitation or talking to oneself, but I do not attempt to cover such cases here.

Note that *hearer* and *addressee* are not interchangeable terms (cf. Clark & Carlson, 1982), although it is difficult to define the notion 'addressee' in a non-circular way that distinguishes the addressee of an utterance like (i) from an intended overhearer.

   i. I can't believe that this salesclerk has not even acknowledged our existence.

In any case, when I write *addressee,* I mean the individual(s) to whom an utterance is addressed, and when I write *hearer,* I mean anyone who happens to hear (or read) the utterance in question.

overview of those mechanisms that allow more to be communicated than is actually said.

Linguistic pragmatics as defined here is at the intersection of a number of fields within and outside of cognitive science: not only linguistics, cognitive psychology, cultural anthropology, and philosophy (logic, semantics, action theory), but also sociology (interpersonal dynamics and social convention) and rhetoric contribute to its domain. This volume does not pretend to do justice to the depth of scholarship in all of these fields, but hopes instead to sketch the interrelationships of the phenomena they variously study.

1. WHAT THIS BOOK IS ABOUT

This chapter discusses the foundations of the analysis of language use. Subsequent chapters treat topics encompassed by successively broader interpretations of the domain of pragmatic theory. Chapter 2, therefore, concerns the narrowest interpretation of *pragmatics*: the interpretation of INDEXICAL expressions (words or phrases like *me, here, then* whose REFERENCE cannot be determined without taking into account the context of the utterance of a linguistic expression). Minimally the context required for the interpretation of indexical expressions includes the time, place, speaker, and topic of the utterance. Chapter 2 also discusses the interpretation of anaphoric expressions like *he* and *next day*. Chapter 3 concerns problems of reference, generally: how a speaker knows what an expression like *grass* or even *Bill* refers to. Ultimately, this leads us to consider also what the conditions for the use of the definite article *the* are, and even how one understands the use of common nouns and verbs like *newspaper* and *baste* or *drink*. Chapter 4 addresses two aspects of meaning that interact with the propositional content of utterances: illocutionary force (what a speaker is doing in making an utterance) and presupposition.

Chapters 5 and 6 focus on means which speakers have available to manage how what they say will be interpreted and strategies for the exploitation of logical relations in arranging the content of one's speech. Chapter 5 begins with a discussion of principles that speakers regularly use to convey more than they actually say. The rest of the chapter illustrates how the exploitation of these principles can be invoked in accounts of discourse coherence, illocutionary force, presupposition, and the relation of literal meaning to metaphor. Chapter 6 deals with how a speaker's discourse goals and attitudes may be reflected in the syntax of the utterances that constitute a discourse.

Finally, in chapter 7, we look at conversational interactions, and some of the devices speakers use to regulate control of conversation and maintain or alter social relations among participants, via patterns of discourse. The discussion treats topic manipulation, politeness strategies, uses of questions, and other exploitations of linguistic form to control the course of the interaction.

2. BELIEF AND INTENTION

The broadest interpretation of pragmatics is that it is the study of understanding intentional human action. Thus, it involves the interpretation of acts assumed to be undertaken in order to accomplish some purpose. The central notions in pragmatics must then include belief, intention (or goal), plan, and act. Assuming that the means and/or the ends involve communication, pragmatics still encompasses all sorts of means of communication, including nonconventional, nonverbal, nonsymbolic ones as, for example, when a lifeguard throws a volleyball in the direction of a swimmer struggling in the ocean.[3] The lifeguard believes that the swimmer wants assistance, and that the swimmer will understand that the volleyball thrown in his direction is intended (by the lifeguard) to be assistance, and that the swimmer will know how to take advantage of the volleyball's property of being lighter than water. That makes at least three beliefs and one intention on the part of the lifeguard, including two beliefs about the swimmer's beliefs, and one about the swimmer's desires.

Reflexive beliefs and intentions (i.e., speaker's and addressee's beliefs and intentions about each other's beliefs and intentions) of this sort are typical of the most ordinary, straightforward uses of language, and such uses cannot be understood without reference to them. For example, belief is what makes the difference (obviously) between a lie and a mistake. When people say something false that they believe to be false, they are lying, but if they say something that is false, but that they happen to believe is true, they are merely mistaken. Belief is also the core of the difference between informing and reminding. If a speaker, S, says to an addressee, A, "The Koreans have a holiday that commemorates the invention of their alphabet," and believes that A does not already know this, S most likely intends to inform A; if S believes that A does already know it, S most likely intends to remind A. Sometimes speakers are content to be vague about this belief, hoping that the remark will be taken as a reminder if A already knows, as information if A does not. Other times, speakers may want to make their position clear (for example, to avoid insulting A by implying that A did not know something that A feels everyone should know that A does know). For example, *As you know, I remind you,* and *Of course* preface utterances that

---

[3]Or to borrow an example from Jerry Morgan (1978): When I deposit my quiche in the dog's dish to express my opinion that it isn't fit for human consumption.

are intended to be taken as reminders; they indicate the speaker's belief that the addressee already knows that the proposition expressed by the sentence is true. Similarly, *Actually* and *In fact* preface utterances that the speaker believes represent information new to the addressee.

Likewise, intent makes the difference between a lie, and a joke or a figure of speech, between a promise and a prediction. Uttering something false like "She phones her mother everytime you say 'Boo!' " is a lie if the speaker intends her addressee to believe that she believes it, a figure of speech if she intends him to understand that it is an exaggeration for effect (hyperbole). Uttering "Johnny will be on time tomorrow" constitutes a promise if the speaker intends to be taken as guaranteeing that it will be true, but it constitutes a prediction if it is only intended to represent her current belief. The nature and interrelationship of beliefs and intentions are explored in the study of philosophy of mind (for an introduction, see Bechtel, 1988).

3. PLANS AND ACTS

Beliefs and intentions are not the whole story, of course. The proverb, "The road to hell is paved with good intentions" means that intentions count for naught unless acted upon. A speaker with an intention and a set of beliefs about her audience acts rationally on that intention by forming a plan to effect it. Typically such plans are hierarchical, and involve subgoals and mediating intentions as well as an ultimate goal. Issues such as these have been investigated in relatively recent artificial intelligence (AI) work on understanding plans associated with language use (e.g., Allen 1983; Pollack 1986).

For example, I might have the ultimate goal of having you have a low opinion of a certain mutual acquaintance. Since I cannot just will this to happen, I must form a plan which will cause you to have this opinion. I could tell or order you to have a low opinion of him, but given my belief that you are rational, and that you believe that I believe this, I know this is unlikely to be effective. I have to choose a plan (from an infinity of possibilities) which will take advantage of your rationality in causing you to conclude that our acquaintance, call him Eks, is a sleaze. For example, I might choose to tell you that he has instituted a policy in the office he manages which I believe you will find offensive, and having decided that, I must choose exactly how to say this. Shall I just blurt out, "He refuses to hire qualified Blacks, Jews, and women!" Or shall I tell an anecdote which gives evidence, with real names and quoted dialogue, which I can expect you will take as indicating that Eks is a despicable character? Or maybe just a single sentence with statistics and one or two names? Once this is decided, the construction of each individual sentence requires many similar decisions (cf. Green, 1982a). And all of this usually takes place without the speaker being aware of even thinking about it. In uttering a single sentence, more decisions have to be made than there are words in the sentence (cf. Green, 1982a), so it is obvious that these decisions must be made very quickly, and below the level of consciousness, or the flow of speech would be considerably more intermittent, and exponentially slower than it is.

The task of the discourse-interpreter is (a) to understand what the speaker has said, that is, to construct a mental model of the situation which the speaker is indicating exists; and (b) to evaluate that model and use it to update his own model of the world. The first task is exemplified by the acts involved in understanding what statement, imperative, question, wish, (or whatever) a speaker has made. The second involves drawing conclusions which add to one's knowledge of the world and to one's model of the speaker: for example, inferences about what the speaker knows; what the speaker believes that the addressee knows; what the speaker believes that the addressee believes to be false; how the speaker feels about individuals, situations, and events that have been referred to in the conversation. This is also done largely subconsciously, and ordinary competent speakers are rarely able to reconstruct and articulate the logic involved.

Pragmatics, as described in this section, is the study of action deliberately undertaken with the intention of causing the intended interpreter to re-assess his model of how things are, including his system of values and his model of the speaker's beliefs, attitudes, and intentions. To narrow our study to linguistic pragmatics, or the pragmatics of language use, we need only stipulate that the principles of pragmatics must account systematically for acts involving linguistic expressions.

4. LINGUISTIC EXPRESSIONS
AND THE DETERMINATION OF MEANING

A language (natural or artificial) consists of (a) a set of basic (i.e., unanalyzed) expressions, termed a LEXICON; (b) a set of rules for combining those expressions in well-formed constructions, termed a SYNTAX; and, according to the standard view, (c) a set of rules for deriving the meaning of each construction from the meanings of its parts, called a COMPOSITIONAL SEMANTICS (Dowty, Wall, & Peters 1981; Montague 1970, 1973). All of these components are conventional, which means that principles of logic and laws of physics do not force the rules to be exactly as they are[4]. Rather, at least

---

[4]Strictly speaking, the syntax and the semantics are arbitrary and conventional as well, but the syntaxes and semanticses of natural languages are so similar, and so restricted (in the face of all the conceivable possibilities) that the principles constraining them (the so-called rules of

some of the rules are arbitrary to at least some degree, and by custom, speakers act in conformity with them. The issue hardly ever comes to consciousness, but using the language in a way that failed to observe the rules would greatly decrease the likelihood of successful communication. For example, there is no logical reason why English adjectives must go before the nouns they modify (e.g., *united states*) rather than after, as in French (*états unis*). Likewise, the semantic rules that guarantee that *John* is understood as the object of *please* in *John is easy to please* (i.e., that make it equivalent to *It is easy [for people] to please John*), might have been otherwise, allowing *John* to be understood as the subject (making the sentence equivalent to *It is easy for John to please [people].*)

In addition to being conventional, the semantics is COMPOSITIONAL and basically TRUTH-CONDITIONAL. It is standard to distinguish between what a sentence means and what a speaker intends to convey by the utterance of that sentence (Grice 1957), and to restrict the role of semantics to explicating the meaning of a sentence in terms of conditions which must be fulfilled for it to be used to truthfully describe a situation. Aspects of the interpretation of utterances which do not involve truth conditions are commonly considered to be outside the domain of semantics, and that is the approach followed here. Thus, whether an utterance is a promise, a prediction, or a question, and how metaphorical utterances like *India demanded compensation* are understood are considered matters of pragmatics, not semantics (cf. chapters 3–5).

To say that the semantics is compositional means that the meaning of a complex expression will be related in a predictable way to the meanings of the parts from which it is constructed. This is usually expressed by saying that the meaning of the whole is a function of the meanings of the parts, where *function* has its technical, mathematical sense. Consequently, the parts of every structure defined by a particular syntactic rule must be related in the same way, because they are related by a single function[5]. This means that, for example, whatever semantic relation a syntactic subject like *Sandy* bears to its predicate in a sentence like *Sandy cooks potatoes,* the syntactic subject in parallel constructions like *Dana eats turnips* must represent the same semantic relation to its predicate.

To say that the semantics is truth conditional means that the meaning of

---

universal grammar) must be a consequence, ultimately, if not directly, of the human genetic make-up (cf. Chomsky, 1965, 1968, 1980).

[5]As a consequence of this principle, noun–noun compounds and expressions like *religious affairs* and *public beaches,* where the adjective is taken as relating to the noun in different ways ('affairs concerning religion,' 'beaches for the public'; cf. *religious person, public intoxication*) must be considered either ambiguous, having a plural but finite number of meanings, or vague, having a single meaning, but an indefinite number of potential intended interpretations. This is an interesting and complex matter, and is taken up in more detail in chapter 5.

sentences (and therefore of their parts, since the semantics is compositional) is explicated in terms of conditions under which they would be true. In other words, the meaning of an expression in a compositional semantics represents a state of affairs that would have to hold if the sentence containing that expression is to be considered true. Although we do not speak of nondeclarative sentences such as questions and commands as being true or false, analyses in modal logic[6] involving such notions as knowledge, necessity, and obligation make truth-conditional analyses of even such sentences possible.

The meanings of the basic expressions are conventional, and arbitrary except for the vagaries of history. That is, there is no particular reason that apples are called *apples,* other than the fact that that is what people are accustomed to calling them. In a seminal paper, Grice (1957) referred to conventional meaning of this sort as NONNATURAL MEANING, and distinguished it from NATURAL MEANING, which he reserved for uses of the word *meaning* which are more akin to 'natural consequence.' Thus, the fact that *apple* "means" 'fruit of a plant of the sub-genus *malus*' is much more like the fact that green (in a street light) means$_{nonnatural}$ 'go' than it is like the fact that 'Sandy is allergic to pollens' means$_{natural}$ that she will not want flowers in her office. The arbitrary, conventional nature of language is evident in the fact that we call fire *fire* (i.e., [fayr] because the folks from whom we learned to talk called it [fayr], or something like that, while our German cousins call it *Feuer* (i.e., [foyr]) because somewhere back in history, our respective ancestors began to follow different pronunciation rules. Swahili speakers call it [moto] because that is how they learned it at their mothers' knees. To put it another way, we call fire *fire* because that is what everybody else (in our speech community) calls it. We know that if we call it something else, we cannot expect people to understand that we are talking about fire.

But it is a mistake to assume just because a language has a conventional syntax, semantics, and defined lexicon, that utterances constructed in accordance with them will be understood as intended.

Up until the 1960s, it was widely assumed among linguists that a theory of meaning framed in terms of conditions under which a sentence would be true (truth conditions) would be able to account for first, the relation between a sentence and the logical proposition it expresses (i.e., to explicate why the sentence *Snow is white* refers to a claim that snow is white (and not to white snow, or Snow White), and second, the relation between a referring expression and its referent (i.e., to account for how it is that *Snow White* refers to Snow White, or how *the president of the United States* refers—in

---

[6]See, for example, Von Wright (1963), Rescher (1966, 1967), Lemmon (1965), Åqvist (1965, 1971), Harrah (1961), Hintikka (1974), Karttunen (1977), and Lewis (1968).

1986—to Ronald Reagan). It was also taken for granted that the same theory of meaning would account for the illocutionary force of sentences (that aspect of their meaning which distinguishes statements from promises or various sorts of pronouncements; cf. Austin, 1962) and in some cases, for the discourse value of expressions as exemplified by the difference between (1) and (2) or between (3) and (4), or between (5) and (6).

1.   Sandy walked in.
2.   In walked Sandy.
3.   Dana's in prison.
4.   Dana's in the slammer.
5.   Luke killed an imperial guard.
6.   Luke caused an imperial guard to die.

For instance, example (2) contributes a narrative effect (most likely resolving a narrative tension) not evoked by (1). Example (4), in contrast to (3), refers to the place of Dana's incarceration with an expression associated with populations intimately familiar with such places, with the implication that the speaker is familiar with that world, and perhaps that the speaker believes that the addressee is also. The circumlocution in (6), as opposed to (5), implies that Luke's action caused the guard's death in a manner less direct than, say, Luke's mortally wounding him (cf. Horn, 1978a; McCawley, 1978a). But it eventually became apparent that these different aspects of what people were used to calling "meaning" were not the same sorts of thing at all. A more current view is that a highly restrictive truth-conditional semantic component must interact with principles of pragmatics that fix or limit what a sentence will convey on an occasion of utterance (Gazdar, 1980). It is often assumed that the pragmatics is independent of the semantics, and takes the "output" of the semantics as "input," the semantics having provided a truth-conditional interpretation of a syntactically well-formed expression.

But even this view is unrealistic if taken literally. There are many cases where a truth-conditional semantics cannot operate independently of pragmatic aspects of meaning (Gazdar, 1979, chapter 7). To take a simple case, consider what a truth-conditional semantics could tell us about the meaning of sentence (7).

7.   He fell down.

A truth-conditional semantics could tell us that it asserts that some sentient male entity came abruptly to be at a point in space lower than its former position at some point in time prior to the asserting of (7). Reference to "the asserting of (7)" is necessary to give truth conditions for the past tense morpheme. This indicates that for a truth-conditional semantics to determine (in the technical sense 'define, specify') the propositional content of a sentence, it must make reference to an agent who is uttering the sentence and to the time of its utterance. (This was recognized early; (cf. Bar-Hillel, 1954.)

But even this "liberal" account of the truth conditions of this sentence does not determine (i.e., specify) a proposition, because *he* does not determine a referent. It might refer to the last-mentioned entity which meets the description 'male, sentient,' but very often it does not.[7] Often, language users have to guess at the referent intended by the speaker of a pronoun (or indexical) like *he,* and this is what makes it impossible to claim that a pragmatics in conjunction with a truth-conditional semantics, could determine what a sentence conveys on an occasion of utterance. There is no way of knowing who the underlined *he* in passages like those in (8) is intended to refer to, short of being able to read the speaker's mind.[8]

8a.   When Luke pushed Adam in to give the photograph to Humphrey, *he* fell down in surprise on seeing the golden charm again.

8b.   The dean expelled John because *he* discovered his secret.

The fact that fully competent language users are not always able to tell what the intended referent is would seem to preclude the devising of principles which could compute this mechanically. Since natural language discourse is governed by guesses as well as knowledge, and some of these guesses are themselves based on guesses about what one's interlocutor knows, thinks, or feels, a model that determines (i.e., specifies) a unique interpretation or even a finite range of interpretations from a finitely describable context and a truth-conditional semantics of the usual sort is not a model of natural language processes. To simulate the pragmatic capacity of an ordinary speaker, we would have to build a device that not only would infer which of many possible referents (or illocutionary forces, etc.) a speaker intended, but also would infer a speaker's discourse intentions. For example, a speaker might be intentionally ambiguous

---

[7]As in an example like (i), where *his* could refer just as easily to the mugger, Robert or Alex, or in well-known examples like (ii), where *they* is much more likely to be correctly understood to refer to the farther potential antecedent.

   i. A mugger attacked Robert, and Alex broke his arm.

   ii. The deans refused to let the students picket, because they feared violence.

[8]More exactly: short of being able to know exactly what the speaker expects the addressee to know about the subject under discussion.

(cf. Weiser, 1974), and content to be taken either way. We saw one example of this above, in the discussion of reminders. To take another, A may say (9) to B, hoping the utterance will be taken as a request (cf. chapter 4) if B is willing to talk, but as a mere statement of interest if B is not.

9.   I'd love to know what went on in the hearing today.

Situations like this are probably pretty rare in scientific text, but surely abound in social conversation, in advertising, and in political speech (cf. Myers, 1984). Myers emphasized that part of the politician's art is in saying things in such a way that they will be interpreted in different (favorable) ways by different special interest constituencies. In slightly more complex cases, a speaker may intend to be taken as being intentionally ambiguous, as in one computer company's slogan, "We put people in front of computers."

A more realistic claim about the relation of semantics and pragmatics would be that, given certain contextual conditions or defaults, a pragmatics in conjunction with a truth-conditional semantics could define a ranking of likely candidates for the intended interpretation of an utterance (n.b. not a sentence), but short of claiming clairvoyance, it could never claim to be able to specify the actual (intended or constructed) interpretation of an utterance.

5. VAGUENESS AND INTERPRETATION

It is commonly assumed that language provides a vehicle for thought, that words, or at least connected words (sentences), express thoughts, and do so uniquely. You have a thought, you put it into words which will carry the thought, and any sane and sober person who knows the language will be able effortlessly to behold your thought, to get your idea. But this assumption is mistaken, and for cognitive science, it is a mistake of major proportions.

Reddy (1979) has discussed this assumption under the rubric "the conduit metaphor," and presented evidence that it is utterly pervasive in our speech about language and communication. According to the conduit metaphor, linguistic expressions (words, sentences, paragraphs, books, etc.) are compared to vessels or conduits into which thoughts, ideas, or meanings are poured, and from which they can be extracted, exactly as they were sent, accomplishing a transfer of possession. References in the previous paragraph to *vehicle, put . . . into words, carry, behold, get* are all instances of this conduit metaphor. When we accept the conduit metaphor, we commit ourselves to a view that communication is achieved as easily as serving a glass of milk or sending a package, that any failure to communicate must be due to carelessness or inattention in choosing or construing linguistic expressions, and that properly chosen linguistic expressions do all the work.

Reddy offered an alternative metaphor, which he called the toolmakers' paradigm. Six individuals live in separate environments. None knows what any environment but his own is like, nor even that they are different from each other. The individuals have no common language, but can send each other blueprints of tools they develop to make it easier to cultivate their various terrains. Each one is proud of the tools he invents, and of the blueprints he carefully drafts to instruct the others on making such a tool for themselves. The toolmakers are generally disappointed, disgusted, or angry, not to mention bewildered, when their careful blueprints for their prized tools are returned with what seem to be senseless or even counter-productive modifications, so much so that it is an event for celebration when one is accepted as is.

As a view of linguistic communication, the toolmakers' paradigm assumes first of all that sentences are more like blueprints, from which much may be inferred, but with no assurance of correctness, than they are like programmed instructions or encyclopedias, where everything is explicit. It implies that speakers may have incorrect conceptions of what their addressees know, and of what "everybody" knows, and may be utterly unaware of it. It suggests that crafting a message so that it will convey what the speaker wants it to convey to the particular addressee to whom it is addressed is an art, and requires assumptions about what that addressee believes. It also implies that correctly divining what the sender of a message intends the receiver to understand involves real work, and a real risk of failure. Toolmaker metaphors in this description include: *crafting, art, divining, risk*. If this is a more correct model than the conduit metaphor, as I believe it is, then communication probably misfires more often than we realize; the experience of discovering minutes, days, weeks, months, or years later that B did not mean 'X' when she said "W," but 'Y,' supports this view.

Reddy argued that the conduit metaphor is not only misleading, but harmfully, perniciously so. For our purposes, however, it is enough to assume that there is more to understanding utterances than parsing them and deriving representations of their propositional meanings in terms of intensional logic or model theory (cf. Dowty et al., 1981). It is necessary also to make inferences about what the utterer believes about what the addressee believes, and about what effect the utterer intends the utterance to have.

A simple demonstration of the necessity of this comes from the work of the psychologists Bransford and Johnson (1973). They asked subjects to read the following paragraph.

The procedure is actually quite simple. First you arrange things into different groups. Of course, one pile may be sufficient depending on how much there is to do. If you have to go somewhere else due to lack of facilities that is the next step, otherwise you are pretty well set. It is important not to overdo things. That is, it is better to do too few things at once than too many. In the short run this may not seem important but complications can easily arise. A mistake can be expensive as well. At first the whole procedure will seem complicated. Soon, however, it will become just another facet of life. It is difficult to foresee any end to the necessity for this task in the immediate future, but then one can never tell. After the procedure is completed one arranges the materials into different groups again. Then they can be put into their appropriate places. Eventually they will be used once more and the whole cycle will then have to be repeated. However, that is part of life.

Subjects found the paragraph difficult to understand and hard to recall, although there is nothing difficult about any of the words or sentences, or even about the way the sentences are connected to each other to make coherent discourse. When subjects were given the information (by means of a two-word title) that the author intended his text as a description of doing laundry, the text was comprehended and recalled much better. What had been missing was information about what the author expected to be taken as intending to refer to: The paragraph itself is vague in not mentioning washing or clothes.

In fact, most natural language utterances are vague (recall example (7) above), and require interpretation of this sort: Who is the speaker referring to? What does she mean by *fell down*? In a race? Off a ladder? Down a hill? Is it good, or bad? For "him," or for her, or for me? How does she know? Does she think she is reminding me or informing me? All of these issues can be addressed explicitly in an utterance of this sort, but they rarely are. The problems posed here are addressed in more detail in chapters 3–5.

Pragmatic "ambiguities" of this sort abound in natural language use. The oral instruction to write your name backwards sounds clear enough, but which of the following is a correct response?

a.   writing the last name first: Green Georgia
b.   writing the name with the letters within a word in reverse order: aigroeg neerg
c.   writing the name as in (b), but last name first: neerg aigroeg
d.   writing the name in mirror writing: NEERG AIGROEG
e.   writing the name from right to left, last letter first:
     Georgia Green
          ⟨ ——
f.   rotating your body so your back is facing your addressee and writing your name

g.   writing the words "your name backwards"
h.   writing the words "your name" as in (a)
i.   writing the words "your name" as in (b)
j.   writing the words "your name" as in (c)
k.   writing the words "your name" as in (d)
l.   writing the words "your name" as in (e)

This looks like a finite, although large, number of distinct interpretations. But there are also cases where the number of likely intended interpretations is indefinitely large. For instance, a sentence like *Tom became the tallest man in Columbus, Ohio* might be intended as a claim that Tom grew taller than all other Columbusites, as a claim that Tom turned into Mike, the tallest man in Columbus, or as a claim that all the other tall men died, moved away, shrank, became women, boys, or frogs, and so on. Apparently, this last one is a vague statement about Columbus, Ohio, or an indefinitely "ambiguous" statement about Tom. Examples like these are strong evidence for the correctness of the view of language and communication implied by Reddy's toolmaker metaphor.

6. MUTUAL BELIEF AND PLAN DEDUCTION

We come now to the final notions necessary for a full description of pragmatics—the reflexivity of belief and intention (Grice, 1957; Searle, 1969). When I say to you "He couldn't get mortgage insurance," intending to refer to Captain Frank Furillo, it is not enough for me to just intend it to be taken that way. For communication to be successful, you must recognize my intention, that is, recognize that *he* is intended to refer to Captain Furillo. If I intend it to make a reference to Captain Furillo, and you assume it is intended as a reference to Officer Renko, I have not succeeded in communicating, in sharing my opinion with you.

Similarly, on a larger scale, if I ask you to open a window, saying, for example, "Open the window, would you?" I must believe

1.   that you know what window I mean you to open
2.   that you are capable of performing what needs to be done to get that window open
3.   that the window is not now open
4.   that the window will not open without the intervention I request
5.   that you realize I'm addressing you
6.   that you understand the language I'm speaking, that you are awake, etc.

Still, my believing all this will not by itself guarantee that my request is communicated to you. For that, you must believe that I believe all that. (If I'm addressing you, and believe that you understand that I am, but you believe I'm addressing the child sitting in your lap, I won't have communicated.) Furthermore, you must believe that I believe you believe it. (If you think I believe that you think that the window is already open, you'll conclude I am — perhaps jokingly, or sarcastically — asking you to do something you think is impossible — like touching your chin to your elbow — when in fact it is a perfectly sincere and feasible request.) If you know that the window is operated by a timer set to open it momentarily, and do not know that I do not know it, you will find my request extremely puzzling, and conclude either that I am not in my right mind, or am operating on some other wave length, or have different beliefs, or that I mean something else by my utterance than a request to open a window (what it might be I'm not sure).

Understanding a speaker's intention in saying what she said the way she said it amounts to inferring[9] the speaker's plan, in all of its hierarchical glory, although there is room for considerable latitude regarding the details. To take a trivially straightforward case, when you understand my saying to you, "Close the window, why don't you" as a request addressed to you, you infer (a) that I want the window closed, (b) that I want you to do it, (c) that I want you to do it because I've asked you (and not, for example, because you think the open window might annoy me), and (d) that I want you to realize that I want you to do it by understanding my utterance as a request as specified above (cf. Bach & Harnish, 1979 pp. 3–18), and all without being aware of inferring anything. Schematically,

GOAL STRUCTURE: Get window closed
  by getting X to close window
   by requesting that X close the window
    by saying "Close the window, why don't you."

PLAN RECONSTRUCTION

Speaker has said, "Close the window, why don't you"
Therefore, Speaker is making a request to close the window.
Therefore, Speaker wants the addressee to close the window.
Therefore, Speaker wants the window closed.

---

[9]In the AI literature, this is referred to as plan deduction (Allen & Perrault, 1980). I reserve the term *deduction* for deductive inferences in a system with a closed, specified set of axioms, which natural language understanding certainly isn't.

Similarly, I might try to get you to decide not to vote for Eks by causing you to have a low opinion of him, by telling you that he has done something which I believe will do this (by showing that his values conflict with yours), by telling you he indulges in discriminatory employment practices, by saying "Eks refuses to hire qualified Blacks, Jews, and women." I will preface my remark with *You know,* in order not to come on too strong: I will make it appear that I am reminding you of something I believe you already know, and know that I know you know. And I may well have arrived at this set of intentions without ever consciously considering any of them. Schematically, this plan looks like this:

Get Y to decide not to vote for Eks
    by getting Y to have a low opinion of Eks
        by causing Y to realize something bad about Eks
            by letting Y know that Eks has done something Y will disapprove of
                by telling Y that Eks engages in discriminatory employment practices while allowing Y to believe I give Y credit for already knowing this
                    by saying "You know, Eks refuses to hire qualified Blacks, Jews, or women."

Notice that the speaker may not want all of his intentions recognized (for example, his intent to influence the addressee's voting behavior), and that some intentions may not be recognized (e.g., the one just mentioned). Indeed, certain intentions (e.g., rhetorical deceits like using *you know* to diminish the inference of informational superiority implied by the speaker's telling the addressee something; cf. chapter 7) are such that their being recognized will make the communication less successful than if they go unnoticed.

Plans of intermediate complexity, such as plans to let someone know, by changing the topic, that he has made a faux pas, or plans to achieve actions by indirect requests like *Can you see the time?* are discussed in chapter 5.

Plan reconstruction may start, as in the example of *Close the window, why don't you* with the eventual utterance, or with the goals, if the addressee believes that he and the speaker share a lot of beliefs and are familiar with each other's values and ultimate goals. Either way, knowledge of this sort is constantly necessary as a check on the validity of the inferences made in plan reconstruction: if the inferences conflict with what is believed about the speaker's beliefs, values, and goals, either the inference or the background belief has to be modified.

2 Indexicals and Anaphora: Contextually Identifiable Indeterminacies of Reference

The narrowest interpretation of the term *pragmatics* is that it refers to the study of indexicals, expressions whose reference is a function of the context of their utterance. In this chapter, we examine the adequacy of this interpretation, focusing first on indexical pronouns like *I* and *you*, and adverbs such as *here* and *yesterday,* and then extending the discussion to related phenomena such as tenses, demonstratives like *that,* and anaphoric pronouns like *he, her,* and *their,* which refer to entities previously mentioned in the discourse. Far from indicating that the domain of pragmatics is narrowly circumscribed by observable contextual phenomena, the interpretation of indexicals and related anaphora is shown to require assumptions or inferences about the speaker's beliefs and/or intended referents, and thus requires a broader interpretation of *pragmatics.*

In his classic 1954 paper "Indexical Expressions"[1], Bar-Hillel argued that indexicality is an inherent and unavoidable property of natural language, and speculated that more than 90% of the declarative sentences people utter are indexical in that they involve implicit references to the speaker, addressee, time and/or place of utterance in expressions like first and second person pronouns (*I, you*), demonstratives (e.g., *this*), tenses, and adverbs like *here, now, yesterday*. Thus, utterances of sentences like those in (1–5) cannot be fully understood (i.e., understood enough to judge whether they are true or false) without an indication of who uttered the sentence (1, 2), and when (1, 3, 4, 5), and where it was uttered (4).

---

[1]This must surely be regarded as one of the seminal papers in pragmatics, though many important points made there have had to be rediscovered and made again repeatedly.

1.   I am hungry.
2.   This is good for coughs.
3.   It's raining in Madrid.
4.   It's begun to rain.
5.   The president of the United States had an audience with the Pope.

Actually, it is an oversimplification, one that it is not clear whether Bar-Hillel appreciated, to suppose that having that information is sufficient to guarantee evaluatability. Strictly speaking, it is irrelevant where the sentence is uttered. What is relevant is what place the speaker intended to be taken as referring to. Sitting in Urbana, Illinois, I can say, "It's raining," referring to the weather in the city where a football game I am watching (or listening to) is being played. Similarly, for uses of tenses: historical presents (e.g., "I try to crawl to safety, but my leg is broken") use a present tense to refer to a past time. Bar-Hillel (1954) may have recognized essentially this problem with *this*:

> 'This' is used to call attention to something in the centre of the field of vision of its producer, but, of course, also to something in his spatial neighborhood, even if not in his centre of vision or not in his field of vision at all, or to some thing or some event or some situation, etc., mentioned by himself or by somebody else in utterances preceding his utterance, and in many more ways. (p. 373)

However, it is probably worth noting that Bar-Hillel did not use the term *intention* or *intended referent* in his description of the phenomenon. Morgan (1978) gave an example[2] that illustrates nicely the problem of identifying the referent of an indexical:

> imagine a jar of sugar with a glass lid, on which the word *sugar* is painted in blue; and imagine that someone puts her fingertip just under the letter *u* of the word *sugar* and says, "What's that? "Our answer might be, among other things, *the letter u, the word sugar, paint, blue paint, blue, English, a lid,*

---

[2]There is an unwitting example in Bar-Hillel's own paper. He says:

> A clear understanding of the functioning of indexical expressions can be helpful both in avoiding pseudo-problems and in solving genuine philosophical problems (though the borderline between these two cases is somewhat vague). (p. 376)

Does "these two cases" refer to pseudo-problems and general philosophical problems, or to avoiding pseudo-problems and solving genuine philosophical problems?

glass, a glass lid, a jar, sugar, a jar of sugar, and so on, depending on our interpretation of the person's interests—is she learning English, the use of seasoning, physics, or what? (p. 264)

1. INDEXICAL PRONOUNS

Although the first person singular pronoun is the paradigmatic example of an indexical expression, the issue is not so clear with first person pronouns as Bar-Hillel may lead us to believe. Dismissing the case of an actor speaking his lines, where the understander has to know how to distinguish between the actor's references to himself, and the persona's references to himself (a task that can get difficult in certain plays by Pirandello and Thornton Wilder), Bar-Hillel (1954) took utterances of *I* to refer to whoever utters them (p. 363), and displayed the supposed universal absurdity (p. 377) of the assertion of sentences like (6) as corroboration.

6.   I am dead.

But whenever an agent speaks for a counterpart (G. Lakoff, 1968; Lewis, 1968) in another "world," the possibility of a non-absurd utterance of a sentence of this form arises, for example, an actor in "Hamlet" referring offstage to the last scene, or Scrooge or Marley's ghost in Dickens' *A Christmas Carol.* Marley's ghost's line, "In life I was your partner, Jacob Marley" presupposes (6), even if it does not assert it, and in his utterance "I wear the chain I forged in life," the first *I* refers to the (speaking) ghost, while the second refers to the then dead Marley.

Still, the reference of the first person singular pronoun is determined (largely) pragmatically as the utterer of the form *I.* This makes the indeterminacy of reference isolatable (in the form *I*), and contextually resolvable, up to counterparts and assumed identities. The second person pronoun poses different problems. It is similar to the first person pronoun in that the form *you* isolates the referent as the individual or individuals whom the speaker is addressing, but there are no linguistic or external clues to who the individual addressed might be. The addressee is whoever the speaker intends to be addressing, and does not have to be physically present where the utterance is made (as in the case of letters, telephone calls, etc.). The addressee does not even have to exist at the time the utterance is produced, as in the case of documents or speeches sent to a recipient light years away, or intended for publication or broadcast 50 years after their production. All that is necessary is that the speaker intend and/or expect that at the time of reception, there will be an appropriate addressee.

Even assuming a contemporaneous, physically present addressee, there may be no linguistic clues to identify which of several candidates is intended. For example, (7a) appears to be addressed to every individual in hearing distance of the speaker, but it surely would not be intended to include casual overhearers (cf. Clark & Carlson, 1982), and might not include individuals allied with the speaker (e.g., henchmen who were expected or required to be present). All we really know about the referent of *you* in (7a) is that it is plural, and we know that from the phrase *all of you*. Without such a clue (as in (7b)), it is not at all clear whether the intended referent is the whole group or some subset containing one or more members.

7a.   I'm glad that all of you received my invitation.
7b.   I'm glad that you received my invitation.

Finally, different tokens of *you* may have different referents in an utterance like (8), and the only clue to who the various referents are may be changes in the direction of eye-gaze or body-position of the speaker.

8.   You$_1$ can vacuum while you$_2$ wash the dishes, and — keep your$_3$ hat on — I'll get the groceries.

Naturally, all the counterpart and assumed persona complications that arise with first person pronouns arise equally here, and with third person pronouns.

First person plural pronouns have all of the indeterminacies of second person pronouns. *We* can refer to the speaker and any number of other individuals, present or not, and not necessarily existing at the time of production. Cases where the addressee (and possibly others as well) is included in the intended reference of *we* (inclusive *we*) must be distinguished from cases where the intended reference is to the speaker and one or more others, not including the addressee (exclusive *we*). Some languages (e.g., Malagasy) have different forms for these two sets of cases.

In all of these cases, it is knowledge of (or beliefs about) the speaker, including beliefs about his beliefs and intentions, at all levels, that enables an interpreter (addressee or otherwise) to divine the intended referents of indexical pronouns. Their reference is some function of the spatio-temporal coordinates of the utterance, but is by no means uniquely entailed by them.

2. TENSES

Bar-Hillel indicated that tensed verbs also make sentence tokens indexical in that their reference and truth cannot be determined without an indication of their "context of utterance," here, crucially, the time of utterance. Although Bar-Hillel's examples include only true present tenses (e.g., *I am hungry* as opposed to *Water is a compound of hydrogen and oxygen*), which define the time of reference as the time of utterance, past and future tenses are equally indexical, referring to times that are a function of the time of utterance (but see below). Thus, if I utter (9a) at time t_0, I mean that I am hungry at t_0; if I utter (9b) at t_0, I mean that I was hungry at some point before t_0, and if I say (9c) at t_0, I mean that I will be hungry at some point after t_0.

9a. I am hungry.
9b. I was hungry.
9c. I will be hungry.

Notice, however, that although (9a) indicates a unique time, (9b) and (9c) refer very vaguely to some time before or after t_0; one does not know if it is on the order of minutes, days, weeks, years, decades, or millenia distant. Furthermore, it is not clear whether the "time" indicated by (9a) is a moment, or an interval of indefinite duration that includes the "moment" of utterance. Although on hearing me say (9a), you would not assume my hunger began when I began to speak or ceased when I stopped speaking, one might want to say that it is a moment, and the fact that (9a) is understood to refer to an interval containing moments before and after t_0 is just the same vagueness that is inherent in the past and future time references. This turns out to be a very complicated issue, however (see Dowty, 1979, for further discussion).

Previously I said that the time reference of a tensed sentence was a function of the time of utterance of the sentence, but in fact, this is not the whole story. Depending again, on the intentions of the speaker, if there is a significant interval between the time of utterance and the time of (assumed) receipt of the utterance, the time reference of a tensed sentence may be partially a function of the assumed/intended time of receipt. For example, if I write a letter, I most likely will index time references to the time of writing: "It's 3 degrees Fahrenheit here; we are thinking of going to St. Maarten," but the commander of an earth-invasion force from Alpha Centauri might write to earthlings, "There are thousands of Alpha Centaurians among you, disguised as trucks, tripods, and tape recorders," long before the situation described came to pass, knowing or believing that by the time the message was received, it would have come to pass.[3]

---

[3]The following sentence from Parade magazine (1-5-86) illustrates the problem of writing for a future audience.

i. Any day now (if not already), Mrs. Thatcher's administration will have abolished

3. ADVERBS

Virtually the same things could be said about time adverbs as were said about tenses[4]: ordinarily *today* refers to the day of its utterance, *now* to the moment of utterance, *yesterday* to the day before its utterance[5], *last month* to the month prior to its utterance, *next week* to the week after the week of utterance, and so on, but all of these could, under the circumstances described in the previous section, be indexed to the assumed time of reception.

Place adverbs like *here* likewise determine reference indexically, as at the place of utterance, and present the same problems of vagueness as *now* (does it mean 'this instant,' 'today,' 'this week,' 'this month'?) and *this* (mentioned previously). Whether *here* means 'at this spot,' 'in this hotel,' 'in/on this city/state/country/hemisphere/planet/galaxy etc.' is a function not of context, but of what the speaker intends it to refer to, and interpreters must guess, again basing their guesses on their knowledge and beliefs about the knowledge, beliefs, and intentions of the speaker. What expressions like *this spot* refer to is entirely vague, linguistically, and can only be interpreted with the aid of gestures or knowledge about the speaker's beliefs and intentions (see below on demonstratives).

In the case of utterances which will be received long after they are sent, the reference of *here* does not seem to be relative to the location of the reception. When I write, "It's going to be cold here" in a letter to be sent across an ocean by surface mail, I will not expect *here* to be taken to refer to the addressee's location. The Alpha Centaurian commander may an-

---

the old trading laws, and the British — suffering from a 13%-plus unemployment rate — will join the ranks of the all-day Sunday shoppers, a move calculated to increase retail employment.

Apparently, at the time of writing, the Sunday trading laws were still in effect, although their abolition seemed imminent to the writer. The sentence involves a blend of *Any day now, Mrs. Thatcher's government will abolish . . .* , appropriate if the abolition has not occurred before press time, and *Mrs. Thatcher's government has already abolished . . .* , appropriate if abolition has occurred. But *Any day now Mrs. Thatcher's administration will have abolished the old trading laws* is ordinarily a very odd thing to say, using a future perfect instead of a simple future, since the future perfect is ordinarily used to relate a future event (like abolishing the trading laws) to an event assumed to be farther in the future, as in (ii):

ii. By the time Prince William is old enough to shop, the Administration will have (already) abolished the old trading laws.

[4]Indeed, a number of linguists have proposed that tenses are pronominal forms of time adverbs (e.g., Kiparsky, 1968; McCawley, 1971a; Partee, 1973). For a more recent treatment, see Hinrichs (1986). Articles accompanying Hinrichs' provide a variety of perspectives on the pragmatics and semantics of tense and aspect in discourse.

[5]In some languages (e.g., Hindi), 'tomorrow' and 'yesterday' are expressed by the same word, which must refer to a time one day removed from the day of utterance.

nounce to earthlings his invasion of Earth with the message, "I have been monitoring activities on Earth for some time, and have sent an invasion force disguised as trucks there to control widespread corruption." If he used *here,* it would be taken to mean he was speaking (or writing) from a location on Earth. A message sent from Alpha Centauri saying, "An invasion force from Alpha Centauri will land here in the next 24 hours," could be understood as heralding an invasion of Earth, but interpreters would understand the announcement as a message not from the commander, but from the public address system, cassette player or whatever broadcast the message. On the other hand, it seems that if the Alpha Centaurian commander characterizes the activities he has been monitoring as *your activities,* then *here* can mean 'on Earth' without assuming that the commander or his spokesman is on Earth.

Contrary to what might be expected, *there* does not ordinarily refer to a location indexed with reference to the addressee; *there* refers to a place not including what *here* would refer to, a place which the speaker expects the addressee to be able to identify. It may refer DEICTICALLY (i.e., by visual or gestural pointing) to something closer to the addressee than to the speaker (cf. example (10)), or just to something farther from the speaker than some location identifiable by the speaker as being 'here' (as in (11)), or it may refer ANAPHORICALLY (i.e., by reference to something mentioned or implied in previous discourse), the way third person pronouns do (see below), as in (12).

10. Hand me that pen over there, will you?
11a. There it is.
11b. There comes the bus.
11c. Put 'er there. [An invitation to shake hands.]
12a. Sandy wants to go to the park, but doesn't know how to get there.
12b. We're supposed to see Dr. Gesundheit today, but Sandy refuses to go there unless she gets a balloon.

Thus, deictic reference involves a relation between an object in the world and a linguistic form with no semantically determined reference (the form X is used to refer to A), while anaphoric and cataphoric (see below) reference involve relations between such a form and some other linguistic expression (the form X is used to refer to the same thing as its antecedent).

Place indexicals in other languages often carve up the world differently. For example, Japanese has three, one for places close to the speaker, one for places close to the hearer, and one for places distant from both, like archaic English *yonder.*

4. DEMONSTRATIVES

Bar-Hillel (1954) described *this* as indexical (p. 36), requiring knowledge of the spatiotemporal coordinates of the speaker for interpretation of its reference, although he goes on, as quoted above, to show that that is generally not sufficient. An utterance of (13a) could be intended (a) deictically, to refer to an indicated photograph of the earth as seen from the moon, (b) anaphorically, to a just completed discourse presenting evidence that the earth is round, (c) CATAPHORICALLY, to such a discourse to follow shortly (as in (13b)), or (d) "META-PHORICALLY", to refer to something evoked by whatever is indicated and deictically referred to (cf. Nunberg, 1978 and discussion in chapter 3), as in (13c), where the reference is not to the single copy of the newspaper, but to the corporation that published it.

13a. This proves that Columbus was right.
13b. OK, this will prove that Eks is irresponsible: when we were on a committee together, he fell asleep during every meeting that he managed to attend.
13c. [indicating a particular copy of a midwestern daily newspaper] An Australian publisher bought this for $5 million.

In terms of the pragmatic properties discussed here, cataphoric expressions are not much different from anaphoric, and I use the latter term to cover both.

That likewise has a deictic and indexical use, as in (14).

14. Put that in the wastebasket, please.

That in (14) is deictic (strictly speaking, spatiotemporally deictic) when some kind of gesture by the speaker is required for the interpretation of its reference; it is indexical in that it is appropriately used in (14) to refer to an object considered to be outside the speaker's domain. I would not say (14) to someone if I was touching or had in my physical possession whatever *that* refers to; I would use *this*. Note that a speaker could use (14) to refer to an item that was physically closer to the speaker than to the addressee, as long as the speaker was not in physical possession of it, if the speaker believed that there was a mutual belief that the addressee has or would take responsibility for it (i.e., that it was, metaphorically speaking, outside the speaker's domain). I could say (14) to one of my children, or even to a guest in my home, but because of the implications of imputing responsibility, I think a prisoner would be more likely to use (15) than (16) in trying to get assistance from his jailer.

15. This needs to be washed.
16. That needs to be washed.

Most uses of *this* and *that,* however, are probably anaphoric, indicating their referent as something referred to in previous discourse, as in (17).

17. Columbus reached the New World in 1492, but this/that did not convince anyone that the earth was round.

And, not surprisingly, *that* can be used meta-phorically, just as *this* can; *that* could be substituted for *this* in (13c) with the same interpretation. For further discussion of *this* and *that* see R. Lakoff (1974) and Prince (1981a).

Table 2.1 summarizes and exemplifies the kinds of indexicals treated in this chapter and elsewhere in this book. The ones discussed so far are enclosed within the box.

TABLE 2.1
Indexical Expressions

Type	Deictic	Anaphoric	Metaphoric
Pronoun	*I, you, we,* . . .	*he, her,* . . .	*he, her,* . . .
Time expression	tenses, *then, today,* . . .	past tenses, *then*	*then*
Place expression	*here, there,* . . .	*there*	*here, there,* . . .
Demonstrative	*this, that,* . . .	*this, that,* . . .	*this, that,* . . .
Epithet	—	*the idiot*[a]	—
Definite description	—	*the gray sweater*[b]	*the Times*[c]
Pro-predicate	*do it*	*so, as, such, other, more, do it,* ellipsis of verb and verb phrase, . . .	—
Pro-adverbial	*thus, again,* . . .	*thus, therefore, however, more-over,* . . .	—
Conjunction	—	*and, but, yet,* . . .	—
Ellipsis	of noun phrase	of noun phrase and verb phrase	

[a]To refer to someone who is not categorically an idiot
[b]To refer to a gray sweater
[c]To refer to a person, building, corporate body, etc.

5. ANAPHORIC REFERENCE

Anaphoric reference, as I have previously indicated, is reference to an entity referred to in preceding discourse. Some writers have thought that the reference of anaphoric elements like third person pronouns was indexical in that it was determined by the "context of utterance," but it should be clear from examples like (8) in chapter 1, repeated here as (18), that their reference is indexical only in that it is determined by the speaker's intention.

18.   The dean expelled John because *he* discovered his secret.

Of course, a considerate or calculating speaker will be careful to use such pronouns only when his estimate of the "context," including the addressee's assumed beliefs, suggests that there is a reasonable likelihood that the intended referent will be correctly inferred. It is often convenient to speak of the reference of a term like *I* or *here* or *he* as being dependent on context, but ultimately, and most generally, it is what the speaker intends to (be understood to) refer to that determines what a form refers to (strictly: is used to refer to) on an occasion of use, and elements of the external context of an utterance (the time, place, speaker, addressee, previous discourse, etc.) only provide clues as to what that intention is likely to be.[6]

Third person pronouns are the prototypical anaphoric expressions, but demonstrative pronouns and adjectives (as illustrated above), and expressions of many other grammatical categories, are distributed and interpreted similarly. Prescriptive grammars often imply that the explicit reference that is taken to indicate what a pronoun will refer to must precede the pronoun, but in normal language use, this often is not the case, as the possibility of coreference between pronoun and following "antecedent" in sentences like (13b) and (19) indicates.

---

[6]One could define *context* to include speakers' intentions, but in fact, if it included speakers' intentions, that would be enough; *I* would refer to whomever the speaker intends it to refer to—most likely, the speaker herself, but perhaps the addressee, as in Samuel Delaney's novel *Babel 17* (a science fiction novel (Ace Books, 1966) which linguists and computer scientists will find either amusing or irritating), and similarly for other indexical expressions.

However, this does not strike me as a useful move, since it obscures the relevance of genuine "environmental" aspects of context in determining how rational it is to use a particular expression to refer to a particular individual in a discourse with a particular addressee about a particular subject. The range of referents likely to be inferred to be intended for a word like *this* (or even a name like *Bob*) is limited by the content of the physical environment of the speaker at the time of utterance, and by the history of discourse among the participants in the speech event. The speaker's intentions are not enough; a three-year-old who wants to call marking pens with permanent ink *pregnant markers* has to be told that it is unreasonable for him to expect others to understand what he intends the phrase to refer to, no matter how intense or sincere his referential intentions might be. See Chapter 3, Sec. 4 for further discussion of what is involved here.

19.   Before he got out of bed, James decided that today would be a good day to leave for Crisfield.

It is essential to distinguish between the referent of a form and the antecedent of a form. The REFERENT of a form is what the form refers to— some actual thing in the real world, or at least some entity, concrete like a table, or abstract like a form of government, in some possible world.[7] The ANTECEDENT of a form is a different linguistic expression which has the same referent as the form. All referring expressions have referents (in some possible world), but not all have antecedents in discourse. Not even all third person pronouns have antecedents, since they can be used deictically with a gesture to refer to some entity for the first (and possibly the only) time in a discourse. Sometimes writers refer to the coreferent antecedent of a pronoun as its referent, but this is an error. A pronoun does not refer to a noun phrase or other linguistic expression[8]; it refers to whatever object in the world its antecedent noun phrase (also) refers to. This is why they are called "coreferential"—they refer to the same thing.

Linguistic research in the late 1960s (Langacker, 1966; Ross, 1967, 1969) attempted to discover simple linguistic conditions for the distribution of pronouns relative to their (semantic or pragmatic) antecedents which would predict that *he* and *James* could be coreferential in (19) but not in (20).

20.   He decided that today would be a good day to leave for Crisfield before James got out of bed.[9]

The most comprehensive discussion of syntactic conditions on pronoun-antecedent relations is Lakoff (1976), which circulated in manuscript form in 1968, but it offers no simple solution. In later research, Kuno (1972, 1975) sought discourse conditions to account for the possible relations of pronoun and antecedent within and across sentences, arguing that in general, BACKWARD PRONOMINALIZATION (as in (19)) was possible only if the referent of the pronoun was determinable from preceding discourse, and that even the possibility of ordinary forward pronominalization within a sentence depended on the discourse role of the noun phrase to be "pronominalized." He mentioned, for example, such variables as whether the noun phrase represented predictable information or an exhaustive answer to a question. He did not explain what made reference determinable or information predictable.

---

[7]Cf. chapter 3 for discussion of the notion 'possible world.'

[8]Except of course in writing about linguistic forms, as in (i):

    i. The first noun phrase in that sentence is singular, and *it* contains four words.

[9]In fact, one occasionally runs across sentences of this form, where the pronoun and full noun phrases are intended coreferents, but in all of the cases I have seen, the sentence does not contain the first reference in the discourse to the referent of the pronoun, and the real linguistic antecedent of the pronoun is a full noun phrase in a previous sentence.

Later, Kantor (1977) argued that the ease of comprehending that a pronoun was intended to refer to the same entity as the closest preceding candidate noun phrase (one which matched the pronoun in number and gender) depended on the degree to which the interpreter expected a reference to something other than the referent of the pronoun. Although Kantor showed how this expectation could be manipulated by both syntactic structure and discourse structure, calculating the interpreter's (or addressee's) expectation has not been comprehensively modelled (but cf. Nunberg, 1978, pp. 90–117 on a parallel problem, and chapter 3 for further discussion).

Contemporary syntactic and semantic work on coreference is addressed to stipulating conditions under which a pronoun and a given candidate noun phrase cannot be coreferential, and to extending that analysis to other anaphoric devices (cf. Bach & Partee 1980; Reinhart, 1983; and other articles in Kreiman & Ojeda, 1980).

Personal pronouns are the stereotypical anaphoric expressions, but many other expressions pose the same sorts of problems of determining what previously mentioned entities or constructs they are intended to refer to. Reference may be direct, as when an anaphoric expression is used to refer to the same entity that a different expression (usually a FULL or LEXICAL noun phrase, sometimes a clause) was previously used to refer to, as in most of the previous examples, or it may be less direct, as when a pronoun or other anaphoric device is used to refer to an idea expressed in an entire clause (as in (17)), or to an entire line of thought, expressed in a paragraph-sized or larger stretch of discourse, as in (21).

21.   Of all the preparations, the most stupendous was the portable wooden town to protect and house the invaders upon landing. A huge camp enclosing a place for each captain and his company, it was virtually an artificial Calais to be towed across the Channel. Its dimensions epitomized the fantasy of omnipotence. It was to have a circumference of nine miles and an area of 1,000 acres surrounded by a wooden wall 20 feet high reinforced by towers at intervals of 12 and 22 yards. Houses, barracks, stables, and markets where the companies would come for their provisions were to be laid out along prearranged streets and squares. William the Conqueror had brought a dismountable wooden fort to England in aid of his landing 300 years before, and similar devices had been used many times since, but nothing so daring in concept and size as *this* had ever before been attempted. (Barbara Tuchman, *A Distant Mirror,* p. 426 (New York: Alfred A. Knopf, 1978))

Demonstrative phrases, epithets, and definite descriptions (i.e., descriptions of the form "the so-and-so," such as *the gray sweater*) are used to refer to a previously mentioned entity, subject to the same pragmatic conditions for interpretation as personal pronouns:

22a. No man or woman of style was fully dressed without a snuffbox; and on *that appendage* the goldsmith, the jeweler, the enameler, and the miniaturist exercised their most delicate craft. (Will and Ariel Durant, *The Age of Voltaire,* p. 79 (New York: Simon and Schuster, 1965)

22b. Philip stopped by yesterday. *The bastard/idiot/son-of-a-bitch* can't seem to keep from fooling around with other people's wives.

22c. Philip stopped by yesterday. *The man* can't seem to keep from fooling around with other people's wives.

22d. William "Refrigerator" Perry was called a "wasted draft pick" at the start of the 1985 season, but *the rookie defensive lineman* has blocked, rushed, and caught for Bears touchdowns, and once even tried to carry the ballcarrier into the end zone.

Strictly speaking, such phrases are of course ambiguous between coreferential uses and noncoreferential uses, but so are ordinary personal pronouns. The possible linguistic antecedents of the anaphoric devices illustrated in (22) are limited by constraints which personal pronouns are not subject to, however. Unlike pronouns, if these expressions are in a complement *that*-clause, they cannot be coreferential to an antecedent in the main clause: although *Sandy* can serve as an antecedent for the pronoun in (23a), *Eric Dickerson* and *Philip* cannot be antecedents for the italicized expressions in (23b) and (23c).

23a. Sandy realized that *he* could get into serious trouble.

23b. Eric Dickerson thought that *the Rams' running back* would rush for at least 100 yards.

23c. Philip doubted that *the man/bastard* would be caught.

The particles *so* and *as* are also anaphoric devices, only they refer to properties of entities, not to entities themselves, and their antecedents are adjective phrases or verb phrases (occasionally prepositional phrases), not noun phrases:

24a. Sandy was afraid of the dark, as was Dana.

24b. James got hot lunch at school, and so will his brother.

24c.   Jan is in France, but so is Dale.

As (24b) indicates, the referent of *so* is not the verb phrase *got hot lunch at school* but the predicate 'get hot lunch at school.' Or 'get hot lunch'—like other anaphoric devices, PRO-PREDICATES like *so* and *as* are ambiguous or vague and may require interpretation as to their intended referent. It is only a knowledge of history that allows us to reject as an interpretation of (25) the claim that Eisenhower, Kennedy, and Johnson supported the equal rights amendment in Nixon's 1968 election campaign.

25.   President Nixon supported the Equal Rights amendment in his 1968 election campaign, as did former Presidents Eisenhower, Kennedy, and Johnson. (from a 1969 newspaper)

Many other lexical items that are not typically counted among the anaphoric expressions nonetheless contribute to the interpretation of a discourse by referring to something mentioned in prior discourse. We cannot understand (26a) without inferring that previous discourse has described an extent of depravity; still, without that description, which the adjective *such* refers to, we cannot tell exactly what sort of environment is being claimed to have nourished the salons. Similarly for the set of cities in (26b) (which one or ones are excluded?), the individual in (26c), and in (26d), the number of individuals (obliquely referred to by the adverb *more*) who took precautionary measures short of leaving town.

26a.   Amidst *such* depravity, the salons flourished.
26b.   In *other* cities, support for the war was diminishing.
26c.   *The former* preferred to stay at home, though no reason was given.
26d.   Thousands *more* left Paris altogether.

Some expressions, notably conjunctions and adverbs like *thus, therefore, nonetheless, notwithstanding* are not considered to be referring expressions like pronouns, but they regularly imply reference to entities evoked or brought into existence by previous discourse, regardless of whether those entities have been explicitly named or referred to. For example, *thus, so,* and *therefore* as clause introducers (as in (27)) are equivalent to the phrase *for that reason* or *for those reasons*; they introduce the conclusions to a reasoned argument, and therefore refer implicitly to previously stated or implied premises of those arguments.

27a.   Therefore Socrates is mortal.

27b. Thus, under this plan, the rich will get richer and the poor will get poorer.

The propositions indirectly referred to may be as close as the preceding clause, as in the use in the sentence introducing the preceding examples; or they may extend over pages (or hours) of text (or discourse), and may even be separated from the anaphor by digressions of some length.

Nonetheless, however, and *notwithstanding* (when it occurs without its object) are similar, except that they are concessive, equivalent to *in spite of that.* Out of context (that is, with no prior discourse indicating what "that" might be), (28) is just as puzzling, incomprehensible even, as (27).

28. Nonetheless, they want you to be their representative.

Adverbs like *moreover* and *too* as in (29) (cf. Green, 1973) function similarly, being equivalent to *in addition to that.*

29a. Moreover, they want you to be their representative.
29b. They want you to be their representative, too.

When conjunctions such as *and, but, or,* and *yet* appear at the beginning of a sentence, they are not grammatical errors (despite what may be taught in grammar school), but serve to conjoin the proposition expressed by the following clause with some proposition or set of propositions expressed or implied in a larger stretch of discourse (usually prior discourse). Thus, in (30a), *and* is used to conjoin references to the reasoning described in the preceding paragraph with the reason alluded to by *another,* and in (30b), *but* contrasts the proposition in the following clause to the affirmative answer which the previous text indicated that the speaker anticipated. Likewise, in (30c), *yet* contrasts the difference indicated in the following clause to the similarities described in the preceding text.[10]

30a. . . . it occurred to him that in fact the arrival of the California police at this exact moment was altogether extraordinary. The Swami had been killed little more than ten minutes before. No one else but himself knew. So how was it that the police were here already?

And hard on the heels of that thought came another. Where

---

[10]Even the lowly semicolon is anaphoric when it serves the grammatical function of connecting two independent clauses in a single sentence. In fact, often simple adjacency of sentences invites the same inference that the semicolon makes more explicit.

was the Swami's murderer? (H. R. F. Keating, *Go West, Inspector Ghote,* p. 84 (New York: Penguin, 1981))

30b. 'Yes,' he jabbed on. 'You are not pure, Nirmala Shahani. There is blood on your hands. Isn't it? Isn't it? That blood.'

He pointed, suddenly and stiff-fingered, at the brownish stain not three yards away from them beside the dark-pink chalk outline that called back to his own mind vividly enough the body that had lain there, its luxuriant black locks outflung.

But Nirmala was slowly shaking her head in negative. (Keating, pp. 184–185)

30c. He sat pretending to be dumbstruck with amazement at the size and magnificence of the houses to either side, at spreading red-tiled roofs that reminded him of a little Catholic enclave he knew in Bombay only multiplied ten or twenty fold, at great white-pillared facades, at wide green gardens under gracefully bending palm trees.

Yet somehow even these palms were different. (Keating, p. 26)

Even though the preceding text in (30c) is only a sentence, the passage quoted in (30c) would have a very different sense if the text were a single sentence and *yet* were a subordinating conjunction (introducing the following clause as a proposition that modified or limited the previous sentence, rather than as an independent proposition). A contrast would be implied between the protagonist's pretending and the difference of the palm trees, and it would be unclear what the palm trees were supposed to be different from.

In the case of elliptical constructions like (31), where the gaps are indicated by "0," the absence of a referring expression where one is predicted by the syntax or the semantics is an anaphoric device, and must be interpreted as having the same referent as a linguistic antecedent somewhere in the discourse.

31a. John wants 0 to be president.
31b. If Dana volunteers, Jan will 0.
31c. Kim bought potatoes and Dano 0 beans.
31d. Sandy picked 0, Dana washed 0, and Kim pickled the tomatoes.
31e. 0 Cooking dinner bores Dale.
31f. Dale likes 0 cooking dinner.

In (31a) it is John himself whom John wants to be president; what Jan will do, it is claimed in (31b), is volunteer; in (31c) Dana is asserted to have bought beans; in (31d) Sandy is claimed to have picked tomatoes and Dana to have washed tomatoes; in (31e) and (31f), it is claimed that it is Dale's cooking dinner that affects Dale. Obviously these constructions require linguistic antecedents;[11] the expressions in (32) could not be sensibly used to begin a discussion, though similar constructions can be independent utterances in a context where another speaker has provided the antecedent, as in (33).

32a. Dana beans.
32b. Jan will.
32c. To be president.

33a. Ann: Kim will bring hamburgers, and Sandy potato salad.
     Jan: And Dana beans.
33b. Mo: I don't know who we can get to volunteer.
     Jo: Jan will.
33c. Jed: What does Sandy want?
     Ned: To be president.

The referents of the gaps in the constructions in (31) are unambiguous, but this is not always the case. In many cases, the more potential linguistic antecedents, the greater the ambiguity. In (34a) the referent of 0 could be Grandpa, or it could be Grandma and Grandpa; in (34b) it is not clear whether Mrs. Smith gave Dana a bond, or whether Mr. Smith gave one to Mrs. Smith; in (34c) the antecedent of the 0 might be *get chocolate ice cream* or *wants to get chocolate ice cream*; and in (34d) there are at least 14 possibilities as to who the suggested dog walkers are, depending on (among

---

[11]In constructions like (i) and (ii), no linguistic antecedent is required.

i. Saw your brother yesterday.
ii. Seen my hat?

In English, if there is no antecedent, the omitted subject of a declarative sentence is always interpreted as the speaker, and the omitted subject of a question as the addressee (Schmerling, 1973). If there is an antecedent, main clause subjects may be omitted with a broader range of referents as long as there is a potential antecedent somewhere in the preceding linguistic context. In English, sentences like (iii) are normally encountered as answers ((iv)) or corrections ((v)) (cf. Morgan, 1973c), or occasionally in narratives in an obsolescent diary style.

iii. Broke his bat.
iv. Jim: What did Danner do then?
    Tim: Broke his bat.
v. Red: I heard Danner broke his back.
    Ted: No, no. Broke his bat.

In other languages, including Japanese and Spanish, such sentences occur more freely, in both relatively formal uses of language, and in ordinary conversation, and subjects may be omitted in dependent as well as independent clauses. In Japanese, nonsubjects may be omitted as well.

other things) the content of the preceding discourse: the speaker, the speaker and addressee jointly, Dale and the speaker, Dale and the address-ee, Dale and the speaker and the addressee jointly, some fourth person (let's call him X), X and the speaker, X and the addressee, X and Dale, and so on.

34a. Grandma said that Grandpa wanted 0 to come into town to watch the Bears game.
34b. Mr. Smith gave Dana a set of encyclopedias and Mrs. Smith 0 a savings bond.
34c. Maybeth wants to get chocolate ice cream if James does 0.
34d. Dale suggested 0 walking the dog.

Some of these constructions are subject to strict conditions on the syntactic position of a coreferent antecedent. In fact, some (e.g., the ones in (31a, 31e, 31f)) are, as Postal (1970) showed, governed by the same syntactic constraints as personal pronouns. Others require no linguistic antecedent for the referent to be inferred, although in the absence of one, they require an extralinguistic indication of a referent. For example, the propredicate *do it,* and "pro-propositional" *it* generally, may have an extralinguistic situational referent, while the propredicate 0 (as in 31b, 32b) requires a linguistic antecedent. Evidence for this claim comes from the fact that the examples in (35), with *it,* would be comprehensible in a situation where speaker and addressee are watching a silent street performer prepar-ing to juggle a telephone, a stapler, a frisbee, a pearl necklace, and a paperback book, while those in (36), with only the gap, would be puzzlingly inappropriate in the same context.

35a. I don't think he can do it.
35b. It'll never work.
36a. I don't think he can.
36b. He won't be able to.

Either of the sentences in (36) would be perfectly OK if one of the conversants (or even the juggler) had provided a linguistic antecedent (e.g., by saying, "I wonder if he'll be able to manage all those things, when they have such different physical properties"). Hankamer and Sag (1976), using *anaphora* in a broader sense than the one adopted here, have referred to this sort of interpretation as deictic or pragmatically controlled anaphora. They show that intersentential anaphora (as in (22) and even (33)) is generally linguistically, not pragmatically, controlled.

6. SUMMARY

This chapter addressed the pragmatic aspect of language as represented by indexical expressions. Some of the semantics literature has implied that the use of indexicals is all there is to pragmatics, and has been interpreted as implying that the use of indexicals involves a small set of terms, and a fairly trivial mapping from the spatiotemporal context of an utterance to a (possibly unique) interpretation for each. We have seen that even in 1954, Bar-Hillel realized there was far more to the interpretation of indexicals than a simple algorithm, and that even the interpretation of indexical expressions like *here* and *you* requires an estimate of the speaker's beliefs and intentions at the time of the utterance.

We went on to examine a selection of the wide range of anaphoric devices that languages provide for speakers to use to refer to entities that are deictically indicated or that have been referred to or otherwise indicated in preceding discourse. In all cases, their use could be vague or ambiguous, resolvable only to the extent that the speaker's intention could be reconstructed. Thus, the set of indexical expressions is not small, and the interpretation of indexical expressions requires, in all but the most fully specified contexts, a means of estimating speakers intentions and beliefs about the world, including the whole Gricean regression referred to in section 6 of chapter 1.

The interpretation of indexicals (both deictic and anaphoric) inescapably involves inferences about the speaker's intended referent. The language provides some constraints on possible antecedents, the linguistic context provides potential antecedents for anaphoric expressions, and the discourse context provides potential antecedents for deictic expressions, but ultimately, it is guesses about what the speaker intended the addressee to assume or infer that determine what a form or expression will be taken to refer to.

3 Reference and Indeterminacy of Sense

In the last chapter, in discussing the reference of indexical and anaphoric expressions, it was taken for granted that the reader would understand what was meant by saying that some form referred (or was used to refer) to a certain entity. It was enough to understand the term *reference* as indicating the means by which a speaker utters a linguistic expression in the expectation that it will enable his addressee to infer correctly what entity, property, relation, event, or the like he is talking about. Now it is time to examine that notion more critically, and to observe the extent to which the pragmatic indeterminacies inherent in it pervade the ordinary use of language.

The modern consideration of the central problem, how one knows what is meant[1] by a referring expression, dates back to the nineteenth century as a philosophical issue.[2] Let us take REFERRING EXPRESSION to refer to whatever kinds of expressions can be used to refer, with REFER understood as in the previous paragraph. In the initial discussions among philosophers (e.g., Frege, 1952; Mill, 1843; Russell, 1905), the class of referring expressions analyzed was usually the set of PROPER NAMES (e.g., *Socrates*) and definite descriptions (e.g., *the author of Waverly*); later on, common nouns referring to natural kinds (e.g., *water, gold*) were added (cf. Kripke 1972; Putnam, 1965, 1970, 1973, 1975a, 1975b). I suggest later that an adequate analysis of these extends to many other kinds of expressions as well, including artifact names, adjectives, verbs, prepositions, and adverbs.

1. SENSE AND REFERENCE

Frege (1952) is generally credited with establishing the necessity of distinguishing between the REFERENCE of an expression, "that to which the

---

[1]This formulation of the question fails to indicate whether it is the speaker or the linguistic expression that is supposed (i.e., believed) to do the referring. This is a serious omission, but typical of many discussions. Many modern logicians (and linguists) write as if linguistic expressions refer even when considered outside the context of any utterance. Others, myself included, treat referring as something that speakers do, often by using linguistic expressions, but occasionally with gestures, vocal or otherwise (cf. Linsky 1966, Green 1984).

[2]Here, as elsewhere, discussion is framed within the boundaries of contemporary questions. Some of the issues touched upon have a history dating back to the Middle Ages, or even to Antiquity, but limitations of space preclude extensive historical discussion here.

sign refers" (p. 116), and its SENSE, an interpretation of the sign, provided by the grammar of the language, "wherein the mode of presentation is contained" (Frege, 1952, p. 116). (The terms EXTENSION, Carnap, 1947; DENOMINATION, and DENOTATION, Mill, 1843) are used by other writers for Frege's *reference,* and the term INTENSION, Carnap, 1947 or CONNOTATION[3], Mill, 1843, for *sense.*) Thus, to use one of Frege's examples, the noun phrase *the Morning Star* would have a sense paraphrasable as 'the star that is seen in the morning,' but its referent would be the planet Venus. The noun phrase *the present king of France* has a clear sense even in 1986, but no reference.

There is some dispute over whether names like *Aristotle* or *George Washington* have sense as well as reference, with Frege and many followers claiming that they do have a sense, namely that of the description of their referent (e.g., 'the teacher of Alexander the Great, the well-known Greek philosopher born in Stagira . . .'; 'the first president of the United States'), which, it was asserted, they "stood for."[4] Others, (e.g., Kripke and Putnam) maintain that proper names and nouns denoting kinds do not, properly speaking, have senses at all, but indicate their referent directly (and arbitrarily), without the mediation of interpreting the sense of the name. According to this CAUSAL THEORY of names, names do not "mean" anything; they are just labels for individuals, given at some more or less remote point in history, and passed on in the course of normal cultural transmission ("That stuff is called *water*"; "I am going to tell you about a great philosopher. His name was Aristotle. He lived . . .").

That is, according to this theory, *Aristotle* can be used to refer to Aristotle because the actual fourth century B.C. philosopher who Mr. Bagnoli told me was (called) Aristotle [on the grounds that his teacher Miss Jones had told him that that man was (called) Aristotle] is the same man as the man your teacher(s) told you was Aristotle. These chains of transmission, ultimately leading back to an assumed initial "dubbing" are called CAUSAL or HISTORICAL CHAINS. Thus, the causal chain via which such names

---

[3]Mill's uses of *denotation* and *connotation* do not correspond to their current ordinary uses. Mill used *connotation* to refer to the "meaning" of a term, the means by which it referred to its denotation (a thing in the real world). This chapter deals with ordinary-language "denotation", or "meaning", as well as reference. Ordinary-language "connotation" will be touched on in Chapter 4.

[4] It is undeniable that some names (e.g. Johnson, Green) are morphologically analyzable; *Johnson* is analyzable as *John's son, Green* is in some sense related to the color name. However, any meaning that the morphemes in a proper name may have in other contexts is irrelevant to the concerns of compositional semantics: defining the conditions under which a sentence may be said to be true of a situation. A sentence like (i) will be true just in case some one identified as "Johnson" did something that can be described as speaking, regardless of whether or not that person happens to be the son of anyone named John.

i. Johnson spoke.

designate their referents involves deixis or ostension (pointing to the intended referent) or anaphora, and therefore indexicality, ultimately. The causal (historical) connection is that kinds and individuals are called what they are called because somewhere, sometime, someone called them that, and it stuck. Who, or when, or where makes no difference. All that is required is that there be a continuous chain, and this requirement is really no more than the claim that language is a social, cooperative institution. As Kripke (1972) said: "the way the reference of a name is fixed is of little importance; what matters is that there be a chain, and that for each name, speakers understand the same referent" (p. 331).

2. SOME OTHER DISTINCTIONS

Donnellan (1966) showed that definite descriptions like (1) can be used to talk about something in two quite distinct ways, referentially and attributively.

1a.   the 1984 Democratic presidential nominee
1b.   the man with the martini

On the REFERENTIAL use, the noun phrase is used to refer to a particular person whom the speaker chooses to describe this particular way, even though countless other ways, including perhaps a proper name, may be available and equally likely to succeed in enabling the addressee to know who is being referred to. An individual referentially indicated will have been previously indicated, independently of the referential expression now being used. The ATTRIBUTIVE use is equivalent to 'whoever fits this description' (i.e., in the case of the expressions in (1) 'whoever the Democratic Party nominated for president in 1984' and 'whoever that is with the martini'). In the attributive use, what is referred to depends strictly on the description, and it may be that no alternative description is available to the speaker. If (1a) was uttered prior to the spring of 1984, it would have to be intended to refer attributively, because no one knew who the Democratic nominee would be. After the Democratic national convention, it would have been used referentially by anyone who knew (and believed that her addressee knew, etc.), but it might have been used attributively by someone who forgot, or was so out of touch that he didn't know who had been nominated. (Someone who knew that it was Mondale, but couldn't remember Mondale's name, would be using (1a) referentially, however, if they meant to refer to Mondale).

Because referential uses are independent from the actual identity of the intended referent, a referential use may involve a (mistaken) description that is false of its intended referent, or is in fact true of no one. Even in such a case, it may still serve to pick out that intended referent. If you and I are in a crowd where only one man is holding a stemmed glass, and I refer to him with (1b), you may be able to tell who I am referring to even if the drink he is holding is not a martini, but rather a Shirley Temple or some other drink, and even if you know that it is no martini in his glass. But if an attributive use involves a mistaken description, it will refer to no one, or be taken to refer to a referent not intended by the speaker. Suppose a detective is instructed that his suspect drinks martinis, and tells his operative to go to a certain restaurant and "shadow the man with the martini." If no one in the restaurant has a martini, then even if the suspect is there, there will be no one whom he has been told to shadow. If someone other than the suspect has the only martini, the operative will be shadowing someone not intended by his employer when he used (1b) to describe the suspect. In many cases, a noun phrase may be used either attributively or referentially in a given context, and successfully refer to the same entity, although the two uses may be intended and understood in different ways. Whether this difference is semantic or pragmatic (and if semantic, how it should be represented) is still a matter of some controversy. See Russell (1905), Quine (1953, 1956, 1960), McCawley (1971b), Keenan (1972), Montague (1974), Cole (1978), Kaplan (1978), and Over (1985) for some proposals.

Kripke (1972) distinguished between RIGID DESIGNATORS (referring expressions with a single descriptional sense) which would pick out the same referent in all possible worlds in which that referent existed (like *the Pope,* or *the president of the United States*), and NON-RIGID designators, that pick out different individuals in different worlds. Before continuing with the discussion of how reference is accomplished, it is necessary to clarify what is meant here by "different worlds."

There is a large philosophical literature on the logic and semantics of POSSIBLE WORLDS (cf. Kripke, 1959; Lewis, 1968 — McCawley, 1981 provides a good overview), including some critical of the notion (v.g., Copi & Gould, 1967, Scott, 1970), although it is by now so standard a notion among logicians that references are not made to its origin. For our purposes, it is enough to understand that a possible world is not a place, but a possible way the world could be, or could have been. There are an infinite number of possible worlds. For example, there are possible worlds exactly like the real world, except that the Panama Canal had never been dug, or the United States in 1950 had a population of 50 million, or I had red hair, and so on.

There are many linguistic expressions and constructions which are used to define worlds other than the real world, or at least to indicate that reference is being made to such a world. Among these are conditional clauses, both indefinite as in (A), and counterfactual as in (B), clauses with modal auxiliary verbs, as in (B) and (C), complements of certain "world-creating" terms (words whose sentential objects describe possible states of affairs which need not correspond to what the speaker believes is true in the real world) as in (D), clauses introduced by adverbs indicating potentiality as in (E), and no doubt many others.

A1. If it rains tomorrow, that will be 25 days of rain in one month.

A2. If Dylan has finished his homework, he may watch TV.

A3. If that book is where it belongs, it's in the middle of the third shelf from the top.

B. If number 10 hadn't fouled out, the Wildcats might/could have won the game.

C. The Cubs might/could/may/will win the pennant next year.

D1. I dreamed/imagined I discovered three new rooms in my house.

D2. Alice wondered whether pigs knew how to fly.

D3. Suppose you're on a desert island.

E. Perhaps/Maybe there is life on Mars.

Expressions like *the Pope* and *Miss America* are non-rigid designators, because who they refer to depends on what world (or "context") is being discussed. In (2a), *the Pope* refers to Pius XII[5]; in (2b), to John-Paul II. Similarly, the two occurrences of *the King* in (2c) refer to two different kings.

2a. Before 1945, the Pope had discussed the situation of European Jews with many world leaders.

2b. The Pope survived an assassination attempt shortly after his election in 1978.

2c. The King is dead. Long live the King!

Proper names are rigid designators, however. The name *John Stuart Mill* refers to the 19th century British philosopher and political economist, no matter what sort of context is indicated[6] (e.g., in all of the examples of (3)).

3a. John Stuart Mill published several important books before Karl Marx was born.

3b. John Stuart Mill must be turning over in his grave.

3c. If John Stuart Mill were alive, this would amuse him.

---

[5]With no other context, anyway. It could be taken to refer (referentially) to any individual who was pope prior or subsequent to 1945 (including whoever is pope at the time of uttering (2a), if that individual was established as a topic of the discourse in which (2a) occurs, and was (mutually believed to be) old enough to talk before 1945.

[6]Except, of course, where it is intended and understood to refer to another individual with the same name, in which case it refers exclusively to the latter; its reference still does not change according to what possible world is intended in the context of its utterance.

3d.   If John Stuart Mill had been drafted to go to Vietnam, he would
never have written *A System of Logic.*

Note however, that although a name like *Joe* will (be used to) refer to
different individuals on different occasions of use, that does not make it a
non-rigid designator. Rather, since there are many individuals who have
been named or dubbed *Joe,* on each occasion of use, *Joe* is a rigid
designator whose successful use to refer depends on speaker and addressee
taking it to be a name of the same individual.

Rigid/non-rigid and referential/attributive are similar distinctions in
some ways, but they are not the same. A non-rigid designator such as *the
Pope* or *the tallest man in Ohio* can be referential as in (4) or attributive as
in the most likely interpretation of the sentences in (5).

4a.   The Pope visited India in 1986.
4b.   The tallest man in Ohio came to the ball game.
5a.   If you have an audience with the Pope, you must kiss his ring.
5b.   Since 1805, the tallest man in Ohio has been allowed to live in the
house rent-free.

3. MODERN TREATMENTS

In most modern semantic theories, including various intensional logics (cf.
Dowty et al., 1981, for further discussion of this term), the sense of an
expression is supposed to determine its reference, and the goal of the
intensional logic that makes explicit the mechanism by which this can
happen is to determine the possible sorts of functions from possible INDICES
(coordinations of worlds, times, speakers, etc.), to their EXTENSIONS or
DENOTATIONS (the entities or sets of entities denoted by an expression at an
index). These functions are taken to represent the senses of linguistic
expressions in such a way that the meaning of a composite expression is a
function of the meanings of its parts. This sounds very complicated, and it
is, but more by involving long sequences of operations than by being
conceptually difficult. Dowty et al. (1981) provides an excellent introduction. The point is that it is a fundamental assumption that linguistic
expressions indicate (denote) extensions in the real world, and they do this
compositionally, with one subpart of the intension extending or delimiting
the extension indicated by another. For example, in Montague semantics
(cf. Dowty et al., 1981; Montague, 1970, 1973, for an introduction), a name
like *Aristotle* is treated as if it denoted the (infinite) set of Aristotle's
properties, whatever they may be; a definite description like *the gray
sweater* gets an analysis paraphrasable as 'the unique thing which is gray

and is a sweater' (and essentially equivalent to the one Russell proposed). Common nouns (and adjectives and intransitive verbs) are taken to have extensions equivalent to sets of individual concepts, while their intensions are properties. Thus, the intension of *sweater* is paraphrasable as 'the property that makes something a sweater' and the intension of *gray* is paraphrasable as 'the property necessarily shared by gray things.'

Kripke and Putnam provide a view of the way common nouns refer that avoids reference to properties. According to the causal theory of names, names are just names; they are not abbreviations for descriptions, and they do not "mean" anything, not even 'the man called Aristotle' (or whatever). Giving someone or something a name, or transmitting that name does not define a meaning for the name, but simply fixes or determines its reference. Both Kripke and Putnam extend this analysis to the names of natural kinds (e.g., water, gold, tigers, horses, beeches, elms, lemons, etc.). Thus, in this analysis, *water* does not "mean" H_2O; it is the name of some stuff which happens to be a liquid at temperatures between $32°F$ and $212°F$, chemically analyzable as containing two parts hydrogen and one part oxygen, and so on. And *horse* is the name of a certain sort of animal, just as *Aristotle* and *Jimmy Carter* are the names of certain individual men. *Horse* does not mean a large, short-haired, vegetarian quadruped with solid hooves and flowing mane and tail, used for drawing or carrying loads, and so on, even though horses generally have those properties.

In this view of things, it is important not to confuse the analysis of the name of a kind such as *fish* or *water,* with analysis of the kind itself, or with people's knowledge, beliefs, or understandings about that kind. The first is part of the study of language (specifically, semantics or pragmatics); the second belongs to biology, chemistry, mechanical engineering, or whatever; and the last is part of cognitive psychology (cf. Rosch & Mervis, 1975; Smith & Medin, 1981) or anthropology (Conklin, 1972). It is as nonsensical to do a semantic analysis of the word *horse* as it would be to do one of *Fred* or *Panasonic,* even though inferences, including inferences of relations among sets referred to, may be derivable from the USE of the term, for the inferences are about the sets, not about the words. I cannot emphasize this point enough; most of the enormous literature on semantic memory by psychologists (e.g., Collins & Loftus, 1975; Collins & Quillian, 1972; Meyer, 1970; Smith, Shoben, & Rips, 1974; Tulving, 1972) is really not about words but about the kinds which words name.

Saying that common nouns like *water* or *lemon* are literally names for kinds of things implies that they are semantically unanalyzable although the concepts of kinds of things which they designate may be analyzable to some degree. Just because a concept is analyzable, it does not follow that its name is analyzable. It is, I think, uncontroversial that we categorize the world, and classify objects into kinds. That is how we know that Fido and Sam and

Skipper and indeed, poodles, and huskies and mongrels generally, are all dogs. However, it does not follow from our ability to do this that in doing so we assume each entity or type of entity to be of only one kind. Our classifications may be, as in the example just given, hierarchical, but they may also (instead, or in addition) cut across each other: Running is a kind of exercise, a kind of sport, and a kind of locomotion. A particular species of bird may be a kind of shore bird, a kind of sexually dimorphic bird, and a kind of migratory bird. In both cases, the categories which subsume the activity or object mentioned are neither proper subsets of each other, nor mutually exclusive with each other.

It also happens that the same word may be used to refer to quite diverse kinds, even ignoring metaphorical uses, just as different individuals may have the same personal names. Thus, *plant* is the name of a large category of organisms, of a kind of building, and of a kind of activity involving seeds and an intention that they grow. *Bank* is the name of a kind of financial institution, of a part of a river or creek bed, and of a kind of maneuver involving causing a projectile to ricochet off a fixed surface toward a target.

Of course, our classifications are not exhaustive, either; we may encounter an object and not know what sort of thing it is (e.g., a westerner encountering tofu or peastarch noodles for the first time). We might be unable to classify the novel object because we do not know what its characteristics are; this is an empirical question, and is, in principle at least, easily resolved. On the other hand, we may know what its properties are, but still not know if it is a member of a kind we have previous knowledge of, or perhaps, of a novel kind.

Thus, just as any interpreter of a discourse has to make a calculated guess about what is intended by the use of indexical terms, he or she must guess at what kinds were intended by the utterance of various lexical referring expressions. It is clear enough that this sort of guessing is required to interpret anaphoric terms like *he,* a little less obvious with proper names like *Bob,* but it is equally required with kind names in definite and indefinite noun phrases such as *the ham sandwich* or *an elm.* Despite this, communication through language succeeds to a satisfactory extent, and it succeeds to the extent that it does because language use is a social and cultural phenomenon. It is in the best interests of the members of a linguistic community to act as if there were a social contract, and to assume more or less standard references for standard words in the language, even though strictly speaking, it is impossible for there to be standard references for standard words because what a word is used to refer to depends on what the speaker intends it to be taken to be intended to refer to, and it is impossible to know what is in another person's mind, and know what he or she uses, say, *drug,* to refer to. We return to this issue in the next section.

There is no reason not to extend the analysis of natural kind words to nonnatural kinds (artifacts) such as pencil, table, clock, robot, plastic, corduroy, and the like; and to what Putnam (1962) called physical magnitudes: heat, kinetic energy, straight line; and even to what might be called social magnitudes: democracy, prayer, aggression. Indeed, Putnam suggested that artifact names, and at least some verbs (e.g., *grow*) and adjectives (*red*) refer as rigid designators, connected to their referent by some causal/historical chain, and Kripke suggested the same for at least the adjectives that correspond to natural kinds or phenomena (e.g., *hot, wet*). In fact, a case can be made (cf. Green, 1984) for treating names for kinds of activities (e.g., running, basting[7], drinking, cramming), states (intending, jealousy, cleanliness), properties (tall, dark, handsome), and situations (giving, growing) as rigidly designating the kind of activity, state, property, and so forth that they refer to.

Not all referring expressions refer by virtue of being names for their referents. Some (e.g., *orphan, weed*) refer by (implicitly) describing their referents. And there are other sorts of words which are not used to refer at all, and so are logically neither names nor descriptions: *and, all; ouch, damn, hello* (cf. Green, 1984, for discussion).

If we adopt the view that in general descriptive terms are rigidly designating names for kinds, we can say[8] that a use of the expression *the gray sweater* indicates a thing of the sort called *sweater* which has the (color) property of the sort called *gray*. How about *the*? Is it the name of some kind also, maybe the property of being unique? Probably not; at least, nobody appears to have advanced this position. As previously hinted at, Russell (1905) and subsequently many other logicians have treated it as an operator which asserts the existence of a unique individual with the properties indicated by the other components of the noun phrase it introduces. The problems with this analysis are that (a) uniqueness is relative, and (b) so is existence. The first problem is demonstrated by an infinite number of ordinary sentences like (6).

6a.   If you don't hang your coat up, *the* cat will make a puddle in it.

6b.   Water *the* plants before you go out, please.

6c.   *The* mailman thinks that those five mailmen are throwing mail in the lake.[9]

One can use (6a) without assuming that there is only one cat in the universe, and (6b) is not an order to water all the plants in the universe. If *the*

---

[7]Whether in sewing or in cooking.

[8]Probably assuming some more or less elaborated form of predicate calculus, with the property designated by *gray* being a function applied to the kind represented by *sweater*.

[9]Example like this attributed by Morgan (1975a) to J.D. McCawley.

involved an assertion of uniqueness, (6c) would contain a contradiction, but it does not. The cat, the plants, and the mailman are not assumed by speaker or addressee to be unique (cf. also Kantor et al., 1982, p. 262).

The second problem is illustrated by sentences like (7), where the speaker and the addressee do not have to suppose that there are unicorns, or that a northwest passage was discovered.

7a.   *The* unicorn is a mythical beast.
7b.   *The* unicorn does not exist.[10]
7c.   *The* discovery of a northwest passage to the Pacific was the goal of many early explorers.

In fact, as (8) shows, the supposition of existence may be explicitly suspended.

8.   Place *the* remaining stitches, if any, on a stitch holder.

In light of these difficulties (and others; cf. Morgan, 1975a), a more attractive analysis, suggested by Strawson (1950) and again by Morgan (1975a) (cf. also Kamp, 1981 and Heim, 1982), is that *the* is neither a name nor a semantic function or operator, but merely a linguistic sign prefixable to the beginning of noun phrases, which a speaker uses to indicate that she has a definite referent in mind that she expects the addressee to be able to identify from whatever clues are available.[11] This is what makes it possible to understand sentences like (6) correctly in context. Out of context, of course, where the interpreter has no way of knowing what cat, plants, or mailman may be intended, such sentences cannot be fully understood, in that the interpreter cannot correctly infer exactly when they would be true.

---

[10]It might be thought that examples like (i) also illustrate the absence of an existence claim inherent in the use of the definite article.

i.   The cat didn't make that mess; we don't have a cat.

However, it is the phenomenon of contradiction that makes (i) acceptable; *the cat* here quotes a previous utterance where the existence of a cat was taken for granted. See Horn 1985 for full discussion of this phenomenon and its consequences for semantic theory.

The analysis of definite noun phrases in "intensional" or "referentially opaque contexts" (cf. Dowty, Wall, and Peters 1981:143ff for discussion of this notion) like (ii) where a possible world is invoked which may be different from what the speaker believes to be the real world presents a major problem for contemporary logic and semantic theory (cf. e.g., Quine 1960, Montague 1970, Kaplan 1977, Stalnaker 1978).

ii.   The unicorn Dana is looking for is supposed to have golden hooves.

[11]This might be an individual, as in *the gray sweater,* or a species as in (7a). Cf. Nunberg & Pan, 1975, and Carlson, 1978, for discussions of the treatment of generic noun phrases.

The has the pragmatic function of aiding the addressee in inferring the speaker's intended referent, but no semantic function in fixing or delimiting truth conditions. The role of *the* in enabling an interpreter to infer the intended referent is actually quite small compared to the extent to which it is necessary to rely on the interpreter's ability to utilize assumptions about the topic and context of the discourse. Thus, even in a context where, out of the millions of cats presumed to exist, there are two which are equally familiar to speaker and addressee, sentence (6a) could be successfully used to refer to a unique cat, if only one of the two cats has an acknowledged reputation for making puddles in inappropriate places.

4. REFERRING FUNCTIONS: GETTING FROM KINDS TO REFERENTS

The question is not what the writer meant, but what he conveyed to those who heard or read." (Gatley, *Libel and Slander,* quoted in Frederick Philbrick, *Language and the Law* (New York: Macmillan, 1949), p. 29.)

So far, I have suggested that the mechanism by which referring expressions enable an interpreter to infer an intended referent is not strictly semantic or truth-conditional, but involves the cooperative exploitation of supposed mutual knowledge: The speaker must suppose that the addressee knows some proposition P and assumes that the speaker knows that the addressee not only knows P but will use that information in inferring the intended referent. Since there are many more kinds (an infinite number, actually) than kind names, sometimes a kind name is used as the name of more than one kind, as was mentioned in the previous section. In fact, this situation arises much more often than it comes to our conscious attention, and exponentially compounds the number of potential inferences that an interpreter might make. But by considering it at more length, we can see in more detail how that inferencing mechanism might work.

We noted above the ambiguity of *bank*. The usual lexicographic analysis of this ambiguity is that *bank* is HOMONYMOUS, that is, that there are separate words, with distinct meanings and origins, which coincidentally have the same pronunciation, [bæŋk]. But not all words that can be used to refer to two or more kinds of referents are treated as homonyms. For example, lexicographers treat the two uses of *chicken* in (9) as two senses of a single POLYSEMOUS word (a word with more than one sense).

9a.　The chicken ate the grubs, and also the lettuce seedlings.
9b.　I had chicken for dinner yesterday.

The difference between polysemy and homonymy appears to be psychologically real, but it is clear that in the vast middle ground, speakers may differ on whether two senses of some phonologically unique form are senses of the same polysemous word, or two different homonymous words. For some people, the 'novel' sense of *original* may be unrelated to the 'initial' sense, but to others, the relationship may be clear. The relation between *cheap* 'inexpensive' and *cheap* 'tawdry' may be obvious to many people, but come as a revelation to others. Generally, whenever one sense can be taken or reconstructed as a metaphorical extension of another (cf. Chapter 5.4 below), the two senses are polysemously related, although it is possible for relationships that are originally clear to become obscure over time, and senses that were once polysemously related may become grammaticized as senses of homonymous words (cf. Morgan, 1978).

The distinction is syntactically real as well, in that in constructions which presuppose linguistic identity[12] (cf. Chapter 2, Sec. 5), homophones like *pear* or *pair,* and homonyms like *bank* and *bank* exhibit different syntactic behavior from distinct senses of polysemous items. In particular, syntactic constructions such as relative clauses and pronominalization treat different senses of polysemous items (as in (10)) as being the same, homonyms (as in (11)) as different. Thus, in (10a), it is a container that is to be picked up, but its contents that must be deposited in the pitcher, and in (10b) what Jan is reading is a copy of an issue of a newspaper, but it was the corporation that publishes the newspaper that nearly went bankrupt. But if we can interpret (11a) at all, we do not understand that land is eroding and a financial institution is closed on Saturday. Rather, if we can make any sense of it, we must understand either that a financial institution is (in some sense) eroding, and closed on Saturday, or that some land is eroding, and (in some sense) closed on Saturday. Similarly, we do not understand (11b) to be about both a leather carrying container and a set of legal arguments. To make sense of it, we have to understand it to be about either a container or (less plausibly) a set of arguments.

10a. Pick up the glass, and pour it into the pitcher.
10b. The newspaper Jan's reading almost went bankrupt in 1983.
11a. Dana's bank is eroding, but it is closed on Saturday.
11b. The lawyer's case(,) which was made of genuine leather(,) suffered from logical flaws.

Many ordinary nouns have the property of being usable to refer to quite

---

[12]The identity is not identity of intended reference, for if it were, the uses of *newspaper* and *chicken* in (10b) could not count as identical, nor is it identity of form, for then *bank* and *bank* would have to count as identical in (11a), and (11a) would have to be acceptable, which it isn't.

a variety of distinct kinds of referents, as illustrated with the noun *newspaper* in (12).

12a. The newspaper raised the price per inch for its classified advertising.
12b. The newspaper fell from my lap.
12c. "Dear Abby" isn't in that newspaper on Saturdays anymore.
12d. The printers' union wants to buy that newspaper.
12e. That newspaper has always supported a Republican candidate for president.

In fact, most ordinary common nouns, and even many proper nouns have a multiplicity of senses of this sort.

13a. Pour a glass of water into the pitcher.
13b. Put a glass of water on the picture.
13c. Put a glass of water in the picture.
13d. France protested the investigation.
13e. France is hexagonal.

Does this mean that all of these words (and names!) are polysemous? If nouns like *glass* and *newspaper* are names, and names do not have senses, then there is no difference between polysemy and homonymy. We would have to say that there are as many different words *glass,* as there are kinds which that word is used to name. If names do have senses, we would have to say that there are that many distinct senses. There are two problems with this conclusion.

First of all, there IS a difference between polysemy and homonymy. As illustrated above, there are demonstrable differences in the syntactic behavior of homonyms and the senses of polysemous terms.

Second, it is possible to show that virtually every noun is polysemous (indeed, virtually every verb, adjective and preposition as well), and possibly infinitely so. If every distinct sort of use is a distinct sense that has to be learned, there is no way to account for our ability to understand sorts of uses we have never encountered before. Thus, almost all nouns taken to refer to concrete objects can be used to refer to particular individual objects as in (14a), or to the TYPES of which such individual objects are exemplars (or TOKENS), as in (14b).

14a. Dana bought a convertible.
14b. In the fall, GM will market a convertible for the first time since 1970.

Many nouns have several less universal sorts of senses as well (cf. Nunberg, 1978, chapter 2). Nominalizations like *manufacture, nomination, opposition, construction, approval, election,* and other abstract nouns (*committee, culture, adventure*) are multiply polysemous, as evidenced by their behavior with relative clauses and pronouns; they can refer to, among other things:

- the fact that something has been done, or is a certain way, as in (15a),
- the extent to which something has been done, or is a certain way, as in (15b),
- whether or not something happens, as in (15c),
- the act of doing something, as in (15d),
- the product of some action, as in (15e),
- the way something was done, as in (15f).

15a. $\left\{\begin{array}{l}\text{The construction of the building} \\ \text{(which took ten weeks)} \\ \text{His opposition (which was vehement)} \\ \text{His presence} \\ \text{His nomination}\end{array}\right\}$ meant that the bill would never pass.

15b. $\left\{\begin{array}{l}\text{The inadequacy of the report} \\ \text{The opposition to the report} \\ \text{The court's construal of the law} \\ \text{The construction in Kuwait}\end{array}\right\}$ surprised the senators.

15c. $\left\{\begin{array}{l}\text{The nomination of Sen. Leffingwell} \\ \text{The approval of the bill}\end{array}\right\}$ depends on there being a quorum.

15d. $\left\{\begin{array}{l}\text{The nomination of Sen. Leffingwell} \\ \text{The construction of the building}\end{array}\right\}$ took four days.

15e. $\left\{\begin{array}{l}\text{Dana's construction} \\ \text{Dale's cooking}\end{array}\right\}$ won awards from international organizations.

15f. $\left\{\begin{array}{l}\text{The construction of the building} \\ \text{The 1986 elections}\end{array}\right\}$ shocked the investigators.

The same sort of evidence shows that even proper names are extensively polysemous. *Shakespeare* is the name of a man, but in (16a) it refers to his works, and then to the man himself, and in (16b) it refers to books containing those works. *Chicago* is the name of a city, but in (16c) it refers

to an athletic team. *Xerox* is the name of a corporation, but in (16d) it refers
to shares of stock in that corporation (cf. Borkin, 1972).

16a. Shakespeare can be difficult for eighth graders to read, although
     he didn't use difficult words.
16b. Shakespeare takes up five feet of Dale's bookshelves.
16c. Chicago beat Dallas, 44–0.
16d. I bought Xerox at 49.

Furthermore, in context, just about any noun can be used to refer to just
about any sort of thing. A waitress might identify a customer as what he has
ordered (giving new meaning to the observation that you are what you eat),
as in (17a); a member of a woodwind ensemble might identify another
member by her instrument, as in (17b); a detergent might be identified in a
TV commercial by the garment it is being used to remove soil from, as in
(17c).

17a. The ham sandwich wants a side order of fries.
17b. The clarinet had to go to the powder room.
17c. Now, the T-shirt is fortified with enzymes, and the apron has
     phosphates.

The potential uses of this sort are infinite. There is no limit to the kinds of
uses (or PSENSES, to use a term Nunberg (1978, p. 6) coined to avoid
confusion with the technical use of *sense* in formal semantics) that a noun
like *ham sandwich* or *newspaper* can have; if each kind of use was a distinct
meaning, then *ham sandwich* could "mean" 'person who ordered a ham
sandwich,' or 'person who ate a ham sandwich,' or 'person who said he
hated ham sandwiches,' or 'person who knocked my ham sandwich to the
floor,' and so on, and proper names would be equally ambiguous.

Thus, the multiplicity of kinds of uses a term may have is extensive and
pervasive. Since human memory is finite, all of these "senses" cannot be
stored as part of the mental representation of linguistic knowledge. There
must be some general principles that people use to interpret such terms in
referring expressions. Without a pragmatic theory of how terms are used to
refer, there is no hope of accounting for cases like (17). With such a theory,
cases like (14–16) can be explained as well, without hypothesizing massive
homonymy or polysemy. The rest of this section, therefore, describes the
pragmatic theory of reference developed by Nunberg (1978) to explain how
uses of terms, even apparently novel ones like (17), are readily understood
according to general, independently needed principles.

Nunberg argued that (a) in general there are no basic or standard psenses
for referring terms (although there are psenses which speakers in particular

subcultures take to be normal in some kinds of contexts), and that (b) successful reference is possible because our linguistic competence includes the ability to derive additional psenses from a given psense using a fairly small number of recursively combinable functions. He showed that deictic indexicals like those in (18) have much the same range of reference as descriptive terms designating the same intended referents.[13]

18a. *That* tastes good. [pointing to a picture of a grilled tomato]
18b. Hearst bought *that* for $3.5 million. [indicating a copy of a newspaper]

This means that the particular intended psense cannot inhere in the individual terms *ham sandwich* and *newspaper,* any more than it can inhere in a pronoun like *he.* Nunberg proposed that speakers make use of REFERRING FUNCTIONS which relate one psense of an expression to another. These are to be understood as functions in the mathematical sense, from psenses (kinds of uses) to other psenses. Thus, in (10a), the two uses of *glass* are related by the function 'contents of' (or 'container of'), and in (10b), the two uses of *newspaper* are related by the function 'publisher of' (or 'product of'). Nunberg suggested that speakers have the ability to relate objects by means of such functions as 'type of' (e.g., (14b), 'cause of,' 'possessor of,' 'location of,' and the like, plus the trivial combinatorial ability to recursively construct an infinite number of composites of these functions, such as 'location of possessor of' (as in (16c)), or 'cause of type of,' and so on. From this perspective, the problem of reference is to determine which of the vast number of potential referring functions relate what is indicated (some object, or some basic concept[14]) to what is intended as the referent of one's remarks. Nunberg described several principles which

---

[13]Nunberg has pointed out (personal communication) that deictic pronouns in sentences like (18) are selected on the basis of properties of the intended referent, not the indicated object. Thus *He* (not *That*) is used in (i) to refer to a customer, and *That* in (ii) refers to a phenomenon (e.g. a sound) or the event which produced it, as shown by the fact that a sentence like (iii) would not be possible in the same situation.

  i. He wants more coffee. [indicating a ham sandwich]
  ii. That must be my piano teacher. [indicating a ringing doorbell]
  iii. That taught me piano.

Notice also that, used in the same situation as (i), (iv) would seem to imply an inanimate customer, or impute to the bread and meat, a desire for more coffee.

  iv. That wants more coffee.

Thus the function relating the demonstratum and the intended referent is not strictly an identity function.

[14]This is an oversimplification in that Nunberg argues that the assumption of basic senses is unjustifiable. See page 54 below.

speakers must use to narrow down the set of referring functions that might be relied upon in a given situation.

First, the demonstratum (whatever is pointed to) must be what it appears to be, and appear to be what it is. You cannot point at candy made to look like a newspaper and expect it to be recognized as candy. The addressee has to know that it is candy, and know that he is expected to know, and so on. This holds even for the identity function (i.e., when the speaker points at an object to refer to that object, rather than something it evokes). Second, the addressee has to be assumed (etc.) to know that there are values of the candidate referring function in the set to which the intended referent belongs. If I point to a ham sandwich and say, "He's a conservative, invoking the referring function 'orderer of,' I have to believe that you believe (etc.) that the set of all ham-sandwich-orderers includes some individual male human beings.

Third, it has to be possible to distinguish the demonstratum from other things like it for which the candidate referring function has different values. Borrowing Nunberg's example, automobiles manufactured in different years are sometimes distinguishable enough to allow a speaker to point to a car and use it to indicate a date, as in (19a), but cars of the same make, model, and year are pretty much indistinguishable, so I could not point to a 1975 Chevy Nova and expect you to use the referring function 'location of manufacture' to derive the city I intended in an accompanying utterance like (19b).

19a. I was in Germany then.
19b. We visited some lovely parks there.

Fourth, when the demonstratum could be the referent, it must be. I cannot expect to be understood to be talking about someone who ordered a ham sandwich when I say either of the sentences in (20), if it is plausible for me to be intending to refer to the sandwich itself.

20a. The ham sandwich fell on the floor.
20b. The ham sandwich needs mustard.

This may be what accounts for the fact that when one reads the following passage, it is difficult not to understand *the little blue flowers called faeries'-eyes scattered across the coverlet* as a reference to embroidered decoration on the coverlet, using the common referring function 'image of' (the one that relates, for example, real dogs to drawings, photographs, statuettes, manufactured miniatures of dogs, and stuffed toy dogs) to interpret *flowers*. The passage, from a modern fairy tale, occurs at the point where a princess discovers that her sister has been kidnapped by faeries.

The little blue flowers called faeries'-eyes scattered across the coverlet were not more dreadful to her now than the fact of the empty bed itself. (McKinley, 1981, p. 12)

It is only a reference, two sentences later, to "a faint mysterious smell from the bruised flowers she had lain on" that suggests that the intended interpretation is natural flowers.

Referring functions were previously described as if they were functions from a basic psense of a descriptive term to a more secondary psense, although it was indicated in footnote 14 that this is an oversimplification. The oversimplification is this: for many descriptive terms or referring expressions, none of the obvious potential psenses is rationally more basic or standard than the others. To demonstrate with some of Nunberg's examples, does *window* refer "inherently" to a kind of hole, or to the framed apparatus that goes in the hole, or to the (usually) transparent material that is part of that apparatus (the part you're referring to when you say, "Casey's home run broke a window")? Is *newspaper* the name of a kind of regularly published document, or an organization that publishes that kind of document regularly, or of paper they print it on? For many nouns it is not clear which is more basic: the mass use as in (21), or the countable use as in (22).

21a. Fire destroyed the garage.
21b. Night is 15 hours long at the winter solstice.
22a. A fire destroyed the garage.
22b. Nights are 15 hours long by mid-December.

Even more generally, which is more basic, the type use of a common count noun, or the token use; the species cat, or individual cats?

Nunberg suggested[15] that in these cases, and therefore in general, neither use is basic. Applied to descriptive referring expressions[16], referring func-

---

[15]Not for nothing did Nunberg coin the term *radical pragmatics* to refer to his view of reference. This view contrasts with the traditional view of word meaning as wholly conventional, but it is entirely consistent with the claim that semantics is compositional. Whether or not semantics is compositional is independent of how reference is determined, but determination of reference is unavoidably pragmatic in any case, for indexicals like pronouns. Names have the same referential vagueness as pronouns, and it has to be resolved the same way, independently of whether common nouns are typically names and similarly vague. The pragmatic determination of reference depends on semantics being compositional in that knowing what is predicated of what is invoked in conditions (cf. below page 57) on inferring referring functions from presumed designata, and thus in assigning referents to referring expressions.

[16]Applied to a demonstrated physical object, the same referring functions relate potentially intended referents to the primary demonstratum. The indeterminacies here are the familiar ones of determining what has been demonstrated (cf. Chapter 2, section 0), and of selecting the referring function intended by the speaker.

tions relate potentially intended descriptions, but to each other, not to any privileged, inherently designated referents. To quote Nunberg (1978):

> A rational speaker, even in a linguistically homogeneous speech-community, may never be able to determine the form of the conventions governing the uses of words; the best he will be able to say is that, say, "*w* is used as if it designated *a* or *b*." (p. 74)

Verb uses display the same broad and pervasive variety we saw with nouns in examples (9–17). The intransitive verb *run,* for example, names a kind of goal-directed locomotive activity (23a), and regular participation in a sport consisting of that activity (23b, 23c). Sometimes the goal-directed activity is not even locomotive (23d). *Run* also describes the excursus of a liquid from a source (23e, 23f), and probably by extension, the flow of electric current (23g) and the functioning of engines or batteries powered by electricity, and machines powered by them (23h, 23i). The execution of computer programs is also called running (23j), perhaps by a further extension. And by extension from one or more of these uses, the goal-directed swimming of fish is also called running (23k). In a related use, any machine with moving parts may be said to run when it is operating (23L). And related to its use to refer to the coursing of a river (23f), *run* can be used for other kinds of trade routes (23m). (Anyone who knows Latin may have noticed the Latin word for 'run' showing up in these descriptions in *current, excursus, coursing.*) This discussion does not even begin to exhaust the senses of *run* that are listed in desk dictionaries, but it should suffice to show the depth of the problem.

23a. Dale ran to the grocery store.
23b. Dale runs with the cross-country team.
23c. Dale runs every day.
23d. He ran for president.
23e. The water is running.
23f. The Mississippi runs from Minnesota to the Gulf of Mexico.
23g. The electricity is running again.
23h. The engine/car/refrigerator is running.
23i. A quartz watch will run for a year before the battery needs to be replaced.
23j. Your program won't run until you correct the typos.
23k. The salmon are running.
23L. A wind-up alarm clock will run for 26 hours.
23m. Highway 136/The railroad runs through San Jose and Havana, Illinois.

There are causative senses ('cause to . . .') of transitive *run* as well. Some refer to locomotive activity (24a–24c), others to directing the operation of a complex organization (24d–24f), perhaps by application of the causative function to the machine operation senses of intransitive *run* in (23h, 23i). Perhaps by analogy to a different sense of intransitive *run* as in (23g) or (23m), transitive *run* is used for extending something from one place to another, as in (24g). Transitive *run* is also used to refer to encountering (24h) and overcoming (24i) obstacles.

24a.   They ran a race.
24b.   They ran her ragged.
24c.   They ran Eks out of town.
24d.   They ran the company for 12 years.
24e.   They ran the company into the ground.
24f.   They ran a clean campaign.
24g.   They ran a wire from the upstairs to the basement.
24h.   They ran the risk of exposing the whole operation.
24i.   The ship ran the blockade and got through to the open sea.

Notice that, within the limits imposed by requirements on parallel syntax, these uses of *run* count as the same for syntactic constructions which require identity of sense, as illustrated by the acceptability of sentences like (25).

25a.   This program will run if your computer will.
25b.   It's a good thing the salmon are running, because the refrigerator isn't.
25c.   The Mississippi has run down to the Gulf for millions of years, the river road for only a hundred or so.
25d.   The captain ran the blockade, and in doing so, the risk of losing his entire cargo.

Furthermore, practically every verb is subject to a multiplicity of uses of this sort.[17] *Slap* is used to refer to an act of striking something with a flexible, flat surface; you can slap something with a hand or a rolled-up newspaper, but not a hardback book or a rock. But the motion gestalt involved in back slapping is not the same as for face slapping. Slapping handcuffs on someone does not involve striking or a flat surface at all, and slapping someone with a sentence or a subpoena only involves motion to the extent that every interpersonal interaction involves motion. *Write* refers to the act of inscribing letters (26a), to the act of inscribing cursive letters (as opposed to printing) (26b), to making visual representations of linguistic expressions (26c, 26d), and to producing a document (26e).

---

[17]As evidence for the pervasiveness and creativity of extended uses, a survey of three arbitrarily chosen 200-word passages from works of modern American fiction revealed that an average of 15% of the nouns, verbs, and adjectives in them were used in senses that are not covered by the entries in a large desk dictionary. (The range was 7% to 29%.)

26a. Write your name on the top line.
26b. Write it; don't print.
26c. He wrote a word/sentence/formula on the blackboard.
26d. He wrote his name in the air.
26e. He wrote a book/a three-page letter to his mother.

Finally, there is a parallel to the fact that in context any noun can be used to refer to an individual associated with something that noun designates (example (17), and accompanying discussion), in that almost any verb that can normally be used to refer to an action can apparently be used (metaphorically) in the context of athletic competition to describe the outcome of a contest.[18] Teams or individuals do not just beat, defeat, overcome, and win over their opponents. They walk over them, roll past them, crush them, stomp them, tip them, skin them, bruise them, and so on. If a game involved a dispute over rules that involved display of a rule book, a sports reporter would probably be understood if he reported the outcome of the game by saying that the winners read the losers their rights.

Prepositions are notorious for rampant "polysemy," although it rarely leads to confusion. The preposition *in,* for example means something different in *in town, in the road, in the sidewalk, in March, in time, in tune, in red, in trouble,* and the like (cf. Green, 1985a).

Many adjectives demonstrate extensive multiplicity of use also. *Red,* for example, refers to different hues when applied to hair, bricks, human skin, mucous membranes, or marking pens. *Rich* refers to different properties when applied to economic entities, nutritional substances, and prose.

If most ordinary words have such an extensive multiplicity of ordinary uses, and no single basic use or psense, how do language users ever figure out what is being referred to?

Nunberg (1978) described two conditions (pp. 97–100) which serve to limit the number of normal interpretations the use of a word can have in a NULL CONTEXT, that is, in an isolated sentence, assuming beliefs assumed to be (a) normal in the community (Nunberg, 1978, pp. 94–97), and (b) relevant in aiding the interpreter in selecting the best referring function for the interpretation of that use. In Nunberg's use, a NORMAL belief is one included in the body of beliefs that a speaker takes "to constitute the

---

[18]For example: (i) headlines a story about the Clemson University baseball team getting nine hits and five runs from the pitching of University of Illinois player Boo Champagne.

   i. Clemson uncorks on Champagne

This feat is also described with metaphorical expressions *(jump on x for, rock x for),* whose pragmatic nature is taken up in Sec. 4 of Chapter 5. Similarly, example (ii) is the headline from an article describing a 10-6 Illinois victory over EIU in which Illinois player Darrin Fletcher hit a grand slam home run.

   ii. Illinois' Fletcher slams EIU

background against which all utterances in a community are rationally made" (pp. 94–95).[19] A normal use is then one which speakers judge to be consistent with the system of normal beliefs. The first condition is that if a word is used to designate an object a in such a way that some predicate ϕ is predicated of it, then if ϕ can be rationally predicated only of members of some set R, the use is normal only if there is some member b of R such that b is best identified as being the value of some function f applied to a, given the system of normal beliefs (Nunberg, 1978, p. 99). In other words, a use of a word w is normal if and only if there is something which is best identified (in the community, on the basis of the system of normal beliefs) as the value of some referring function applied to the designation of that word, and it is rational to predicate of that thing whatever is predicated of the designatum of w. Thus, the use of a newspaper name as the subject of *endorse* (as in *The Herald endorsed three Democrats last year*) is normal because publishers are readily identifiable as the value of the referring function 'publisher of,' applied to 'newspaper,' and it is rational to speak of a publisher as endorsing political candidates.

This condition says that uses which presuppose beliefs foreign to the system of normal beliefs are not normal uses. For example it rules out any normal interpretation for a sentence like *That idea slept late,* because there is no plausible entity (b) that intends to awaken before a certain time (a member of the set R which the predicate *sleep late* (ϕ) is rationally predicated of) which is best identified as the value of any function (f) from the set (a) of abstract propositions (normally taken to be) designated by *idea*.[20]

A second condition allows uses of a word w to refer to things that are not normally the argument of the predicate predicated of w only if there is no good function from what w designates to something that can be the argument of that predicate. Thus *chicken* could refer to chicken feathers in a discussion of substances to fill pillows with, as in (27a), because there is a good function from feather-bearing creatures to their feathers, and having loft can be rationally predicated of its output.

27a. Chicken doesn't have much loft.
27b. Chicken is tasty.

But in a discussion of edibles, as in (27b), *chicken* could not rationally be expected to be taken to refer to chicken feathers, because there is a function

---

[19]Thus, *normal* as used here has nothing to do with statistics, and makes no claims about clinical psychological fitness.

[20]One could also take *idea* literally, and say that *sleep late* is not a normal use since logically, *idea* represents a predicate predicated of something in the set of things that sleep late, and it is not rational to predicate idea-hood of such things.

(from creatures to their meat) whose output, applied to *chicken,* better satisfies the predicate 'is tasty.' The second condition thus predicts that in the null context, neither (28a) nor (28b) will be ambiguous, although *alligator* can be used normally to refer to either a kind of meat or a kind of leather or hide.

28a. Alligator is tasty.
28b. Alligator is waterproof.

With conditions like this, it is not crucial which psense came first; all that matters is that a plausible psense can be reconstructed or inferred.

In addition to normal uses, there are what Nunberg called local uses: uses licensed by systems of beliefs generally considered rational in only a subpart of the speech community (e.g., linguists, musicians, Roman Catholics, New Englanders, people who sail boats, surfers, MTV watchers, etc.). Examples of local uses are (17a, 17b), among many others, and (29), where the name of a corporation is used to designate a representative of that corporation.

29.   IBM was held up in traffic.

(Example (17c) is an example of a nonce use, a use designated for a particular discourse, and conventional in an even narrower "community" than a local use.) Examining this distinction more closely, Nunberg suggested that the difference between normal uses and local uses is just the degree and/or extent to which a use is conventionalized. Starting from the assumption that "a word-use is predictable for a given speaker to the degree that he believes that normal beliefs provide its rationale" (p. 115) Nunberg proceeded to distinguish several stages of conventionalization:

> Given a speaker S, who is aware both of a regular use R of a word *w* to refer to *a,* and of general conformity to another regular use R' of *w* to refer to *b,* we can say that S can expect use R to be assumed if either I or II holds. (pp. 115–116)

Condition I requires, paraphrasing Nunberg, that S believe that it is normally believed that, given use R' of *w* to refer to *b,* use R is licensed by normal beliefs. (The various uses of *newspaper* in (10) exemplify this condition. The relevant normal beliefs are that newspapers are produced with editorials, in regular editions, at manufacturing plants, by corporations that sell advertising, etc.)

Condition II says that S must believe that it is normally believed that, given use R' of *w* to refer to *b,* use R is licensed by beliefs to which members of the community would normally conform, even if they do not themselves hold those beliefs. (This condition covers cases where only experts command all of the details needed to construct the appropriate referring functions; cf. Nunberg, 1978, pp. 113–115 and Green, 1984, for discussion of Putnam, 1975a, 1975b, on this topic. Examples are uses of trade jargon uses by lay people (as when a novice computer user asks, "How much memory does that computer have?"). Here it is assumed that there is a rational connection between the technical use and a more ordinary use, although the speaker need not know exactly what it is.)

Nunberg describes four progressively more conventionalized stages of word use, where S is less and less likely to expect a use R to be understood via a referring function generated from R'. That is, the more convention-alized a use is, the less reasonable it is to expect it to be correctly interpreted just by applying inferential processes to a more widely assumed use. Thus, in stage III, S believes that it is normally believed that given use R' of w to refer to b, use R to refer to a is licensed by beliefs that are considered normal in some subgroup, but not in the community at large. (The example Nunberg gives of this condition is the use of *country* to refer to a kind of music, licensed by the belief of some speakers that that music has rural origins.)

In stage IV, S believes that it is normally believed that given use R' of w to refer to b, beliefs that license use R are normally reconstructable, although they are not necessarily assumed to be held by any members of the community. [Examples would be transparent idioms like *make book* or *book* (a suspect) which would involve belief in the existence of books in which bets or the names of accused criminals were entered.]

In stage V, S believes that it is normally believed that given use R' of w to refer to b, there are beliefs which would license use R, though S may have no idea who might hold those beliefs. (This condition licenses the use of idioms that look analyzable, like *let the cat out of the bag* or *kick the bucket*, about which one can make up stories which are plausible, but which no one can actually verify.)

Stage VI is characterized by S's belief that it is normally believed that given use R' of w to refer to b, there is no reason why w is used in use R to refer to a. (This condition covers purely arbitrary idioms, like *beef* for 'complaint.)

5. SUMMARY

When a speaker uses a word w to refer to some intended referent a, he must assume that his addressee will consider it rational to use w to refer to a in that context; he must assume that if he and his addressee do not in fact have the same assumptions about what beliefs are normal in the community at large, and in every relevant subgroup, at least the addressee will be able to tell what relevant beliefs the speaker imputes to the addressee, including reflexive beliefs, as described in chapter 1. Likewise, the interpreter must assume that she knows or can infer what beliefs about what is normal that the addressee will (reflexively) impute to the speaker. For example, to interpret an utterance like *He bought IBM at 71 1/2,* the interpreter must assume (a) that the speaker assumes that it is normally considered rational to refer to shares of stock in a corporation by means of a referring function from the name of the corporation, or at least (b) that the speaker assumes that the addressee will assume it is rational to do so, or (c) that the speaker assumes that the addressee will assume that the speaker assumes it is rational to do so, and so on. As Nunberg concluded a particularly illustrative discussion (pp. 81–86) of what is involved in our figuring out what he might mean by *jazz* when he says, *Do you like jazz?,* "My theory of jazz is relevant only insofar as it happens to coincide with the beliefs that somebody else might reasonably attribute to me."

4

Non-truth-conditional Meaning: Interpreting the Packaging of Propositional Content

> *"I had an appointment at the lawyers," Gram announced. "At which I was told that you are now, legally and officially and permanently . . . my responsibility."*
>
> *"We're adopted?" James asked.*
>
> *"That's what I said."*
>
> *"No, it's not," he pointed out.*
>
> *"Well it's what I meant and since you understood me it must be what I said."*
>
> —Voigt, 1983, p. 150

As the passage shows, in ordinary usage, the verb *say* is systematically ambiguous, with one interpretation (let us call it *say₁*) referring to the physical act of uttering linguistic forms in intentional communication,[1] and another (*say₂*) to the assertions made in uttering such forms. Gram (idiosyncratically) uses *say* in yet a third sense, to refer to implications intended in uttering such forms with a particular assertion intended. Thus, *say₁* is essentially the same as *utter*, relating to the actual form of what was uttered. *Say₂* is roughly *assert*; it relates to the proposition that constitutes the face value, or literal meaning of what was uttered. But Gram's use of *said* has to do with the meaning intended to be conveyed by an utterance,

---

[1]The verb *go* is reserved for the act of uttering nonlinguistic forms, as in (i) (and also for imitation of nonlinguistic and noncommunicative acts), though the use of *go* is becoming common among young people for linguistic communication as well, as in (ii).

i. When she said that, we all went [apico-labial trill]/"Bleeaaugh!"/"Ssshhh!".

ii. And I go, "So what made you call her?" and he goes, "Oh, nothing. Nothing at all."

and really is not saying at all; it has more in common with the ordinary-language use of *imply*. In this chapter and the two following, we turn our attention from the questions of the intended reference of referring expressions, which occupied us in chapters 2 and 3, to questions of what a speaker intends to accomplish in saying₂ what she says, and saying it the way she says it and at the point in the discourse at which it is said.

We look first at the kinds of acts that are involved when one says something (speech acts and illocutionary forces), and then turn to implications conveyed by the choice of word or phrase (presuppositions and connotations) and to the implications (technically, the implicatures) of saying₂ something with its particular propositional content and presuppositions. We consider the latter in some detail in chapter 5, tracing how a single, general, nonlinguistic principle and its linguistic corollaries provide a means to explain how people can mean (and convey) more than they say₂. This enables us to account for such conversational strategies as understatement, damning with faint praise, and intentional vagueness. At the same time, it provides the foundation for understanding the phenomenon of textual coherence—what makes individually comprehensible sentences into more or less coherent texts or discourses when they are strung together. Finally, this principle and its corollaries are shown to provide solutions to a number of problematic questions in semantic and pragmatic theory that are treated in this chapter. We will see that implicature is far from being a rhetorical trick that only clever and accomplished writers and conversationalists use, as is sometimes thought, but rather is indispensable to an understanding of how even the simplest, most ordinary connected text is understood as intended.

1. SPEECH ACTS AND ILLOCUTIONARY FORCE

When James says, "We're adopted," in the passage quoted above, he performs, simultaneously, a number of different kinds of SPEECH ACTS, all of them intentional and goal-directed, although the execution of several is undoubtedly subconsciously controlled. First, he performs what the English philosopher J. L. Austin (1962) called a phonetic act—producing the articulation of tongue, jaw, diaphragm, larynx, and so on that results in connected speech sounds. Presumably, the goal of the phonetic act is to produce an acoustic object that the addressee (Gram) will recognize as speech sounds (and not, e.g., as involuntary vocalizations such as belches or sneezes). Simultaneously, and by means of the phonetic act, James performs the act of uttering linguistic expressions, producing a series of tokens of forms according to the grammar of a certain language, and with a certain intonation (Austin's "phatic act"), with the intention that it be recognized as belonging to that language. At the same time, in order that his utterance be recognized as connected discourse about some proposition, James performs the acts of referring (with *we*), and predicating (with *'re adopted*), intending the forms he uses to be taken as referring to individuals, actions, events, and so forth, according to the conventions of the language and culture of the community he shares with the addressee (Austin's "rhetic act").

Austin referred to these three kinds of acts as constituting a LOCUTIONARY ACT, an act of saying$_1$ something. (In another influential work, the philosopher John Searle, 1969, lumped the first and second together as constituting an "utterance act" and used "propositional act" for Austin's "rhetic act.")

By means of the same utterance, James performs an ILLOCUTIONARY ACT, doing something by means of the locutionary act he has performed. In this case, James' illocutionary act is questioning, but in a different context, and with a different intonation, the same utterance could have had the force of an assertion, an announcement, or an exclamation.[2]

Finally, James performs this illocutionary act for some reason, and to the extent that he expects that reason to be recognized, he is performing a rhetorical act of implicating, a topic discussed in chapter 5. In principle, it could be that in/by asking Gram if they were adopted, James was intending to convey to Gram that she was speaking obscurely, although there is no particular reason to suspect that that is true in this case.

In addition, a speaker might, in performing a given illocutionary act, perform any number of intentional or unintentional PERLOCUTIONARY ACTS, acts which have an effect which is not a universally inevitable consequence of the performance of the illocutionary act. Thus, a person's committing himself to buying six shares of IBM is not a perlocutionary effect of his saying, "I promise to buy six shares of IBM," because that commitment is entailed by his making that promise with those words. On the other hand, a speaker's uttering some warning might (intentionally) alert the addressee to a potential danger; an innocent question addressed to an addressee unaware of the speaker's presence may (intentionally or unintentionally) startle the addressee; a candidate's utterance might (intentionally or unintentionally) convince the addressee that the speaker would make a good leader. All of these are perlocutionary effects created by perlocutionary acts.

---

[2]I do not know how many taxonomies of illocutionary acts list exclaiming, but I take declarative exclamations to be emotional expressions of conclusions, intended not so much to inform the addressee of their content, as to express (exploiting intonation and voice quality) the speaker's attitude toward it.

1.1 Performative Verbs

Sometimes a sentence contains linguistic expressions or intonation that serve to indicate the illocutionary force of the sentence. The expressions may be particles, as in Japanese (Uyeno, 1971, critiqued in Kendall, 1985), or verbs, as in English. For example, *promise* in (1a) tells us that (1a) is a promise (and not, e.g., a prediction),[3] and *order* in (1b) tells us that (1b) is an order, and not a request, plea, or suggestion.

1a.   I promise I'll sit in the front row.
1b.   I order you to put out that cigarette.

By saying *I promise* or *I order,* we thereby promise or order, but only certain verbs, which Austin called PERFORMATIVES, have this property of allowing the speaker to do the action the verb names by using the verb in a certain way (hence Austin's title, *How to Do Things with Words*). Other verbs only name actions, and cannot be used in this way; by saying (2a), one does not thereby believe that it will snow; saying (2b) does not count as an act of driving a white car, but only as a report of one's driving, and although (2c) might be true on occasion, merely saying it cannot accomplish forcing anyone to do anything.

2a.   I believe that it will snow tomorrow.
2b.   I drive a white car.
2c.   I force you to practice the piano.

While illocutionary acts can be performed by performative sentences like (2), perlocutionary acts cannot be performed by naming the act. Even a charismatic politician could not get people to vote for him by saying, "I convince you that I would make a good leader."

Performative sentences, although they look like ordinary declarative sentences, are not simply true or false the way declaratives like (2) are.[4] It does not make sense to ask whether the speaker of (1a) or (1b) is lying or telling the truth, even though the speaker of (1a) might or might not be sincere, and the speaker of (1b) might or might not have the authority to make the order, might or might not want the cigarette put out, and so on.

The performative expressions Austin mentions cover a wide range, from

---

[3]We need to ignore the interpretations available for any present tense verb, which allow them to be used to assert habitual action, to assert that an action is scheduled, or to describe past action (historical present).

[4]In chapter 5 (Sec. 4.2), we see that a case can be made for the claim that performative sentences like (1) are necessarily true, whether uttered sincerely or not.

promise, assert and *order* to *vote, nominate, deny* and *sentence, bet, resign, apologize, curse, bequeath* and *christen.* Austin and Searle devoted considerable attention to describing conditions (involving the sincerity of the speaker and various facts about the context) that have to be met in order for various utterance acts to count as illocutionary acts of one sort or another. They and several others devoted considerable effort to classifying the verbs that could be used performatively (Austin, 1962; Fraser, 1973; McCawley, 1977; Searle, 1975a, 1976a), to the extent that in many people's minds, *speech act* became identified with *illocutionary act,* although in fact the former covers a much wider range of phenomena than the latter. Thus, referring and predicating are speech acts, as are explaining, intimating, and nagging, but none of them can be performed by naming the act: saying "I refer to Mr. O'Neill" does not thereby refer to Mr. O'Neill, although it may indicate that a previous referring expression was intended to refer to him. Saying "I nag you to pick up your clothes" is not nagging.

1.2 The Performative Hypothesis

Austin noted that performative expressions only had performative force in the present tense, with first person singular subjects. Thus, utterances of (3a) and (3b) cannot be acts of promising or ordering, but only reports of acts of promising and ordering.

3a.   I promised I would sit in the front row.
3b.   She orders him to put out his cigarette.

And in general, the performative expression has to be the predicate of the main clause of the utterance, so uttering (4) does not count as a promise, even though it has a first person singular, present tense form of the performative verb *promise,* because *I promise* is in a subordinate clause.

4.   My students are betting that I promise to sit in the front row.

In the late 1960s linguists took note of these properties of performative expressions, and some argued (e.g., R. Lakoff, 1968; Ross, 1970; Sadock, 1974) that the underlying linguistic representation of EVERY sentence contained as its highest clause, a performative verb with a first person singular subject. This clause could be overt as in (1), or "abstract" (i.e., invisible or deleted) as in (5).

5a.   I'll sit in the front row.
5b.   Put out that cigarette!

Thus, a declarative sentence like (5a) would have an underlying representation similar to (1a), and (3a) would have an underlying representation like
(6).

6.   I SAY TO YOU THAT I promised I would sit in the front row.

The performative hypothesis, as it was called, was offered to explain not
only the different illocutionary force of sentences like (1) and sentences like
(2), but also the ambiguity of sentences like (5a), which was attributed to the
possibility of underlying performative verbs of predicting, promising, or
announcing, and so on. As the performative hypothesis was a syntactic
hypothesis, syntactic arguments were offered to support it. They generally
hinged on the fact that certain linguistic expressions occurred only (a) in
subordinate clauses that were introduced by a certain kind of verb referring
to an illocutionary force, with a coreference condition holding between a
noun phrase in the subordinate clause and a noun phrase in the introducing
clause; or (b) in main clauses with a certain illocutionary force and certain
particular sorts of noun phrases.

As an illustration, it was argued that the idiomatic expression *be damned
if,* as used to indicate emphatic negation, could occur in main clauses just
in case its subject was first person and the sentence was declarative, as in
(7). ('#' indicates unacceptability in the sense intended—here, emphatic
refusal.)

7a.   I'll be damned if I'll vote for that man.
7b.   #You'll be damned if you'll vote for that man.
7c.   #Will I be damned if I'll vote for that man?

It was claimed that *be damned if* with the denial reading could occur in a
subordinate clause just in case it was in the complement of a verb of stating
and its subject was coreferential to the subject of the verb of stating, as
shown in (8).

8a.   John says he'll be damned if he'll vote for that man.
8b.   #John fears that he'll be damned if he'll vote for that man.
8c.   #John says I'll be damned if I'll vote for that man.

If the performative hypothesis is correct, and a sentence like (7a) is (in its
underlying structure) the object complement of a clause whose subject
refers to the speaker of the sentence (i.e., is first person), and whose verb is
a verb of stating, as in (9), then these conditions can be reduced to a single
condition, stated as (10).

9. I say to you that I'll be damned if I'll vote for that man.
10. The idiom *be damned if,* with its sense of emphatic negation, can
    occur only embedded in the complement of a verb of stating,
    and the subject of the idiom must be identical in reference to that
    of the embedding verb.

Without the performative hypothesis, sentences (7c) and (11) are treated
as anomalous for entirely unrelated reasons, since they violate entirely
unrelated conditions; under the performative hypothesis, sentence (7c) has
an underlying structure similar to (11), and thus they are anomalous for the
same syntactic reason: both violate condition (10) in the same way.

11. #I ask you whether I'll be damned if I'll vote for that man.

The *be damned if* argument was only one of scores (cf. in addition to
references previously given, Davison, 1970; Peterson, 1969), and although
the performative analysis quickly gained popularity, objections were raised,
not only to the syntactic arguments, but to the assumptions and consequences of the theory itself. Linguists such as Anderson (1971) and Fraser
(1971, 1974) pointed out that, contrary to the claim that performative verbs
had to be main verbs, sometimes performative verbs occurred with
performative force in subordinate clauses, as in (12), where (12a) appears to
announce itself as a request, (12b) counts as an act of sentencing, and saying
(12c) constitutes saying that one has no money.

12a. I'm afraid I must ask you to leave.
12b. Your behavior leaves me no alternative but to sentence you to 20
     years.
12c. I regret to say that I have no money.

On another front, Morgan (1973a) showed that the performative hypothesis
was inconsistent with other hypotheses about the syntactic representation of
semantic properties of sentences. The hypothesis was also attacked as both
unnecessary and empirically wrong (cf. Stampe, 1975; Searle, 1976b;
Gazdar, 1979; Green & Morgan, 1980).

Linguists were also able to demonstrate that several of the phenomena
that Ross (1970) had argued were conditioned by principles like (10) in fact
occurred in syntactic contexts which those principles failed to predict. In
fact, it can be shown (cf. Green, 1981; Green & Morgan, 1976) that many
of the morphological or syntactical phenomena that were argued to imply
an abstract performative on syntactic grounds are in fact conditioned by
pragmatic considerations, not semantic properties or syntactic contexts.
Indeed, the use of *be damned if* is not, strictly speaking, sanctioned by
being in the complement of a verb of stating. Rather, *be damned if*

predicates refusal (by the referent of the subject of *be damned if*) to be responsible for the act[5] that the complement of *be damned if* refers to. Thus, although *know* is not a verb of stating, nor is *want to know*, (13) could be uttered (and most likely would be) to inform the addressee that the speaker would not vote for a certain man.

13.   I want you to know that I'll be damned if I'll vote for that man.

Similarly, the subject of *be damned if* does not have to be first person or coreferential to the subject of the embedding verb (as in (14)), as long as the utterance as a whole is being used to report or make a refusal, as it is if the speaker purports to be a spokesman for the individual named by the subject of *be damned if,* as in (14a) and (14b), but not (14c).

14a.   John'll be damned if he'll vote for that man.
14b.   I know John'll be damned if he'll vote for that man.
14c.   *I wonder if John'll be damned if he'll vote for that man.

The correct condition on the occurrence of *be damned if* thus seems to be a pragmatic usage rule, not a syntactic condition. The idiom is used in verbal refusals to act, which may be conveyed directly as in (7a), in reports of such refusals (8a),[6] or in refusals that are conveyed indirectly as in (13) and (14).

Ross (1970), unaware of facts like these, and data like those cited by Fraser and Anderson, had considered a pragmatic analysis, and rejected it as premature, on the grounds that conditions like (10) were incapable in principle of being extended to pragmatic objects like 'speaker' and 'speaking,' since they were not syntactic objects, and could not stand in syntactic relations to genuine syntactic objects like verbs and subject noun phrases, any more than an actual piece of sports equipment could be part of a program for a computer simulation of a football game. We return to the issue of the possibility of a pragmatic analysis of illocutionary forces in section 4.2 of Chapter 5.

---

[5]This includes acts by the speaker as well as acts by others for whom the speaker assumes responsibility. Thus (i) is acceptable:

  i. I'll be damned if she'll go out with greasers who drive souped-up convertibles.

The reference to acts predicts that states do not occur in the complement of *be damned if*:

  ii. ??I'll be damned if I like rutabagas.

[6]Thus, it is even possible to use *be damned if* in the past tense. Sentence (i) is acceptable in an indirect free style narrative written from the subject's point of view.

  i. John was damned if he'd vote for that man.

The literature on the analysis of illocutionary force is huge, and still growing. Useful bibliographies may be found in Verschueren (1976), Gazdar (1979), and Searle, Kiefer, and Bierwisch (1980).

2. PRESUPPOSITION

There is a rich and broad variety of phenomena that philosophers and linguists have discussed under the rubric PRESUPPOSITION. Briefly, this term is used to refer to propositions whose truth is taken for granted in the utterance of a linguistic expression, propositions without which the utterance cannot be evaluated. For example, it is said that the sentence *It's too bad that Carter lost the election* (or the utterance of *It's too bad that Carter lost the election*) presupposes the proposition 'Carter lost the election,' while *It's believed that Carter lost the election* does not presuppose this. The characterization of presupposition given here skirts all sorts of important issues. For example, taken by whom for granted? Granted by whom? Are the propositions implied by the linguistic object uttered, or by the act of uttering? These questions are addressed in more detail after a survey of the sorts of phenomena that have been called presupposition and their common properties.

2.1 Some Representative Phenomena

Existence Presuppositions

The phenomenon that is probably most uniformly considered to represent cases of presupposition is the existence presupposition of definite descriptions, as in (15), where (saying) (15a) presupposes 'there is a movie on Channel 4,' and (saying) (15b) presupposes 'Jack has children.'

15a. The movie on Channel 4 is rated R.
15b. I've coached Jack's children.

Factive Presuppositions

A close second for the standard example of presupposition would be factive presuppositions (cf. Kiparsky & Kiparsky, 1971, for an early account), of which there are several sorts. One kind is associated with expressions that take a sentential subject or object. The object complements of such EPISTEMIC factives as *know, realize,* and the subject complements of *mean, prove, be obvious* are considered to be presupposed true, as are the complements of such EMOTIVE factives as *regret, be glad, be surprised, amaze.*[7] Thus the sentences in (16) all presuppose 'Taylor has a 42-inch vertical leap'.

16a. Jan knows that Taylor has a 42-inch vertical leap.
16b. That Taylor has a 42-inch vertical leap is obvious.
16c. Jan regrets that Taylor has a 42-inch vertical leap.
16d. That Taylor has a 42-inch vertical leap amazed the scouts.

Change of state, or inchoative verbs also have complements presupposed to be true, as in (17a, 17b), which both presuppose 'Ferd admires Frieda'.[8]

17a. Jan discovered that Ferd admires Frieda.
17b. Jan forgot that Ferd admires Frieda.

Other constructions associated with factive presuppositions are cleft constructions, as in (18), questions introduced by a question word, (called

---

[7]Implicative verbs, as described by Karttunen (1971), involve a presupposition that the proposition represented by the sentence as a whole is a necessary and/or sufficient condition for the truth of the proposition represented by the complement. Thus, (ia) represents a necessary and sufficient condition for (ib), which approximates the gist of the proposition that is the complement of *condescend* in (ia); (iia) represents a necessary condition for (iib), a representation of the complement of *be able* in (iia); and (iiia) represents a sufficient condition for the truth of the proposition which is the complement of *made* in (iiia), as approximated in (iiib).

ia. Sandy condescended to attend the party.
ib. 'Sandy attended the party'
iia. Jan was able to attend the party.
iib. 'Jan attended the party'
iiia. Sandy made Dana attend the party.
iiib. 'Dana attended the party'

There are negative implicative verbs of the three types as well, for example, *fail, refuse,* and *prevent.* These verbs involve a presupposition that the proposition represented by the sentence as a whole is a necessary and/or sufficient condition for the negation of the proposition represented by the complement of the negative implicative verb.

[8]Sentences like (i–ii) have been taken to represent this sort of presupposition also, with (i) presupposing that Ferd has been admiring Frieda, and (ii) presupposing that Ferd did not admire Frieda before 1969.

i. Has Ferd stopped admiring Frieda?
ii. In 1969 Ferd began to admire Frieda.

However these "presuppositions" are not constant under negation (cf. Sec. 2.2); (iii) and (iv) are consistent with Ferd either admiring or not admiring Frieda in 1969.

iii. Ferd didn't stop admiring Frieda in 1969.
iv. Ferd didn't begin to admire Frieda in 1969.

This suggests that there must be some other explanation for the implications of (i) and (ii).

WH-questions by American linguists), as in (19), adverbial and relative clauses introduced by the corresponding subordinating particles, as in (20), and iterative particles, as in (21). Thus, (18–21) all presuppose 'The Sixers beat the Lakers.'

18.   It was in Los Angeles that the Sixers beat the Lakers.
19a.   When did the Sixers beat the Lakers?
19b.   I don't know where the Sixers beat the Lakers.
20a.   When the Sixers beat the Lakers, there was a power failure.
20b.   The arena where the Sixers beat the Lakers needs to have the floor refinished.
21.   The Sixers beat the Lakers again.

In addition, there is a presupposition associated with the COUNTERFACTIVE verb *pretend,* that the complement is not true, as in (22), and the COUNTERFACTUAL conditional has a presupposition that the proposition expressed by the *if*-clause is not true, as in (23). Thus, (22) and (23) both presuppose that Germany did not invade Czechoslovakia.

22.   Sandy pretended that Germany had invaded Czechoslovakia.
23.   If Germany had invaded Czechoslovakia, England would still have entered the war.

"Connotations"

Many lexical items are used in only a subset of the class of situations in which they might conceivably apply, and the restrictions have been claimed to be (or reflect) presuppositions about the situation. For example, use of the transitive verb *play* implies the proposition that the referent of the subject is an organism capable of volitional action, and the proposition that the object noun phrase refers to a game or a musical instrument. Neither of these is likely in (24).

24.   Golf plays John.

The earliest descriptions of this phenomenon (cf. Chomsky, 1965) took this to be a matter of grammatical properties ("selectional restrictions") of the words involved, but McCawley (1968) showed that this phenomenon is not so much a function of the words as of the properties that language users attribute to the presumed intended referents of the words—in other words, that selectional restrictions were pragmatic, not syntactic.

A classic example of a connotation presupposition is *assassinate* (Gallagher, 1970; McCawley, 1975a). *Assassinate* is used to assert that the referent of its grammatical object is killed, but, as with *murder,* there is a presupposition that the killing was intended. Thus, the bizarreness of (25).

25.   John accidentally assassinated the Prime Minister.

In addition, the use of *assassinate* presupposes that the victim had significant political power, from which his death removed him, and that removing that power was the motive for the lethal deed. Thus, powerful political figures, underworld leaders, and powerful charismatic leaders of any sort might be the victims of assassination attempts, but not rock stars or journalists, no matter how famous or threatening to an individual; the murder of a former chief of state who had retired from political activity would not be assassination, nor would murdering a chief of state for some perceived personal injustice.

Another well-known example of lexical presupposition is the verbs of judging discussed by Fillmore (1971a) and McCawley (1975b). Saying that A is accused of or blamed or criticized for doing B all involve the propositions 'A did B' and 'B is bad,' but, Fillmore claimed, *accuse* asserts A did it and presupposes B is bad, while *criticize* asserts that B is bad, and presupposes that A is responsible for it. Similarly, German *essen* 'eat' presupposes that the referent of the logical subject noun phrase is human, *fressen* 'eat,' that it is an animal.

Similarly, to refer to a government leader's *reign* could be said to presuppose that the government is a kingdom or empire, to his *regime* that the leader is a dictator, to his *administration* that he is chief executive in a state where real power is in other hands (e.g., the legislature), to his *government* that he is head of a (parliamentary) government where his tenure is a function of his support in the legislature. Thus, to refer to an elected governor's administration as *Gov. Eks's regime* would imply that Gov. Eks had a dictatorial administrative style, and to refer to it as *his reign* would imply that he acted as if the job was his for life (and maybe by divine right).

To stop (arbitrarily, because one could go on for volumes) with a final example, the quantifier *all* presupposes that the set it is applied to has at least three members. Thus, (26a) implies that Jack has at least three children, and (26b) is a distinctly odd thing for a human being to say.

26a.   All of Jack's children are bright.
26b.   All of my legs hurt.

2.2 Properties of Presupposition

We have discussed a broad variety of cases that linguists have taken to represent examples of presupposition. In Sec. 2.3 we will take up the question of whether presuppositions are something inherent in linguistic objects like words and sentences, or whether they are something that speakers make, something associated with uses of sentences. The first alternative reflects an opinion held by many writers, especially in the period 1969–1975, that presupposition is a semantic phenomenon. The second reflects an opinion common among nonlogicians. Both the second and the third alternatives represent pragmatic approaches to the problem. Here, we only consider in more detail what the earmarks or identifying properties of presupposition have been taken to be.

First, as previously mentioned, a presupposition is semantic material which is taken for granted, that is, entailed (semantic approach) or assumed (pragmatic approach) and not asserted in a declarative sentence, questioned in a question, or ordered in an imperative. A person who uttered one of the declarative sentences in (27) would be understood as taking for granted 'Mr. D. was late for class,' rather than asserting it, so objecting to the presupposition by simply denying it with (28) is not likely to meet with success. In contrast, the main assertion of the utterance is easily denied, as in (29).

27a. The students regret that Mr. D. was late for class.
27b. When Mr. D was late for class, the students demanded an apology.
27c. If Mr. D. had not been late for class, the students would have done their work.

28. No, he wasn't.
29. No they don't/didn't/wouldn't.

Second, the presuppositions associated with a word or construction are constant when the clause containing that word or construction is negated or questioned. The presupposition 'Mr. D. was late', linked to the factive verb, adverbial clause, or counterfactual conditional construction in (27a–27c) is equally present in the negated and interrogative sentences in (30a–30c). Similarly, (31a) still presupposes that Vader was emperor, and (31b) that Jack has children.

30a. The students did not regret that Mr. D. was late to class.
30b. Did the students rejoice when Mr. D. was late to class?
30c. If Mr. D. had not been late for class, the students would not have done their work.

31a. Did Darth Vader's reign begin before the Jedi returned?
31b. Are Jack's children bright?

Third, presuppositions cannot be denied without evident self-contradiction, although they can be suspended. Thus, the sentences of (32) involve self-contradictions, whereas those of (33) do not.

32a. Jack's children are bright, but Jack has no children.
32b. The students regret that Mr. D. was late although Mr. D. was not late.
32c. The students rejoiced when the final score was posted, but it was never posted.
32d. If Mr. D. had been late, the students would have been disappointed, although Mr. D. was late.

33a. I'm sure that Jack's children are bright, if he has children.
33b. The students will regret that Mr. D. was late, if he was in fact late.
33c. I was in the locker room when the score was posted, if it was in fact ever posted.
33d. If Russia hadn't invaded Germany, Poland would be larger today, if Russia did in fact invade Germany.

Finally, presuppositions are relative to an assumed "world." In all of the examples discussed here, it has been taken for granted that the relevant world is the real world (as presumed to be mutually known). However, certain "world-creating" verbs and constructions (cf. Morgan, 1969; McCawley, 1978c, 1981; Dinsmore, 1981; Fauconnier, 1985) can define other worlds as relevant for the evaluation of presupposition-involving constructions. For example, in (34) it is the world defined by a dream, a supposition, and a condition, respectively, where the relevant presuppositions must hold.

34a. I dreamed that the earth was flat, and that a lot of people were glad when Columbus fell off the edge.
34b. Suppose Columbus discovered a passage to India: no one would criticize him for not landing in the West Indies.
34c. If pigs could fly, pork wings wouldn't taste any better than chicken wings.

Notice that *dream, suppose,* and *if* do not establish a new world for the presuppositions in (34) all by themselves; it takes a world-creating word and its complement to establish the world defined by the propositional content of the complement. This is why the presuppositions of (35) are all presuppositions relative to the real world, not to the worlds of dreams or suppositions.

35a. I dreamed that everyone regretted that Columbus fell off the edge of the earth.
35b. Suppose people had criticized Columbus for not landing in the West Indies.
35c. If pork wings don't taste good, don't eat them.

It is also important that the world-defining proposition does not have to be identical to the presupposition it warrants, as indeed it is not in the examples of (34). It is sufficient if the world-defining proposition provides a necessary or sufficient condition for the presupposed proposition, and in fact, not even this much is necessary; in (36) the world-defining propositions provide no more than a suggestive environment for the existential presupposition of *their children* and *our house.*

36a. If Richard and Debra get married, their children will be beautiful.
36b. When we grow up, I hope we get married and move to the midwest — our house will have two stories and a front porch.

This property is the basis for one of the arguments (cf. Morgan, 1973b) that presupposition is not a semantic property inherent in lexical items, but a pragmatic property of utterances in context.

2.3 The Nature of Presupposition

A Property of Sentences, or Utterances?

Presuppositions were originally described by logicians in semantic terms, as propositions associated with such linguistic objects as words or sentences (e.g., Strawson, 1950; cf. also Karttunen, 1973, Katz & Langendoen, 1976). In particular, they were defined as propositions that were entailed by a sentence and by its negation. (A proposition P is said to be ENTAILED by another proposition Q if whenever Q is true, P is also true.) However, problems with taking this description as a definition soon became evident (Morgan, 1973b). First, for noncontroversial entailments, asserting a sentence and one of its entailments results in an argument that is intuitively valid, although trivial (cf. (37)), but asserting a presupposition in this sort of context results in an argument that is intuitively invalid, as in (38).

37.   Jack has 5 children. Therefore Jack has more than 4 children.
38.   Dana regrets that Mr. D was late. Therefore Mr. D. was late.

Second, the description of presuppositions as propositions entailed by a sentence and by its negation is inadequate as a definition of presupposition because it would fail to correctly characterize presuppositions of all the sentence types that don't have negations. There are no acceptable sentences that could be considered the negations of sentences like (39) or (40) in that they correspond to them in the same way that (30a) corresponds to (27a).

39a.   Drat/Damn the pork wings.
39b.   Long live the present king of France.
40a.   Here come the pork wings.
40b.   In waltzed the present king of France.

Furthermore, it is not clear what the logical negation of nondeclarative sentences like (41a) would be, and (41b) seems to presuppose 'someone ate my porridge,' while its apparent negation (41c) presupposes 'someone didn't eat my porridge.'

41a.   Do you regret that you left your swim clothes at home?
41b.   Who ate my porridge?
41c.   Who didn't eat my porridge?

Reformulating the definition to say that a sentence S presupposes a proposition P if whenever S is true P is true, and whenever S is false, P is true does not resolve these problems. Even reformulating it in terms of satisfaction conditions for illocutionary acts, to avoid the problems posed by (41a), fails to distinguish presupposed "entailments" from the tautologies that are trivially entailed by every sentence: since tautologies like (42) are always true, they are true when sentences like (27) (or any other sentence, for that matter) are true, and when those sentences are false.

42.   Things that are red are red.

But (42) is never involved in understanding (27) the way the proposition 'Mr. D was late for class' is. An adequate semantic definition of presupposition would therefore have to include the notion 'relevant'—a quintessentially context-bound and pragmatic notion.

Other arguments against a semantic treatment of presupposition are based on the fact that the context in which a supposed presupposition-involving sentence is used influences speakers' judgments of whether that sentence does or does not carry the presupposition in· question. For instance, speakers agree that (43a) presupposes (43b), but that (43c), which contains (43a) as a coordinate part, does not.

43a.   Jack's children have left home.
43b.   Jack has children.
43c.   Either Jack has no children, or Jack's children have left home.

And some inchoative factives, unlike the examples in (35), do not presuppose their complements in world-creating contexts. Sentences (44a–44c) do not presuppose 'Dana had an appointment with the dean,' although (44d) in isolation is generally considered to.

44a.   Maybe Dana realized he had an appointment with the dean.
44b.   I bet Dana realized he had an appointment with the dean.
44c.   I know. Dana realized he had an appointment with the dean!
       . . . No, that can't be it; the dean's out of town.
44d.   Dana realized he had an appointment with the dean.

And although (45a) presupposes 'John got a parking ticket,' (45b) does not; it does not even presuppose 'John got a parking ticket or something.'

45a.   John regrets getting a parking ticket.
45b.   [Why is John so withdrawn?] Maybe he regrets getting a parking ticket or something.

Examples (34) and (36) illustrate the same point, and additional arguments against semantic presupposition may be found in Stalnaker (1974), Kempson (1975), Wilson (1975), Boer and Lycan (1976), and Gazdar (1979).

Data such as (34–36, 43–45) exemplify what came to be known as the projection problem — the problem of stating when a presupposition of an embedded sentence was a presupposition of the sentence as a whole. A different sort of exemplification is provided by examples like (46), where (46a, 46b) do not presuppose that Jack has children, but only that Mary assumes (or presupposes) that he does.

46a.   Mary asked to be introduced to Jack's children.
46b.   Mary said that Dana realized that Jack had children.

Karttunen (1973) included an attempt at a semantic treatment of the projection problem, but consideration of the problem led most analysts to the conclusion that at least the projection problem, if not the phenomenon of presupposition itself, is a pragmatic phenomenon. Morgan (1973b), for example, characterized presuppositions relative to worlds (e.g., reality as perceived by the speaker, or in the world of a dream, the world of some individual's belief, or some hypothesized possible world), as propositions which could not be false in that world, and hypothesized a "free pass" principle for factive presuppositions. The "Free Pass" principle claimed that for any sentence S, of the form *A F's that p* where F is a factive predicate (e.g., *Albert regrets that Sandy is 40*), p is true in any world where S is true or false. This principle predicted the necessary (nondefeatable) local projections (e.g., the fact that in any world where the sentence *Albert regrets that Sandy is 40* is either true or false, it is true that Sandy is 40. Projections to worlds not covered by this principle Morgan argued were contingent, subject to being overcome in contexts like (36, 44–46), and he showed how several could be accounted for as inferences from what was asserted, according to principles of the sort proposed by Grice (1975)[9] (cf. chapter 5 for detailed discussion).

Gazdar (1979) presented a formalization of this insight. He took presuppositions (in his terminology: pre-suppositions or potential presuppositions) to be conventionally associated with individual lexical items, and argued (1979, chapter 6) that they are filtered out by propositions assumed in the context of utterance of the sentence, by entailments (including what is asserted) and by clausal and scalar implicatures[10] of what is said, in that order, when they are inconsistent with them.

If one adopts an approach to lexical meaning in which ordinary lexical items are names for kinds of things (cf. Green, 1984), then it is hard to see how lexical presuppositions of the sort discussed on pp. 73–74 could be anything but pragmatic. If (most) words do not have senses or definitions, these aspects of their meaning (e.g., *fressen* implying a nonhuman agent) could not be part of any semantic content, and would represent assumptions (not assertions) that the thing referred to had the properties in question.

Granted by Whom? Taken for Granted by Whom?

It is a simple task to show that it will not do to say that presuppositions have to be in fact true, rather than just assumed to be so, for this would

---

[9]Grice (1975) was circulated in prepublication form as early as 1968. Grice's proposal was intended to account for the apparent nonstandard logic of ordinary language, but turned out, as we see in chapter 5, to have many other applications.

[10]Sentence (i) represents a clausal implicature of (ii); (iii) represents a scalar implicature of (iv) (cf. Horn, 1972, 1973).

    i. The proposition that Jack has children and the proposition that he does not are both consistent with all the speaker knows.

   ii. If Jack has children, Jack's children are bright.

  iii. Not all linguists like tofu.

  iv. Some linguists like tofu.

treat sentences like (47) as ungrammatical or semantically anomalous, when in fact they are entirely grammatical and meaningful, and merely reflect their speaker's bizarre view of the world.

47.   Sandy doesn't realize that Tennyson wrote the King James Bible.

Similarly inadequate is the idea that the presupposed proposition must be assumed to be not only true, but common knowledge, because this would predict that sentences like (48) are self-contradictory, although in fact, they are not.

48.   Nobody realizes that Geralda is more qualified for the position than any of the other candidates.

In the simplest pragmatic accounts of presupposition, the notion amounts to no more than the speaker's *assumption* that the proposition said to be presupposed is true. Some writers (e.g., Karttunen & Peters, 1979) have supposed that the proposition must be mutual knowledge, that is, that both speaker and addressee must assume it is true, and that the speaker must assume that the addressee assumes it, and so on. If this were correct, then a sentence like (49) would be an unthinkably bizarre thing to say if the speaker did not think that the addressee knew that the speaker had children, and (50) would never be appropriate, since the addressee could not know that the speaker had a giraffe (cf. Hawkins, 1976; McCawley, 1979; Gundel, 1985).

49.   Sorry I'm late—my children spilled milk on me, and I had to take the time to change my clothes.
50.   Excuse me. You don't know me, but my giraffe has escaped into your yard and is eating your eucalyptus.

But in fact, (49) is a pretty ordinary thing to say, and more likely than (50) only because more people (are assumed to) have children than are assumed to have giraffes.

Does the addressee have to take the presupposed proposition for granted to consider a sentence with a presupposition to be evaluatable as true or false? Of course not. She only has to be willing to infer that the speaker does, and that the speaker expects that she can reasonably infer that the speaker does. This is why sentences like (51a) are commonly understood as intended to convey to the addressee that her slip is showing, why the utterance of (51b) flatters the audience as being assumed to be among those who realize the enormity of the danger mentioned, and why someone to whom (51c) is addressed may be annoyed if she believes that the speaker could not have waded in a frozen creek. In all cases, the explanation is that the speaker is treating the proposition in the presupposition construction as noncontroversial, even though it may, in fact, be controversial and not taken for granted by the addressee, and the speaker may realize this.

51a. Do you realize that your slip is showing?
51b. Not everyone realizes that the passage of Senator Eks' amendment would seriously jeopardize currently protected First Amendment rights.
51c. Although the temperature never went above 15 degrees Fahrenheit, we didn't regret wading in the creek.

2.4 Some Other Phenomena that Have Been Called "Presupposition"

Felicity Conditions

One might think that felicity conditions on the successful performance of illocutionary acts are a sort of presupposition (also vice versa, that presuppositions are a sort of felicity condition). This would mean that the proposition 'Speaker is empowered to pass sentence on the addressee,' representing a felicity condition on (52a) has the same relation to it as the presupposition 'Jack has children' has to (52b).

52a. I sentence you to 10 years imprisonment.
52b. Jack's children are bright.

Similarly, the term *presupposition* has been used to refer to the sincerity and preparatory conditions (cf. Searle, 1969) on felicitous commands, for example, the conditions that the speaker want the action being ordered, and that it be possible to perform the action (e.g., Fillmore, 1971b). Thus, sentences like (53) would be said to presuppose 'Speaker wants the door closed' and 'The door is not closed.'

53. Close the door.

Notice that sentences like (52a) do not have negations with the same illocutionary force, and that (54) (the grammatical negation of (53)), presupposes that the speaker doesn't want the door closed.

54. Don't close the door.

Thus, these phenomena cannot be shown to meet the criteria traditionally taken to be diagnostic of presupposition (see Sec. 2.2).

Pronoun Choice

Another set of phenomena referred to as presupposition involves pronoun choice. One of these phenomena is the assumption of coreference mentioned in chapter 2. A related phenomenon is the assumptions about sex and neuropsychological constitution that are necessary to choose the appropriate reflexive and relative pronouns, as in (55). Thus, in (55a) the use of *herself* reflects a presupposition that the neighbor is female, despite the fact that the word *neighbor* neither carries nor invites any such presupposition; in (55b) we simply have no idea (or concern) what sex the neighbor is. And in (55c), the use of *which* reflects an assumption that Arotovignians (whatever they might be) are a nonhuman species.

55a.   My neighbor hurt herself mowing the lawn.
55b.   My neighbor mowed the lawn.
55c.   The Arotovignians, which eat chocolate, are insensitive to rotenone.

Although Postal (1970) referred to the phenomenon in (55a) as presupposed coreference, he appears to have been using the term *presupposed* in a nontechnical way, and these phenomena are not included in descriptions of presupposition as a semantic phenomenon. These presuppositions are not suspendable the way garden-variety presuppositions are (cf. Sec. 2.2 above), nor do they provoke a reaction of contradiction when explicitly denied. Thus, (56) is more a metalinguistic comment on the appropriateness of the word *him* (cf. Horn, 1985; and chapter 5, Sec. 4.3), than a comment on the conditions under which it could be true or false, like (33a).

56.   I wrote him a letter, if he is in fact a male.

And (57a, 57b) do not sound contradictory, the way the sentences of (32) do.

57a.   The descendants which have simple eyes are human.
57b.   The descendants who have complex eyes are not human.

In both cases, the assumption reflected by the relative pronoun seems to be about as strong as the assertion; the speaker seems to think in (57a) that the descendants really are not quite human, in (57b), that they are almost as human as you can get.

Similarly, the choice of a so-called "familiar" second person pronoun[11]

---

[11]This description oversimplifies the nature of the problem considerably. Thai, for instance,

(French, Spanish *tu*, German *du*) over a "distant" form (French *vous*, Spanish *Usted*, German *Sie*) has been said (Levinson, 1983, pp. 89–92, 128–130, 166) to reflect a presupposition that the addressee is socially intimate with the speaker, or socially inferior (e.g., a young child), and it has been claimed that the use of a vocative proper noun (e.g., *Judy* in (58)) presupposes that the person so addressed is called by that name.

58.   Hey, Judy, give me a hand.

But again, the social relationship presuppositions are not suspendable; (59) does not succeed in suspending the assumption that the speaker considers the addressee to be an intimate.[12]

59.   Je t'ai   vu hier,   si nous nous   connaissons bien.
       I you-fam.-have seen yesterday if we   each-other know   well.
       I saw you-fam. yesterday, if we know each other well.

And using a vocative in a deductive-exclamative context does not cancel the vocative's presupposition, although garden variety presuppositions may be cancelled in such contexts (cf. 44c); in (60), the speaker using the vocative *Rumplestiltskin* still must presuppose the addressee's name is Rumplestiltskin.

60.   ??I know, Rumplestiltskin! Your name is Rumplestiltskin![13]

In fact, there are certain proper nouns conventionally used to address individuals whose name is not known to the speaker: *Mac, Buster, Joe* (GIs). Thus, they are used to address individuals whose name they are

---

has a whole array of first and person pronouns whose appropriate use depends on beliefs about the sex and pedigree of the referent (i.e., whether the referent is male or female, or a king, queen, or royalty), and on the speaker's relation to the addressee (i.e., parent–child, servant–master, monk–ordinary person), as well as on the degree of intimacy between speaker and addressee.

[12]It is possible to suspend a presupposition or speaker assumption that is is appropriate to use the familiar pronoun as in (i); both French and German have special verbs for referring to pronoun use.

i.   Je t'ai   vu hier,   si je peux te   tutoyer.
     I you-fam.-have seen yesterday, if I can you-fam. say-"tu"-to
     I saw you yesterday, if I can call you "tu".

[13]As opposed to (i), where the first instance of *Rumplestiltskin* is not a vocative, but the answer to a question.

i.   I know! Rumplestiltskin! Your name is Rumplestiltskin!

assumed not to be. Consequently sentences like (61a) are not contradictory, and ones like (61b) are a little odd pragmatically.

> 61a. Hey, Mac! I know that's not your name, but your left rear tire's flat.
>
> 61b. Listen, Buster, if that's your name. Your truck is in my way.

Nonrestrictive Relative Clauses

It has been claimed (e.g., by Keenan, 1971) that sentences with nonrestrictive relative clauses as in (62) presuppose the truth of the relative clause, but almost all analysts agree that in fact nonrestrictive relative clauses are asserted rather than presupposed.

> 62. Taylor, who has a 42-inch vertical leap, will be a sophomore next year.

The rational speaker of (62) does not take it for granted that the addressee realizes (or even will infer that the speaker believes that it is common knowledge) that Taylor has a 42-inch vertical leap. Instead, the nonrestrictive relative clause in (62) offers a way of asserting that information, while not making it the main point of his utterance.

Further Remarks on Connotations

It is not always clear what "connotations" should be analyzed as presuppositions lexically tied to a word. For example, as McCawley (1975b) pointed out, the presuppositional properties of *accuse* and *criticize* are not quite as straightforward as Fillmore's analysis suggests. Most importantly, the 'X is bad' presupposition is more accurately characterized as 'Accuser thinks X is bad,' and the 'Defendant is responsible for X' presuppositions are more accurately characterized as assumptions that the criticizer thinks X happened and that the defendant is responsible for X. Thus, they are more like sincerity conditions on illocutionary acts (i.e., acts of saying that someone did something that is bad, and of saying that what someone did is bad) than they are like more standard kinds of presuppositions, in that denying the supposed presupposition does not result in a contradiction, as it does for undisputed presuppositions. Thus, (63a, 63b) report an insincere accusation and an insincere or mistaken criticism, not impossible events, just as (64a, 64b) are merely blatantly insincere, and not contradictory like the examples in (32).

> 63a. The students accused Mr. D. of being late, although they liked his being late.

63b. The students criticized Mr. D. for being late, although he was not late.

64a. It's snowing, although I don't believe that it is.

64b. I hereby reluctantly order you to close the door, even though it is already closed.

Conclusions

Regardless of whether the phenomena just discussed are of exactly the same sort as those discussed in 2.1, it is unquestionable that (a) they are relevant to the understanding of utterances, and (b) they involve the assumptions of speaker and addressee, as well as, in some cases, those of agents named in the utterance. Indeed, in certain speech interactions, it might be more important that the speaker assumes he stands in a social relation to the addressee which licenses the use of a certain pronoun, than whether the speaker does in fact have a giraffe in sentences like (50). In chapters 5–7 we examine other possible sources for such inferences.

5 Implicature

Capt. Renault: *Rick, do you have those letters of transit?*
Rick: *Louis! Are you Pro-Vichy or Free French?*
Capt. Renault: *Ha-ha! Serves me right for asking a direct question. The subject is closed.*

The reader may recognize the dialogue reproduced here from the movie *Casablanca*. Captain Louis Renault (Claude Rains) suspects cafe owner Rick (Humphrey Bogart) of having some stolen letters of transit which will enable a suspected Free French spy to escape from Vichy-controlled Casablanca. Captain Renault asks Rick a straightforward question, no doubt with utter sincerity. Rick responds with another question, and we can believe he does not know the answer to it any more than the captain knows the answer to the question he asked Rick. The Captain responds to Rick's question as if Rick has rebuked him for asking about the letters of transit. Why isn't this dialogue incoherent? Why, in fact, is Rick's question many times more eloquent than a plain spoken, "You shouldn't ask me that; if I answer, it will destroy our ability to get along here"? This section deals with a theory of discourse which provides means to answer these questions. Subsequent sections show how this theory has been or can be used in resolving a number of problematical issues in pragmatics, including coherence, indirect speech acts, the range of illocutionary forces, and the nature of presupposition, metaphor, and reference.

1. THE COOPERATIVE PRINCIPLE

In 1967, the philosopher H. P. Grice argued that it was unnecessary to consider the differences noted by logicians between such logical operators as $\wedge$, $\vee$, $\exists$, $\sim$, $\supset$, and their natural language counterparts (i.e., *and, or, some, not, if . . . then*) to be differences in meaning. Grice proposed that the differences were differences in use, and arose from the fact that natural language expressions are used in ordinary kinds of discourse (his term was *conversation*), which is governed by principles irrelevant to the use of the corresponding operators in formal logical proofs. Grice argued that the extra baggage that distinguishes the natural language terms from their counterparts in formal logic is the same sort of stuff that distinguishes saying something (directly) from conveying it, but not saying it "in so many words."

Briefly, Grice proposed that all of this could be derived from the assumption that in conversing (indeed, in behaving rationally[1]; Grice 1975[2], p. 47), human beings follow a behavioral dictum, which he called the Cooperative Principle:

> Make your conversational contribution such as is required, at the stage at which it occurs, by the accepted purpose or direction of the talk exchange in which you are engaged. (p. 45)

Grice went on to describe four categories of special cases of this principle (i.e., applications of it to particular kinds of requirements), and gave examples of their application in both linguistic and nonlinguistic domains. The special cases, which he called maxims, tend to strike the naive reader variously as common sense, wishful thinking, or composition teachers' futile rules, but the attraction of Grice's theory is its ability to explain how in being honored as much in the (apparent) breach as in the observance, the maxims provide explanations for otherwise puzzling phenomena. That is, Grice shows that as long as participants in a mutual enterprise such as a conversation each assume that the other is adhering to the Cooperative Principle, meanings that are conveyed without being said$_1$ follow as inferences from the fact that some particular maxim appears to be being violated. The maxims (Grice, 1975, pp. 45-46) are listed here:

QUANTITY: I. Make your contribution as informative as is required (for the current purposes of the exchange).

---

[1]In fact, one could take adherence to the Cooperative Principle as (part of) the definition of rational behavior.

[2]Dittoed copies of the text of the seven 1967 lectures circulated "underground" among linguists and philosophers for several years. In 1975, Lecture II was published (Grice, 1975), and in 1978, Lecture III (Grice, 1978). Acknowledgment notes accompanying these say that the lectures will be published in due course by Harvard University Press.

   II. Do not make your contribution more informative than
       is required.[3]

QUALITY: Try to make your contribution one that is true.
      I. Do not say what you believe to be false.
      II. Do not say that for which you lack adequate evidence.

RELATION: Be relevant.

MANNER: Be perspicuous.[4]
      1. Avoid obscurity of expression.
      2. Avoid ambiguity.
      3. Be brief (avoid unnecessary prolixity).
      4. Be orderly.

Grice notes that speakers value the maxim of Quality much more highly
than the other maxims[5] — violating it amounts to a moral offense, whereas
violating the others is at worst inconsiderate or rude.

As I mentioned, the maxims derive their explanatory power from what
happens when behavior appears not to conform to them. Grice noted (1975,
p. 49) that they can fail to be observed in several different ways. A maxim
may be just ignored, or quietly violated, in which case hearers will be
misled. Telling a lie, for instance, is a quiet violation of the first maxim of
Quality.

A speaker may be unable to conform to all of the maxims at once; if two
are in conflict, she may have to sacrifice one to the other. It may be

---

[3]Grice expressed some doubt regarding the necessity of the second maxim of Quantity,
pointing to the possibility of subsuming it under the maxim of Relevance. One might also argue
that it is at least an implicature (cf. later), if not an entailment, of the first maxim of Quantity.

[4]I have always thought that Grice was indulging in a private joke in the formulation of this
maxim. Insofar as *perspicuous* and *prolixity* are unnecessarily obscure expressions (compared
to *clear* and *verbosity* or *too many words*), the statement of the maxim and its third submaxim
violate the first submaxim; submaxim (3) violates itself as well with the obscure and repetitious
paraphrase; and submaxim (4) is not ordered well with the others, bringing to mind infuriating
recipes like that in (i).

i.   MATZO BALLS
   2 tablespoons fat   1 teaspoon salt
   2 eggs, slightly beaten   2 tablespoons soup stock or water
   1/2 cup matzo meal

Mix fat and eggs together. Add matzo meal and salt, which were first mixed together. When
well blended, . . . [Manischevitz Matzo Meal package]

[5]In some cultures, anyway. Things may well be different in contexts or subcultures where
narrative style is more highly valued than accuracy.

impossible in some situation, for example, to say as much as is necessary without saying things without adequate evidence. Similarly, in some situations (e.g., in scholarly discourse or testifying in court under oath) a speaker may have to sacrifice the maxim of Manner and be prolix and obscure, or risk violating the first maxim of Quality by saying something she believes to be false. The strong claim is that the Cooperative Principle governs conversational interaction, and rational speakers abide by the maxims insofar as they are able, and expect their interlocutors to. Consequently, in cases where a speaker cannot honor one maxim without ignoring the requirements of another, the hearer/addressee may be misled into thinking that the speaker is being cooperative in every way (that is, that all maxims are being observed) if the speaker does not explicitly opt out of conforming to a maxim, by informing her interlocutor, either explicitly as in (1) or implicitly as in (2), that she is not conforming to that maxim.

1a.	I am not at liberty to say any more.	[Quantity I]
1b.	I probably don't need to say this . . .	[Quantity II]
1c.	I'm not sure if it's true, but . . .	[Quality I]
1d.	I have no evidence for this, but . . .	[Quality II]
1e.	I know this is irrelevant, but . . .	[Relation]
2a.	As you know, . . .	[Quantity II]
2b.	This may be just a rumor, but . . .	[Quality II]
2c.	By the way, . . .	[Relation]

So far, this discussion of the Cooperative Principle and the maxims is little different from the exhortations of the composition or rhetoric teacher, and the reader may be getting impatient to know what there is here that is new. It is this: in addition, a speaker may contribute an utterance which, taken at face value, disregards a maxim (usually Relation), even though the speaker intends the utterance to convey something relevant. Even when speech behavior appears inconsistent with the maxims, the hearer assumes that the speaker is observing the Cooperative Principle—to do otherwise would be to assume that the speaker is irrational and unpredictable, and cannot be expected to participate in rational discourse. Assuming that the speaker is then abiding by the Cooperative Principle (and the maxims, unless this absolutely cannot be reconciled with the speaker's behavior), the hearer will adopt a strategy of interpreting the speaker's behavior as conforming to the maxims, and will consider what propositions must be assumed to make the speaker's behavior patently in conformity with the Cooperative Principle and the maxims.

Since the speaker (as a speaker-hearer of a natural language spoken in a society) expects the hearer to adopt this strategy for interpreting speech behavior, the speaker is free to exploit it, and speak in such a way that his behavior must be interpreted according to it. If the speaker's remark seems irrelevant, the hearer will seek to construct a sequence of inferences which make it relevant or at least cooperative. This exploitation of the maxims is the basic mechanism by which utterances are used to convey more than they literally denote (i.e., say$_2$), and Grice gave it the name IMPLICATURE. In this section, we first examine some examples showing how implicature works, then examine the notion of implicature more closely, and illustrate the varieties of implicature with more examples.

Implicatures are likely to arise or be intended whenever a maxim appears to be conspicuously violated, whether the violation is real or only apparent, and whether or not the maxim is sacrificed for another maxim. For example, in the dialogue in (3), adapted from Grice (1975, p. 51), B's response to A's remark about Smitty appears on the surface to violate the maxim of Relation.

3.   A: Smitty doesn't seem to have a girlfriend these days.
      B: He's been driving to New York every weekend.

But if A assumes that B is observing the Cooperative Principle, he must assume that B's response is as relevant, truthful, complete, and clear, as B considers appropriate. B may intend A to infer (i.e., B may implicate) that (B believes that) Smitty has a girlfriend in New York, or has too many business obligations in New York to have time for a girlfriend, or has so much to do in New York he finds no need for a girlfriend, or some other comment on or explanation for Smitty's apparent girlfriendlessness which preserves the assumption that B is observing the maxim of relation. The implicated proposition might be one which B does not have adequate evidence for, or one which B has adequate evidence for, but does not want to explain how he got it (sacrificing Quantity I so that he can abide by the maxims of quality). By implicating this comment, rather than asserting it, B observes Quality I and Relation, without violating Quality II.

In the dialogue in (4), D would be violating Relation and Quantity I if he did not expect C to be able to interpret his reply as a cooperative response to the question, and infer that D believed the screwdriver was in the red tool box, that the toolbox was accessible, and so on.

4.   C: Have you seen my stubby screwdriver?
      D: Look in the red toolbox.

By responding as he does, D implicates that the screwdriver is in the toolbox and accessible to C. Indeed, to respond 'directly' with *yes* (i.e., 'In my lifetime, I have seen it') would be distinctly unhelpful, a blatant violation of the Cooperative Principle itself. If D infers, as most of us do in such cases, that C really wants to know where the screwdriver is, and is implicating that he wants that, then a *yes* answer implicates that D does not intend to cooperate with C in this enterprise.

As the ordinariness of example (4) suggests, conversational implicature is an absolutely unremarkable and ordinary conversational strategy. The examples in (5–7) all exploit the assumption that the utterance conforms to the relevance maxim. With (5b) and (5c), the speaker implicates an answer to a question (given as (5a)) which she might feel social taboos prevent her from answering directly.

5a.   Q: What would you like for your birthday?
5b.   A: I need a new camera.
5c.   A: Well, my camera's broken.[6]

One ordinarily understands an utterance like (6) as implicating that the proposition expressed by the second sentence is relevant to the proposition expressed by the first, probably by representing an intended effect of the state of affairs which the first sentence describes.

6.   I will rake the leaves that have fallen on Toad's lawn. He will be surprised.

And in (7), exploiting the assumption that she is speaking in accordance with the maxim of relevance, B's answer implicates that because her car is not working, she cannot provide a ride for A.

7a.   A: Can I get a ride with you?
7b.   B: My car's not working.

A speaker may even exhibit behavior which blatantly and conspicuously fails to conform to a maxim with the intention that her behavior be recognized as failing to conform to that maxim, and interpreted as nonetheless being cooperative in the overall scheme of things. For example, a speaker might say much more than clearly is necessary, or say something obviously false or irrelevant, obscure, ambiguous, or prolix. If the hearer

---

[6]As discussed in chapter 6, the initial particle *well* often signals that not everything relevant is being made explicit. Cf. also Lakoff (1973a) and Schourup (1982).

assumes that the speaker is observing the Cooperative Principle, is able to conform to the maxim so clearly ignored, and so is not opting out, or sacrificing the observance of one maxim to preserve that of another, he will have to reconcile this assumption with the fact that a maxim appears to have been violated.

Examples (3–7) illustrate the generation of implicatures, although none involve the conspicuous flouting of a maxim to do so. The next example (after Grice, 1975, p. 52) illustrates how conspicuously failing to conform to a maxim exploits that maxim to generate implicature. Suppose Professor A is asked by his professional colleague Professor B to evaluate for a position at an American university, candidate X, a former student of A's. A writes a letter of recommendation consisting of the paragraph in (8).

8.   Mr. X's command of English is excellent, and he always attended class regularly.

A regular kiss of death recommendation — but how? Since A has responded to the request to write, he is not opting out of cooperating. Since X was his student, A is in a position to abide by Quantity, Quality, and Relation, and to provide a considerable amount (Quantity) of adequately warranted (Quality II) relevant (Relation) information about X of the sort he knows B wants. But all A says is that X speaks English well and attended class regularly. Since A can be supposed to realize (a) that his saying only this obviously violates Quantity I, and (b) that B will recognize this, A must intend for B to recognize it. However, if A is alert, he must also realize that B will try to interpret A's behavior as cooperating with the request, by concluding that it is significant that A did not say more. Therefore, A must intend B to conclude this. A logical reason for A not to say more is that there is nothing to recommend X beyond what A wrote. Since this is obviously an inadequate recommendation for an academic position, if A is rational and alert, he must have intended to implicate that X's qualifications for the position in question are inadequate.

Now that we have some clear examples of the sort of phenomena Grice had in mind we can look at his characterization (1975, p. 49–50) of implicature. In, by, and when saying "P," a speaker implicates 'q,' provided that

1.   the speaker is presumed to be observing the maxims, or at least the Cooperative Principle,
2.   in order to make the speaker's uttering "P" consistent with (1), it is necessary to assume that the speaker believes that 'q,'

3.   the speaker reflexively expects (cf. Ch. 1, Sec. 6) that the addressee is able to grasp intuitively, or actively infer (2).

Grice distinguished between CONVERSATIONAL implicatures, which must be capable of being worked out, even if they are short circuited and grasped intuitively (cf. Morgan, 1978), and CONVENTIONAL implicatures, which can only be "grasped intuitively." Grice (1975) gave only one example of a conventional implicature, the implicature of causality associated with *therefore* in (9).

9.   He is an Englishman; he is, therefore, brave.

According to this analysis, *therefore* differs from *because* in that *A because B* asserts that B is the cause of A, while *B, therefore A* only implicates, takes for granted, or presupposes that B is the cause of A.[7] Indeed, presuppositions associated locally by convention with the use of particular forms (Gazdar's, 1979, "pre-suppositions") are now customarily referred to as conventional implicatures rather than as presuppositions.

Conventional implicatures also differ from conversational implicatures in that conventional implicatures do not crucially depend on assuming the speaker to be observing the Cooperative Principle. The particular conversational implicature that a particular utterance generates in a particular context is a function of the addressee's estimate of the speaker's reflexive estimate of what the addressee assumes and will conclude. Since there is ample room for error here, what is conversationally implicated is somewhat indeterminate: what is potentially conversationally implicated is a large (perhaps indefinitely large) disjunction of propositions (recall example (3)), and the speaker is in a position to rationally deny that a particular one was intended. The conventional implicature of a linguistic expression, on the other hand, is quite specific, and so not cancellable; you cannot deny that you meant them without involving yourself in a contradiction.

Grice also distinguished a class of implicatures as generalized conversational implicatures (1975, p. 56). These are implicatures that in normal (nonspecial) circumstances are regularly associated with a linguistic expression. For example, Grice described a generalized conversational implicature associated with the indefinite article *a,* that the referent of the noun it

---

[7]The causal connection to some previously mentioned circumstance is thus similar to the implication connected with the use of pronouns. Just as *he* doesn't assert 'masculine and singular,' but rather presupposes it, so the "pro-conjunction" (Cf. chapter 2, Sec. 5) *therefore* presupposes rather than asserts a causal relation.

modifies is not closely associated "with some [contextually] identifiable person."[8] This is why (10) implicates that the woman is not John's wife, girlfriend, sister, or mother, and why (11) implicates that it was neither John's car, nor the speaker's or the addressee's, that was involved.

10.   John is meeting a woman this evening.
11.   A car ran over John's cat.

Generalized conversational implicature differs from conventional implicature in that, as conversational implicature, it is cancellable, context-dependent, and not strictly determinate. As Hirschberg (1985) pointed out, the difference between generalized conversational implicature and particularized conversational implicature is only a matter of the degree of dependence on context, and thus, not a categorical distinction.

The reader is cautioned not to take these characterizations of conversational, conventional, and generalized conversational implicatures as defining criteria. Grice did not intend them that way (Grice, 1978, pp. 114–115) and Sadock (1978) outlined serious problems with taking them that way. Kempson (1975), Wilson (1975), Gazdar (1979), and Wilson and Sperber (1979), among others, offer more explicit accounts, based on Grice's principles or extensions of them.

In talking about the observance of the Cooperative Principle as rational, Grice (1975, pp. 47, 49) hinted that he takes it and the maxims to represent values universally assumed in human society. Grice does not actually claim universality for the Cooperative Principle and the maxims (which he takes to be special cases of the Cooperative Principle),[9] but it is clear that the value of the Cooperative Principle and the maxims in explaining linguistic

---

[8]With entities that are inalienably connected with an identified referent, *a* implicates, as Grice noted, the reverse. We would infer from the utterance of (i) that it was Smitty's own finger that he broke, unless we made the (special) assumption that Smitty was (known to be) a gangster or other sort of brute, or such a clutz that it was not unusual for him to injure others.

i.   Smitty broke a finger yesterday.

Naturally, the inalienably connected entity has to be of the sort that individuals typically have more than one of. Example (ii) works more like (10) than like (i).

ii.   John broke a nose yesterday.

Cf. Horn (1984a) for extended discussion of this phenomenon.

[9]Actually, since Grice takes the maxims to be only special cases, and not corollaries, discovering that one of the maxims was not universal would not invalidate claims that the Cooperative Principle was universal.

phenomena is much greater if they are universal (and hence potentially a consequence of some property of human nature or human society) than if they are not. Thus, it is worthwhile to examine Keenan's (1978) frequently cited argument that the maxims do not universally govern human talk exchanges. Keenan claimed that Malagasy speakers regularly withhold information from their conversational partners, and concluded from this that they must lack the first maxim of Quantity, and that therefore, the maxims are not universal. In her discussion, Keenan indicated that it is not uncommon for speakers to withhold information in answering a question. For example, a question amounting to something like (12a) might be answered with the equivalent of (12b), even when the respondent is in a position to give a more precise answer.

12a. A: Where is your mother?
12b. B: She is either in the house or at the market.

But as Prince (1982) noted, Keenan's account indicates that among the Malagasy, information that is not readily available is a highly prized commodity that confers prestige on those who have it. Furthermore, there are cultural taboos about making statements which turn out to be incorrect, or that assign blame. But information that the speaker is not the unique possessor of is readily imparted, as is information whose publication would not make the speaker guilty of a cultural infraction. Thus, when B knows where his mother is, and saying where would not amount to blaming her for anything, interchanges like (12) involve either opting out of the first maxim of Quantity, to preserve one's status, or flouting the maxim, to flaunt it. Either way, the existence of the maxim of Quantity among the Malagasy is entailed; it could not be exploited if it did not exist. Keenan confirmed this in revealing (1976, pp. 76–78) that when providing the information sought does not threaten the speaker's position in the community, even uniquely possessed information is not withheld. Thus, Malagasy speakers are just like western Europeans in abiding by the Cooperative Principle and observing even the questioned first maxim of Quantity, although it is readily sacrificed to Quality (II), and to a Malagasy prohibition against assigning blame. Indeed, they exploit it when maintaining membership in an information elite is valued more highly than other interpersonal goals.

   This case should make it clear how the value of the maxims as an explanatory tool lies in what they induce a rational hearer to infer when she assumes that a speaker is abiding by them, even when what is said appears not to conform. Grice's contribution was thus not the claim that discourse should conform to the maxims, or that a very particular sort of discourse does conform to them, but the observation that assuming that conversation is governed by the maxims explains usages which, taken at face value, appear illogical, yet typically convey much more than is said. This assumption, put as the Cooperative Principle, is in essence the eminently reasonable claim that man is a social animal. As section 4 details, other scholars saw that this same assumption could help to resolve troubling puzzles in syntax, semantics, and discourse theory.

To give the reader some idea of the scope of the phenomena that implicature can be invoked to explain, the next section provides a variety of examples of the exploitation of various maxims to make implicatures.

2. EXPLOITING THE MAXIMS

Probably most of the implicatures we commonly make involve apparent violations of the maxim of Relation, that is, cases where the maxim 'Be relevant' looks like it has been disregarded, but where what is said is correctly understood only by assuming that what is apparently irrelevant is, in fact, relevant.[10] A typical example is the use of a question to respond to a question as in the example from *Casablanca* above, and in example (13).

13.

Garfield   10·25   © 1984 United Feature Syndicate, Inc.   JIM DAVIS

© 1984 United Feature Syndicate, Inc.

In (13) Garfield, widely known to love food above all else, responds to Arlene's question with an apparently irrelevant question. His question is one whose true answer is negative and obviously negative. Arlene realizes this, and apparently infers (as intended) that the relevance of that is that the true answer to her question is likewise obviously negative. Thus, Garfield's question implicates not only "No," but also "as you ought to know." Novel rhetorical questions work as well as cliched ones like this (and their positive counterparts like *Is the Pope Catholic?*). Garfield could have achieved the same effect with *Do alligators grow geraniums?*

But we are all also probably familiar with cases where implicatures are intended to arise from conspicuously disregarding the maxim of Relation.

---

[10]Indeed, Sperber and Wilson (1982, 1986) have taken the maxim of Relevance as central, and attempted to show how the implicatures Grice derived from violations of the other maxims could be derived without them.

Someone may "change the subject" abruptly to indicate to the other conversant(s) that what was being said could put its speaker in an awkward situation (or worse), because the referent of uncomplimentary remarks has just walked into overhearing range, because the room might be bugged by spies or political opponents, and so on. It is usually safer, quicker, and more effective to implicate 'Don't say any more about that. What you said was a faux pas' (or: 'Don't say any more about it. Doing so could endanger our plans') than to openly try to persuade the other conversant(s) of it.

In most cases where a speech act appears not to conform with all of the maxims, the addressee is intended to assume that it IS in conformity with all of them, and interpret it in that light. In cases of genuinely disregarding a maxim, however, the addressee is intended to infer that the speaker is not conforming to a maxim, and to figure out why. This generally induces an implicature which is a metalinguistic comment about the discourse. For example, the violation of Quantity I in (8) implicates 'What I am not saying is significant'; changing the subject abruptly (violating Relation) implicates, 'This subject is dangerous.' Such comments disrupt the discourse, and so are not cooperative with respect to the discourse in progress, although if the speaker is assumed to be rational and cooperative, they will be taken as cooperative with respect to some broader, more global enterprise involving speaker and addressee, for example, maintaining appearances (for instance, that everyone is nice and good, that no one is inferior), or just keeping a private conversation from being overheard.

One can purport to violate both Relation and the first maxim of Quality for effects similar to Garfield's in (13). In (14), B utters an obviously and outrageously false statement which has no apparent relation to A's remark. But if A assumes that B means to be conveying something not false that is relevant, B may be successful in implicating that A's assertion is equally false.

14.   A: You know, I can crush rocks with my bare hands.
      B: Yeah, and I'm Marie of Rumania.
      [Or: Yeah, and the sun rises in the west.]

Grice cited understatement, hyperbole, and sarcasm as also being cases where Quality is apparently violated to implicate something true and relevant while avoiding "going on record" (for whatever reason). Thus, uttering *That was smart!* implicates 'That was stupid!' just in case the addressee can be expected to realize that the speaker believes that the literally expressed proposition is relevant, but doesn't believe it is true (Grice, 1975, p. 53; cf. also Sperber & Wilson, 1981, 1986).

Purporting to blatantly violate the first maxim of Quantity (Say as much as is required . . .) is fairly commonplace as well, implicating, as in (15), that the speaker is unwilling to say more.

15a. A: Where've you been?
      B: Out.

15b. A: Where do you live?
      B: Somewhere.

If speaker B is not intending to be understood as uncooperative, she may intend the addressee to infer further that the contribution he sought is none of his business, or should not have been requested in public, or was rudely requested, or something of that nature. Equally commonplace are violations which, like the example of the letter of recommendation cited earlier, implicate 'There is nothing more positive I can say.'[11] Other familiar examples include the evaluation *It was interesting* of a scholarly paper or an artistic performance, or *He (or she) has a nice personality* of a blind date.

Examples of the blatant violation of the second maxim of Quantity (Say no more than is necessary) are not so easy to find. It is not too uncommon for a participant in a conversation to contribute much more detail than is relevant (usually simultaneously violating Relation and the Manner submaxims against prolixity) in order to show off his knowledge (the opposite of the Malagasy case), but since the violator does not ordinarily intend to be taken to be intentionally disregarding this maxim, this is not an example of implicature arising from flouting the second maxim of Quantity, but of boorishness.

However, it is not too hard to imagine a context (involving espionage and intrigue, say) where a person who is known to be a person of few words deliberately monopolizes the conversation, in order to keep a certain participant from talking (because that person might give the game away, say), with the intention that this ploy be recognized (and abetted) by other participants. This would be a case of implicature arising from blatant violation because the speaker's talking "too much" would be intentional, and intended to be recognized as both intentional and significant.

As with all the other cases of blatantly flouting a maxim, when the maxim of Manner is flouted, the implicature is a metalinguistic comment about the discourse in progress. Thus conversants may be intentionally obscure, communicating in stylistically inappropriate polysyllables, even in a foreign

---

[11]This gloss is ambiguous between 'nothing else positive' and 'nothing with greater positiveness.' Either suits my meaning.

language that neither of them knows well, in order to implicate 'What we are discussing is not for the ears of those who may overhear us' (e.g., the children playing at our feet, the student or colleague at the coffeepot over there, etc.).

Speakers are also intentionally prolix or obscure (sometimes the two co-occur) as in (16a) and (17a) to implicate that a shorter, more direct manner of speaking would be inaccurate, as in (16) or inconsiderate, impolitic, or the like, as in (17). All of the examples in (16–17) are from "Walter Scott's *Personality Parade*"; the examples in (16a) and (16b) addressing the same issues show that this publication is not uniformly obscure about certain topics, and support the hypothesis that the implicatures of (16a) and (16b) are intentional.

16a. Q: Now that he's hit the big time, is it true that Don Johnson of the "Miami Vice" TV show has dumped Patti D'Arbanville, the mother of his 3-year-old boy?

A: At this writing, Johnson and his longtime live-in are reportedly not as compatible as they once were. Johnson has been working and residing in Miami, while Patti has been holding down the fort and caring for their son, Jesse, in Los Angeles. (6Apr86)

16b. Q: How about the rumor that, after she gives birth to her second child in August, Princess Caroline of Monaco plans to drop her young husband for the Argentine tennis star Guillermo Vilas?

A: Caroline, 29, had a fling with Vilas in the South Pacific several years ago, before marrying Italian hier Stefano Casiraghi, but there's little or no chance she would dump Stefano. (6Apr86)

17a. Q: Is Don Regan, the White House chief of staff, a feudist? [. . .]

A: [. . .] Don Regan, 66, is not a feudist, but he is not as well liked as his predecessor, [James] Baker. Somehow, the adjective "ruthless" invariably arises when Regan is discussed. (8Dec85)

17b. Q: [. . .] Did Maria [Shriver] get that ["CBS Morning News"] job because she is a Kennedy family member?

A: Maria Shriver, 30, replaced Phyllis George on "The CBS Morning News" not because she happens to be a daughter of Eunice Kennedy and Sargent Shriver but because CBS

executives believed her well-qualified for the job. A 1977
graduate of Georgetown University, Shriver worked at [. . .]
(6Apr86)[12]

The injunction against ambiguity is often quietly ignored in the service of
politics and politeness, as we saw in chapter 1. But it is also flouted, by
every speaker who makes a (good) pun. In the example below, Bea's remark
is only funny if the ambiguities of *racing* and *running* ('beating rapidly' and
'dripping' versus 'good for racing' and 'good for running') are recognized.

18.   Abe: You're in bed with a cold, and you're still planning to run
                in the marathon tomorrow?
       Bea: Why not? I've got a racing pulse and a running nose.

3. COHERENCE

One consequence of the Cooperative Principle, and of the maxim "Be
relevant" in particular, that Grice never discussed, is that it provides the
basis for a natural account of the problem of the coherence of texts, that is,
of elucidating what it is that makes (19a) a plausible discourse, in contrast
to (19b), which appears to be just a string of sentences related only by
temporal or spatial order.[13]

19a.   The following days were unlike any that had gone before. There
        wasn't a man on the ranch who didn't know of Saturday's race
        and the conditions under which it would be run. They gave any
        excuses to get near the black stallion's corral.

---

[12]The observant reader will have noticed that the answers in these examples do not conform
to the maxims the way answers in face to face oral conversations do. Specifically, if these were
personal, oral answers, they would be considered disorderly and overly informative. However,
the apparent violation of the second maxim of quantity is motivated by the fact that the real
addressee is not the person who asked the question (whose initials and city I have left out), but
the entire readership of *Parade* magazine, so journalistic values and assumptions regarding
optimal discourse structure enter into the writer's notion of "required by the purpose of the talk
exchange." Cf. Green, (1979) for further discussion of unique pragmatic features of journalistic prose.

[13]I use *discourse* to refer to either spoken or written language, and *text* to refer to any written
language segment, whether transcribed from speech or not.

[Walter Farley, *The Black Stallion,* p. 199. New York: Random House (1953)]

19b. The sun climbed higher, and with its ascent the desert changed. There was nothing Lucy liked so much as the smell and feel of fur. One evening, after dark, she crept away and tried to open the first gate, but swing and tug as she might she could not budge the pin.[14]

Some theorists (e.g., Halliday & Hasan, 1976) have claimed that what makes a sequence of sentences hang together to be a text that is more than just a sequence of sentences is LINGUISTIC properties of those sentences: whether they exhibit (a) anaphoric expressions which (could be taken to) refer to (the same entities, properties, etc. as) previous expressions, and (b) whether the same or related[15] lexical items appear across sentences in the text. The reader can see, however, that as far as such linguistic properties go, (19a) and (19b) do not differ significantly. The sentences are structurally similar, pairwise across examples. The third sentence in each contains a pronominal subject which could have the definite noun phrase in the second sentence as its antecedent. In both, the vocabulary items in each individual sentence have nothing inherently to do with the lexical items in any other sentence. And in both, there is no cohesive LINGUISTIC link between the first and the second sentence at all. In any case, Halliday and Hasan insisted that the linguistic properties of a text (termed by them "cohesion") that contribute to coherence are not a function of the reference of the words in the text, but of the forms themselves, and their histories of occurrence. It is difficult to see how a theory like this could account for the striking difference between (19a) and (19b).

There are also theories (e.g., Prince, 1973; Rumelhart, 1975; van Dijk, 1972, 1977) which treat the coherence of text as reflecting a (defining) property comparable to grammaticality for sentences, which all genuine texts have, but random collections of sentences do not have. Morgan and Sellner (1980) and Morgan (1981) critique these theories in some detail.

A more promising approach to what connects individual sentences in a genuine text but not a spurious one is based on the assumption that the sequence of sentences at issue is produced by an individual in accordance

---

[14]These sentences are from Walter Farley's *The Black Stallion Revolts* (New York: Random House, 1953), C. S. Lewis's *The Lion, the Witch, and the Wardrobe* (New York: Macmillan, 1950), and Mary Norton's *The Borrowers* (New York: Harcourt, Brace and World, 1952), respectively. They were chosen to match the excerpt in (19a) for syntax, anaphora, and introduction of noun phrases with definite articles.

[15]It is not clear what criterion of relatedness Halliday and Hasan have in mind, but from their examples, it seems to be topical rather than formal, though they refer to it as formal.

with the Cooperative Principle, and that as a consequence, each sentence is intended to say something necessary, true, and relevant to accomplishing some objective in which (it is mutually believed) the text producer and the intended audience are mutually interested. A coherent text is one where the interpreter can readily reconstruct the speaker's plan with reasonable certainty, by inferring the relations among the sentences, and their individual relations to the various subgoals in the inferred plan for the enterprise understood to be at hand.

With this in mind, let us examine (19a) and (19b) once more. The first sentence of (19a) tells us that certain days were unique. We expect subsequent sentences to tell us what was unique about them, or perhaps, what that uniqueness led to, and we are not disappointed. The second sentence tells us that there was universal interest in a race, and we infer that this is what is extraordinary. We take the days to be days experienced by men on a ranch anticipating a race which will take place under unusual conditions on the next Saturday. We take the *they* in the third sentence to refer to the men, and take the sentence as a whole to be intended to provide an additional example of what was unique about the days mentioned in the first sentence. Finally, we infer from the reference to a black stallion that the race is a horse race, and not, say, a road race, or a drag race.

In (19b), on the other hand, the first sentence describes a desert sunrise. We expect the next sentence to elaborate on that description, or maybe to begin a narration of an event in the desert, or perhaps to state a cause or an effect of the conditions of this particular sunrise. From the descriptive *there*-construction (cf. Milsark, 1977), a guess that the second sentence is an elaboration seems to be the best bet, but it is hard to imagine how a cooperative writer could expect us to infer what Lucy's attraction to fur has to do with a desert sunrise. Maybe (although this is pushing it) Lucy regrets the sunrise, because after sunrise, fur-bearing desert animals will disappear into burrows to keep cool, so maybe a narration will ensue. This inference allows us to infer that the third sentence refers to Lucy's attempt to go out at night in an effort to find some furry animals, but I still cannot think of a rational way to connect the third sentence with the first one, whether it is taken as the beginning of a narrative, or as an exemplification of Lucy's love of fur. Since (19b) is composed of sentences from three different books (cf. footnote 4), it is not surprising that they seem to have nothing to do with each other.

Coherence, in this approach, depends not on properties of the text components themselves, either individually or in relation to each other, but on the extent to which effort is required to construct a reasonable plan to attribute to the text producer in producing the text. This, in turn, depends on how hard or easy it is to take each sentence as representing a true, necessary, and relevant contribution to that plan.

Examination of one more example may prove instructive. In example (20), the first paragraph of a bona fide text by a professional writer, the nature of the connection between the first and the second sentence is not immediately obvious.

20.   One afternoon last fall I found myself unable to leave my car when I arrived at the grocery store. On "All Things Considered" there was an excerpt from a series called "Breakdown and Back," the story of a mental breakdown as experienced by one woman, Annie.
[Jeanie Cheeseman, "Breakdown and back". *Patterns* [WILL AM, FM and TV programming guide] Feb. 1986, p. [4]. Urbana, Illinois (1986).]

The writer of this paragraph has taken it for granted that the reader will recognize "All Things Considered" as the name of a radio program and understand that the writer was listening to it over a radio. Still, that is not enough to understand what the two sentences have to do with each other. Asked about this paragraph, some respondents assume that the relation is just that of contemporaneousness of events, and that the two sentences together set the stage for a narration of what happened to the writer in the car. Others agree that the second sentence is relevant to the first in that it represents the proximate cause of the writer's inability to get out of the car, but vary widely in their interpretations of the ultimate cause. Some infer that the writer was paralyzed by the recall of a breakdown she herself experienced, some infer (correctly, as is clear from subsequent paragraphs) that the excerpts were so fascinating that the writer did not want to miss the rest (by moving out of the range of the car radio's speaker). Others might infer that the writer was afraid to hear the rest of the program in the grocery store, and no doubt there are still other plausible reasons one might infer.

In any case, the variation in understanding provoked by examples like this provide strong evidence that the coherence of text is not a matter of properties exclusively of the text, but of the likelihood that the text's audience will be able to make whatever inferences are necessary to relate the content of the individual sentences to each other in such a way that they support the inference of an orderly execution of an inferred plan to achieve an inferred objective.

It is a mistake, however, to think that because easily inferable connections among sentences contribute to making a text coherent, then increasing the number of explicit connections will make any text better and easier to understand correctly. For example, understanding the passage in (21) requires a certain amount of inferencing.

21.   Suddenly Mrs. Reilly remembered the horrible night that she and Mr. Reilly had gone to the Prytania to see Clark Gable and Jean Harlow in *Red Dust*. In the heat and confusion that had followed their return home, nice Mr. Reilly had tried one of his indirect approaches, and Ignatius was conceived. Poor Mr. Reilly. He had never gone to another movie as long as he lived. [John Kennedy Toole, *A Confederacy of Dunces*, p. 103. New York: Grove Press. 1982]

We have to infer what was horrible about the night. What, if anything, did Ignatius' being conceived have to do with the horribleness? What did it have to do with Mr. Reilly approaching something? Who or what did he approach? Why should we feel sorry for Mr. Reilly? Why didn't he ever go to another movie? I doubt that the average adult reader has difficulty understanding this paragraph, but suppose we spell out some of these inferences, as in (22).

22.   Suddenly Mrs. Reilly remembered the horrible night that she and Mr. Reilly had gone to the Prytania to see Clark Gable and Jean Harlow in *Red Dust*. It was horrible because it resulted in Ignatius being conceived. It happened like this. They had gone home after the show. Mr. Reilly had tried to have intercourse with Mrs. Reilly. This had caused heat and confusion. In the heat and confusion that had followed their return home, nice Mr. Reilly had tried one of his indirect approaches to her. He succeeded, and Ignatius was conceived. Poor Mr. Reilly. He so regretted conceiving Ignatius that he was afraid to go to the movies again because he feared that if he went to the movies he might get carried away by passion. He feared that if he got carried away by passion, he might father another child and suffer as he did with Ignatius. Consequently he had never gone to another movie as long as he lived.

The paragraph in (22) is more explicit than (21), but it does not seem to be any easier to understand, and it certainly is not better writing. In fact, in spelling out the relations among the propositions entailed and asserted by the sentences in (21), (22) raises other questions. If the writer is abiding by the Cooperative Principle, then everything he says should be relevant to the goal of the discourse, and necessary for its achievement. Therefore everything he says must be noteworthy. Is it noteworthy that the Reillys had gone home after the show? Should they have been expected to go elsewhere? Noteworthy that Mr. Reilly succeeded in achieving intercourse? Didn't he usually? Noteworthy that Ignatius' existence was regrettable? The author has provided ample evidence that Ignatius is an extremely unpleasant person in the previous 90 pages. Should it be reinterpreted in light of the fact that he finds it necessary to inform us of this now? Are the details of Mr. Reilly's logic so unlikely that they need to be spelled out in such detail? Or does the author think that we readers are so dim-witted that we could not figure out why Mr. Reilly would attribute the conception of Ignatius to viewing a romantic movie?

Far from making the passage more coherent, spelling out the connections that we have to make in order to account for why the author of the original appears to have left things out distracts our attention away from the author's point and toward tangential issues, even toward ourselves and his opinion of us. If a reader makes even one of these inferences, the passage is thereby less coherent and more difficult to appreciate properly than it would have been without the unnecessary explicit connections.

This points up again the degree to which coherence is a function, not of the properties of the text, but rather of the text-producer's estimate of his audience's beliefs and inferencing capacity, and of his acting appropriately on that estimate.

4. PRAGMATIC ALTERNATIVES TO SYNTACTIC AND SEMANTIC ACCOUNTS OF SOME PHENOMENA

As Morgan (1975b) pointed out, the possibility of accounting for meaning properties and syntactic distributions of uses of linguistic expressions in terms of conversational inferences rather than semantic entailments or grammatical ill-formedness was welcomed by many linguists as a means of avoiding redundant analyses on the one hand, and analyses which postulate rampant ambiguity on the other. The program of resolving syntactic and semantic puzzles via implicature was not without its own problems, but it is worthwhile to examine some of those puzzles, and the contribution that implicature makes to their solution.

Indirect Speech Acts

Investigation of the performative hypothesis brought the attention of linguists (e.g., Sadock, 1970, 1972) to a class of utterances whose syntactic form did not match their apparent illocutionary force. These INDIRECT SPEECH ACTS, illustrated in (23), posed a problem for the performative hypothesis.

23a. Will you (please) pass the salad. = Please pass the salad.
      (Question form, imperative force)
23b. Why don't you pass the salad. = Pass the salad.
      (Question form, imperative force)
23c. I'd like you to set the table now = Set the table now.
      (Declarative form, imperative force)
23d. Is that good! = That is good!
      (Question form, declarative force)

Adherents of the performative hypothesis maintained that (a) illocutionary force was uniformly represented in (underlying) syntactic structure, and (b) that surface form was related in a regular way to illocutionary force. Faced with phenomena like those in (23), they attempted to construct syntactic analyses of these constructions that would be consistent with the performative hypothesis, but found themselves with baroque analyses that had little in the way of syntactic support (Heringer, 1972; Sadock, 1970). Sadock (1972) and Searle (1975b) thus proposed that sentences like (23) represented speech act idioms, forms whose illocutionary force was arbitrarily connected to their syntactic form; in this analysis, utterances of *Can/Could/Would/Will/Won't you VERB PHRASE* and *Why don't you VERB PHRASE* have the force of the corresponding imperative-form (verb phrase) utterances simply by convention.

Gordon and Lakoff (1975), on the other hand, proposed to account for the imperative senses of these question forms as implicatures arising from the fact that the question forms (interpreted as questions) suggest that one or another of the various sincerity conditions involving the addressee of a request is not met. (Recall that the maker of a sincere request assumes that the addressee is able to perform the requested act, would be willing to do so if asked, and has no standing plans to do it; Searle, 1969.) Thus, asking if the addressee can do something implies a belief that he might not be able to, and asking why he does not do something implies a belief that he has no plans to do it. Similarly, they treated cases like (23c) as an implicature arising from the assertion of a sincerity condition involving the speaker — the maker of a sincere request wants the requested act performed, and has a reason for this desire. Gordon and Lakoff's analysis accounts not only for the fact that (23a) and (23c) have the illocutionary force of imperatives, but also for the fact that (24a) and (24b) can be understood as (or, in their terms, entail) requests to close a window (Gordon & Lakoff, 1975, pp. 84, 86).

24a. It's cold in here.
24b. I assume you can close the window.

This generality, however, is a weakness as well as a strength of the analysis, for it is unable to distinguish between indirect speech acts that seem at worst ambiguous, like those of (23), and ones that are vague, like (24a) or (25).

25.   I left my watch at home.

A sentence like (24a) hints at a request to open a window, close a window, turn up the heat, find the speaker a sweater—generally, to do whatever would make the speaker more comfortable if she is assumed, BECAUSE of the utterance of (24a), to be uncomfortable; (25) could be an excuse for being late (or early), or a request for the time, for a watch, for the location of a clock, for notification of the time at some future point, and so forth. Furthermore, forms like (23a, 23c) convey requests much more directly (in English, anyway) than forms like (24) or (25), and curiously, there seems to be much more cross-linguistic agreement about the potential for sentences like (24a) and (25) to be used as hints than there is about the directness with which sentences like (23a, 23c) convey requests (Green, 1975a).

Finally, in order to account for the fact that question forms with certain stigmata such as preverbal *please* (as in (23a)) are always understood as requests, Gordon and Lakoff were forced to introduce a novel kind of grammatical rule, one which was conditioned by utterance context. (Cf. Green, 1975a, and Morgan, 1977, for more detailed discussion of these and other issues, and Clark, 1979, for demonstration of the psychological reality of distinctions of the sort made here.)

The situation with indirect speech acts typifies the problems that Morgan (1975b) outlined: A purely syntactic analysis neutralizes pragmatic distinctions that otherwise correspond to syntactic differences, but syntactic idiosyncrasies complicate a purely pragmatic analysis. Morgan (1978) attempted to cut through this Gordian knot by demonstrating that linguistic expression is governed by two different kinds of convention: (a) conventions of language, like language-specific rules for constituent order in syntax, and meaning postulates for words and idioms, and (b) conventions of use, such as culture-specific rules for the use of expressions for answering the phone, or for the use of forms like *God bless you*, or, according to Morgan, for the use of forms like (23), which in his analysis SHORT-CIRCUIT an implicature. A short-circuited implicature is a kind of conversational implicature. As with other conversational implicatures, what is intended to be conveyed is readily derivable from the assumption that it was uttered in conformity with the Cooperative Principle and the maxims. However, because of known conventions of usage (including even known idiosyncratic habits of the speaker), the intended effect can be recognized immediately, although it can also still be calculated.

Morgan's (1978) description of short-circuited implicature involved the elaboration and subsequent truncation of means-ends chains of the sort schematized in (26).

26a. In situation X, one does Y.
26b. In situation X, one does Y by indicating Z, which one does by expressing A, by saying, "P."
26c. In situation X, one does Y by saying "P."
26d. In situation X, one says "P."

Assuming that the means in (26) are implicatures, (26c) represents a short circuiting of the implicature represented in (26b), while (26d) is an arbitrary convention of use. The fact that *dog* is an English word, whereas *dgo* is not, and the fact that yes–no questions begin with an auxiliary verb in English are conventions of English; the fact that Americans answer the phone by saying *Hello* or by identifying themselves by saying the name of some unit they represent, like *Cognitive Science Program* and the fact that we regularly use forms like (23a–23c) to implicate requests are conventions of the use of English.

Illocutionary Force

One effect of linguists being introduced to Austin's ideas and the performative hypothesis was to focus attention on performative verbs and on their classification into their various kinds. In many quarters there was an identification of the general notion 'speech act', with 'illocutionary act'[16] (or even with 'illocutionary force)', and one wondered whether there were as many distinct illocutionary forces as there were distinct performative verbs. After all, an utterance like (5a) in chapter 4 (repeated here as (27a)) can have the force of a promise or a prediction, and an utterance like (27b) seems to have a different force when it is understood as intended to remind the addressee than it has when understood as intended to straightforwardly inform the addressee; the "tag" *you know* can only follow the reminder.[17]

27a. I'll sit in the front row.
27b. You have an appointment with Dean Brown at 3:00.

---

[16]To my mind, the identification is mistaken. Searle took 'speech act' to include a variety of acts accomplished with language, including uttering, referring, and predicating. I would include also implicating, reciting, imitating and other such complex acts.

[17]Naturally, a speaker can use *you know* with a sentence intended to inform, *implicating* that the sentence is a reminder rather than new information. A speaker might do this in order not to appear to know more than his addressee. See chapter 7 for a discussion of the values and assumptions involved in this sort of choice.

Does the performative hypothesis imply that these two uses have distinct illocutionary forces and distinct underlying forms?

In a paper that seems to have been about 10 years ahead of its time, Stampe (1975) argued against the conventionalism of the Searle–Austin performative hypothesis on the grounds that it was not by virtue of any rules, linguistic or otherwise, or Illocutionary-Force-Indicating Devices, overt or abstract, that promises, for example, were promises, and when uttered sincerely, required or entailed an intention on the part of the speaker to act accordingly. Rather, Stampe argued, it is the speaker's intending an utterance as a promise, reminder, suggestion, or request that makes it one; whether it will be so understood depends on the addressee's ability to infer that it was so intended. Sometimes parenthetical "tags" like *you know, why don't you,* and *please* will be present and provide a sufficient clue to the speaker's intention; overt main clauses of the sort Austin called performative, in Stampe's view, assert the intended force of the utterance (1975, p. 29)[18] so the addressee can make no mistake. But in many cases, the addressee will have only her estimate of the speaker's goals and plans to base her inference of the intended illocutionary force on. In this view (suggested also in Morgan, 1976, and recently formalized in Cohen & Levesque, 1987), the number of potential illocutionary forces is not limited (to around four) by the number of basic sentence types, or (to a couple of thousand) by the number of verbs in a language that can be used "performatively," but only by the number of different kinds of intentions (in saying what she says) which a speaker might have and which an addressee assuming that the speaker is abiding by the Cooperative Principle could be intended and expected, given the utterance in its context, to infer that the speaker has. Probably there are an infinite number of such intentions. Thus, in this view, there are illocutionary forces for which we do not have conventional names, such as those intended in utterances like those in (28), suggested by Larkin and O'Malley (1973).

28a. Gotcha! [said as Speaker tags Addressee]
28b. Hello?/Cognitive Science. [picking up the receiver of a ringing telephone]
28c. You put the shirt with the check in it in the washing machine?!
28d. She's your mother, not mine.
28e. Hey, you reached over the net!
28f. Well, that's done. [to co-worker, finishing a difficult task]

Another set of data which support the claim that illocutionary force is conveyed as an inference the addressee is expected to make from the "literal" sense of the expression exactly as uttered and the mutually assumed

---

[18]And so, contra Austin, have a truth value.

context in which it is uttered are utterances like those in (29), which were described by Yanofsky (1978, 1980) as NOUN PHRASE UTTERANCES.

29a. Police!
29b. Lunchtime!
29c. The laundry!
29d. My car!

Although what is intended to be conveyed by the utterance of a noun phrase utterance is generally clear in context, in principle there is no limit to what a speaker could reasonably expect one of them to convey. Thus, in different contexts (29c) might successfully convey what any of the more explicit expressions in (30) could be depended on to convey.

30a. That thunderstorm is wetting my laundry that's hanging out to dry!
30b. I/You have to pick up the laundry before the cleaner closes in 15 minutes!
30c. I/You have to remember to do the laundry today.
30d. I forgot to do the laundry!
30e. What have you done to the laundry!?
30f. We can't have the leading lady exit with her arms folded; that will leave the laundry onstage, and it will seem very strange when Sir Richard comes on stage and doesn't say anything about it.

Under the performative hypothesis, utterances like (29), if they have any illocutionary force at all, have an indefinitely large number of them. The pragmatic alternative is to say that the noun phrase utterance merely MENTIONS its referent. The noun phrase utterance itself has no illocutionary force, but as long as the hearer assumes that the speaker is being cooperative, uttering a noun phrase will implicate that its referent is relevant to the speaker's and/or addressee's goals (whether or not these goals correspond to goals of the ongoing conversation). Unless the speaker has misjudged the addressee, the addressee will be able to infer how merely mentioning the referent of the noun phrase is relevant in the context.

Similarly, one could argue (although I do not know that anyone has) that the fact that a certain syntactic form represents an imperative is merely an inference derived from the mention of a kind of action.[19] The fact that utterances consisting of tenseless verb phrases are just as ambiguous or vague as (27a) or (27b) would follow as a consequence of such an analysis.

---

[19]It is also, of course, vague or ambiguous as to what kind of directive it might be; it could be a command, a demand, a plea, a request, a suggestion, etc. Cf. Green (1975a) for some discussion of these different types.

Thus, (31) could be a directive[20] to give Eks the keys to the city, but it could also be an expression of disgust at the absurdity of the suggestion that someone give Eks the keys to the city, or dismay or astonishment or glee that plans are in effect to do that, and so on.

    31.   Give Eks the keys to the city.

Which one of these will be inferred would depend on what the speaker and addressee mutually assume about plans to bestow the city keys, and what they mutually believe about the speaker's attitudes toward Eks, among other things (cf. also Cohen & Levesque, 1987) although there may be default use-conventions which favor imperative interpretations for verb phrase utterances, interrogative interpretations for inverted sentence constructions, and so forth.

Presupposition

The question of whether presupposition is pragmatic or semantic in nature seems no longer to be a live one. There seems to be agreement on the one hand, that by convention, all other things being equal, the use of certain expressions of a language implies a state of knowledge or justified true belief on the part of the utterer concerning the propositional complements of certain predicates or the referents of noun phrases that are introduced by certain articles.[21]

---

[20]Similarly both (i) and (ii) could be used to indicate glee, or disgust.

    i.   give Eks the key to the city
    ii. giving Eks the key to the city

The fact that (i) is more readily understood as a directive than (ii) would have to be taken as a reflection of the fact that its implicature is regularly short circuited, and it is understood directly, like *Can you please pass the salt.*

The validity of such an analysis, however, depends on the existence of cases where (ii) is clearly used to implicate a directive. While (iii) might provide such a context, since both (i) and (ii) would be acceptable and essentially equivalent responses, uses of forms like (ii) as directives are limited to cases where *-ing* phrases are licensed as subject or object of a salient expression in the immediately preceding context, and this diminishes the significance of their interchangeability with forms like (i) in contexts like (iii).

    iii. What do you think would induce Eks to locate his factory here?

Thus (ii) is not nearly so good an answer to (iv) as it is to (iii), and this suggests that it represents a reduced sentence, rather than the mere mention of an action (cf. Morgan 1973c).

    iv. How can we get Eks to locate his factory here?

[21]Thus Karttunen and Peters (1979) identify epistemic factive, counterfactual, and focus factive presuppositions (e.g., *too/either*; cf. Green, 1973; Karttunen 1973), *also, even, only* (cf. Horn, 1972), clefts and pseudo-clefts) with Grice's conventional implicatures, and propose apparatus, including projection principles, for incorporating them into the framework of

On the other hand, because sentences are instruments used intentionally by agents in the context of the execution of particular plans relative to particular addressees presumed to have particular beliefs and attitudes, all other things are not equal, and there is general agreement that there is a conditional, pragmatic, conversational, discourse structural aspect to what has been described as presupposition also. Thus, Gazdar (1979, pp. 129–135) articulated a means by which potential presuppositions of a sentence (his "pre-suppositions") are projected as actual presuppositions of an utterance of that sentence only if they are consistent with entailments of the sentence and implicatures of its utterance in its context. Similarly, McCawley (1978a, 1978b) showed how supposed presuppositions of particular lexical items are better analyzed as involving implicatures from the maxim of quantity, and Horn (1978a, 1984a) elaborated on this theme more generally.

On another front, a pragmatic approach offers an account of what is going on in negative sentences which deny propositions they allegedly presuppose, like (32). The fact that such sentences are acceptable, interpretable, and not nonsensical had plagued adherents of semantic presupposition, but Horn (1984b, 1985; Horn & Bayer 1984) accounts for the negation in (32) as not linguistic negation, which simply denies a proposition, but as a METALINGUISTIC device, which denies the appropriateness of the WAY something was said.

32a.   The king of France isn't bald; there is no king of France.
32b.   John doesn't regret failing the exam, because in fact he passed.

Horn showed that metalinguistic negation can be used to register objection to an utterance on any grounds whatever, including the way it was pronounced (as in (33c)).

33a.   I'm not his daughter; he's my father.
33b.   I don't like coffee; I love it.
33c.   I didn't [míyənɨj] to read it; I [mǽnɨjd] to read it.

Finally, to take one last example of work elucidating the pragmatic nature of the presuppositions of utterances, Horn (1986) demonstrated that the discourse role of the content of an expression affects whether or not presuppositions are associated with that expression in a given utterance. He presented an account of why definite noun phrases are more *likely* to convey a presupposition of the existence of their referent when in subject position, as the contrast in (34) shows, and why the complements of factive verbs are more likely to be interpreted as presupposed true when in subject

---

Montague semantics. Similarly, Gazdar (1979, p. 124) codified them as pre-suppositions, propositions associated by convention with particular lexical items.

position, as in (35), than when extraposed to the end of the sentence or in object position, as in (36).

34a. But for the grace of God, the first king of the U.S.A. would have been Nixon.
34b. But for the grace of God, Nixon would have been the first king of the U.S.A.

35a. That Kim is a vegetarian is obvious.
35b. That her guests are vegetarians may be worrying her.
35c. That Pat was involved hasn't yet been discovered by Lee.

36a. It's obvious that Kim is a vegetarian.
36b. She may be worrying that her guests are vegetarians.
36c. Lee hasn't yet discovered that Pat was involved.

The relevant factor, Horn showed, is not actually subject position, but whether or not the clause or phrase in sentence-initial position represents what the sentence is about (i.e., represents the theme, or topic, of the sentence); when the initial phrase or subordinate clause is not a topic, then it is not necessarily presupposed, as in (37).

37a. The king of France does not exist.[22]
37b. ??That apartheid is doomed, Ed was muttering.[23]

Since sentence topics are typically material familiar to both speaker and addressee, and preferentially either salient or presupposed, sentence interpreters will tend to take initial subjects (and other initial phrases, as in (37b) — cf. chap. 6) as presupposed if they can be interpreted as representing sentence topics. Some early psychological studies suggesting this are reported in Clark and Haviland (1977).

---

[22]The following passage provides another example of the same phenomena, a nontopic definite noun phrase (italicized) failing to presuppose the existence of a referent. The narrator is a female detective investigating the death of her cousin, Boom-Boom, a hockey player for the Chicago Blackhawks. The passage describes her contemplation of a calendar she has found in his desk, with certain dates circled each month.

I . . . stared fixedly at the dates circled in the front of the book. I keep track of my period by circling the dates when I get it in my desk calendar, but that wouldn't be true in my cousin's case. I grinned to myself, picturing Boom-Boom's reaction if I'd suggested that to him.
The dates might not track *Boom-Boom's menstrual cycle,* but maybe they indicated some other periodic occurrence.
[Sara Paretsky, *Deadlock,* p. 97. (New York: Ballantine Books, 1984)]

[23]Sentence (37b) is odd because the clausal complement of a manner-of-speaking verb like *mutter, whisper, shout,* etc. is always predicated, and thus is always the point or focus (or comment) of a sentence, never the topic or theme.

Reference, Compositionality, and Metaphor

It was claimed in chapter 3 that most ordinary predicative expressions (e.g., nouns, verbs, adjectives, prepositions) exhibit an extensive multiplicity of uses, or intended senses, and the question was posed, how do language users ever figure out what is being referred to by the use of such expressions? As mentioned in that chapter, the problem of reference is to determine which of the vast number of referring functions is to be used to identify the speaker's intended referent from the referring expression she used on that occasion of utterance. In this section, I demonstrate that inferences which depend on the Cooperative Principle and the maxims (mostly Quality and Relevance) are instrumental in making this determination. A natural conclusion from this is that metaphorical uses of language are basically more extreme examples of the same phenomenon (cf. Rumelhart, 1979).

Reference

How does a hearer tell which of the several normal uses of a referring expression a speaker intended? And how does he get from an intended use to an intended referent? To answer these questions, we must assume that the hearer (H) assumes that the speaker (S) is abiding by the Cooperative Principle. If he fails to make this assumption, he must assume that the connections between what S says and what she means are arbitrary, and not rationally inferrable—rather like the child who believes he has the right to call a marking pen with permanent ink a *pregnant marker* if he chooses.

Let us take a relatively simple case first. Suppose that faced with the task of interpreting (38), H assumes that the Cooperative Principle is being adhered to.

38.   Sandy bought IBM at 71.

Now, what can H infer about what S meant by *IBM*? H must assume that S assumes that the initials *IBM* abbreviate the same thing he assumes they abbreviate. It might be International Business Machines, or it might be Indiana Building Materials, or Idaho Bulk Minerals, and so on. This is essentially the same problem as guessing/inferring which Sandy that H might know is intended by S's utterance of *Sandy,* or what a gesture indicates (recall the problem posed in the introduction to chapter 2). H must also identify what referring function for *IBM* S assumes H will assume S assumes (etc.): 'corporation called x,' 'share of stock in corporation called x,' 'goods produced by corporation called x,' and so on. In addition, H must infer what the number 71 refers to. Probably a quantity, but a quantity of what: dollars? thousands or millions of dollars? percentage points (as in *They got their mortgage at 8 1/2*)? years (as in *At 46, Phil Niekro is the oldest active player*)? home runs (as in *Roger Maris got in the record books at 61*)? Importantly, while H must come to conclusions on all of these issues, there is no factor determining a priori which one must be resolved first, and in some cases the resolution may need to be simultaneous. Let us look in more detail at how this might work.

Given the assumption that S is observing the Cooperative Principle, and the fact that S has chosen to use the cryptic/vague/ambiguous referring expression *IBM,* H infers that the explicit expression those initials are supposed to invoke is assumed by S to be salient enough for S to say that little. In other words, H utilizes the belief that S is saying as much as is necessary (abiding by the maxim of Relation and the first maxim of Quantity) to infer that the most likely explicit expression is the intended one. If H has no reason to believe S is concerned with Indiana Building Materials or Idaho Bulk Minerals (or to believe that S believes that H is so concerned), H will be rational in assuming that *IBM* refers to the corporation that makes computers and other office machines. (Otherwise, of course, S's utterance may be functionally ambiguous, and H will want to seek clarification if he realizes this, and may be misled if he does not.)

Suppose S meant International Business Machines, and H took her to mean this. What is S claiming Sandy bought? Suppose further that S and H mutually know that Sandy wants to take control of the IBM corporation, and that this is a matter that is on their minds. Considerations of relevance and quantity (or avoiding ambiguity) similar to those cited above will make such referring functions as 'goods produced by' and 'a spokesman for' unlikely candidates. But does S mean that Sandy bought shares of stock in IBM for $71 a share, or that Sandy bought the whole corporation for $71 billion (overbidding Lee by, say, $2 billion)? How could H narrow down the choices to just these? If H knows that both Sandy and IBM are under 71 years of age, and can safely assume that S knows this and knows that H knows it, and H assumes further that S is abiding by the maxim of Quality, and telling the truth, H can assume that *at 71* is not a temporal phrase locating the event in time by referring to the age at the time of the purchase of the purchaser or the purchasee. H may infer then that *at 71* refers to the compensation necessary to effect the transfer of ownership that *bought* entails. Because H takes it for granted (and takes it for granted that S believes H takes it for granted) that the usual sort of compensation is monetary, he can infer from the fact that S did not specify 71 of what that *71* represents some sum of money; if S had meant percentage points, or years of servitude, or home run obligations or possessions, she would have said so under the circumstances if she was being cooperative and abiding by the maxim of Quantity, and so saying as much as was necessary to communicate what she wanted to communicate. The use of a minimally specified expression implicates that the action was effected by the means assumed most likely. If some other form of payment than money was involved, it would have been relevant to say so; if S was abiding by the

Cooperative Principle and the maxim of relevance, she would have said so. Since she didn't specify the form of payment, it must be what H would (be expected to) take as normal: money.

Now, shares of stock for $71 per share, or a whole corporation for $71 billion? (H can assume it was $71 per share and not $71,000 or more, and $71 billion and not $71,000 or less for reasons similar to those adduced in inferring that the consideration was monetary; H assumes that shares of stock are not normally assumed to sell for more than $1,000 per share, or huge corporations for less than $100 million.) In addition to knowledge that H may have about S's financial resources, S's use of the preposition *at* in this discussion of a purchase provides a valuable clue. Because the price per share of regularly traded stocks fluctuates in a regulated and regularly charted way, it is conventional to use the preposition *at* in naming the price per share. Strictly speaking, a sentence like (39) must mean that the subject bought 31 shares of stock when it was at $71 per share. Sentence (39) merely implicates that Lee bought the stock FOR $71 per share—with a shady broker, he might have actually paid more or less than that.

39.   Lee bought 31 shares of IBM at 71.

Since to refer to the sale of a corporation as if it had a price that fluctuated publicly in response to pressures other than what the owners decide to ask or demand would provoke implicatures that this was indeed the case, in the absence of any independent evidence that it was a corporation that Sandy would be purchasing (and not stock in one), or that the price of the corporation did indeed fluctuate publicly, H can assume that it was stock that S is saying Sandy bought.

Again, H cannot reach this conclusion without assuming that what S says is all relevant, true, and necessary to inferring what S means to convey. The mental processes involved in interpreting an ordinary utterance like this are not necessarily exclusively inferential ones; obviously inference is not the only mechanism involved in understanding what must have been meant by an utterance of an ordinary sentence like (38). Salience and attention, and assumptions about them are intrinsic to the process as well, as described above. Nonetheless, the interpretation process is governed, limited, and especially, made tractable, by the assumption that speakers conform to the Cooperative Principle and the maxims. I refer the reader to Horn (1984a) for a comprehensive discussion of a wide variety of discourse consequences of the interaction between the assumption that the speaker is saying as much as is necessary and the assumption that what she intends to convey is relevant.

This example illustrates a very important fact about natural language understanding: parsing, determination of the sense and reference of uses of linguistic expressions, and evaluation of the truth of the propositions that an utterance expresses, entails, and implicates are interdependent processes. I mean by this that the information which represents the resolution of an indeterminacy in one area may equally well be crucial for, or dependent on, the resolution of an indeterminacy in another. How human beings or efficient machines actually manage the necessary integration is an open question.

Compositionality

It was observed in footnote 5 to chapter 1 that the interpretation of complex noun-like constructions poses a problem for compositionality. For example, *public beaches* is ordinarily taken to refer to beaches open to the public and not beaches which concern the public, while *religious affairs* is ordinarily taken to refer to affairs which concern religion and not affairs open to the/a religion; *public intoxication* is taken to refer to intoxication in public, and not intoxication concerning the public, and *religious person* to a person who observes a religion, and not to a person concerning religion. Either these forms are idioms, and not compositional at all, or the usual interpretation is an inference from a compositional but vague sense, or an inference disambiguates (as with *IBM* and *71* discussed previously) among a disjunction of precisely distinguishable compositional senses.[24] Aspects of this general issue are discussed in some detail by Downing (1977) and Levi (1978), with respect to complex nominals like *corporation lawyer, student protest,* and *avocado shampoo,* and by Clark and Clark (1979), who deal with denominal verbs like *to hammer, to party,* and *to bench.*

On the one hand, expressions such as *religious affairs* differ from compound nouns like *flea collar, kitchen carpet,* or *Illinois shirt* only in the superficial syntactic category of the first word,[25] and compound nouns represent an infinitely large class, because they are formed recursively by the addition of a noun to the right of a noun (or compound) which modifies it, thus: *rug shampoo, rug shampoo container, rug shampoo container cleaner, rug shampoo container cleaner salesman,* and so on. This means that IN GENERAL they cannot be treated as idiomatic, that is, lexicalized and conventional, because they are productive, representing a potentially infinite set of expressions, and so cannot be exhaustively listed. If their ranges

---

[24]For convenience, I am using *sense* here (idiosyncratically) to refer to the relation between a word and the kind it is taken to name.

[25]The only restriction is that these nouns can only have adjectival form if they are initial in the compound; a criminal legal education is not the same as a criminal law education, and *corporation legal education* seems not to even parse compared to [[*corporate law] education*]. It seems that in medial position, adjectival forms force a predicating interpretation on the preceding constituent. Cf. Levi (1978, pp. 15–39) for discussion of difference between non-predicating adjectives like *religious* in *religious affairs* and predicating adjectives like *red* in *red Porsche.*

of senses are not determined compositionally, we cannot explain how they are interpreted at all.

On the other hand, we do want to say that some expressions have a conventional, lexicalized "sense." *Sonic boom* refers to a noise heard when a noisy object travels faster than the speed of sound, and not just to a boom which is from or concerns or has sound, and *water bed* is conventionally used to refer to a bed with a water-filled mattress, not to a bed for water, or a bed which is water, and so forth. Yes, the senses normally associated with *water, bed, sonic,* and *boom* are discernible in descriptions of the normal referents of these expressions, but the contribution of those senses to the sense of the referring expression as a whole is no longer regular and predictable, although it may once have been. This is what it means to say that a meaning of a complex form has become lexicalized and conventional (cf. Morgan, 1978).

Let us assume then, that some complex nominals (i.e., Adjective–Noun and Noun–Noun compounds) may have lexicalized and conventional senses. In general, however, complex nominals are syntactically constructed expressions whose reference is a function of the references of their parts. This leaves us with the question of whether they are (a) vague, or (b) ambiguous, their parts related by a finite and relatively small number of distinct semantic functions. Levi's position is that such expressions are multiply ambiguous; there is a small number (12) of distinct semantic functions relating the parts of a complex nominal construction, in addition to (a) lexicalized, conventionalized, idiomatic meanings for some complex nominals (e.g., *venereal disease, blackboard, eggplant*) and (b) metaphor-ical uses of complex nominals (e.g., *wind bag, coffin nails*) which must be interpreted by strategies such as we have previously described.

The Clarks, on the other hand, treat novel ("innovative") constructions not as ambiguous, but as vague (or in their words, as having "an indefinite number of potential senses" (Clark & Clark, 1979, p. 783)). They maintain that "their interpretation depends on the context, especially the cooperation of speaker and listener" (p. 783), and that for this reason, innovative expressions "must be dealt with differently from both purely denotational and indexical expressions" (p. 783).

We have seen, however, in chapter 3 and earlier in this chapter, that under Nunberg's approach, (a) "purely denotational" expressions are gen-erally many ways "ambiguous"—in principle nothing limits the range or complexity of the referring functions a speaker might choose to use[26] in referring to a particular object with a particular expression, and (b) "purely denotational" expressions must be interpreted via strategies very similar to

---

[26]This is why Nunberg refers to his description of what others might call "word meaning" as "the pragmatics of reference."

those needed for interpreting indexical expressions (as described in chapters 2 and 3). That is, there is nothing particularly unique about the wide range of interpretations potentially intended for novel complex nominals or denominal verbs; they simply represent a more extreme case of the general principles for using words of the language to refer to objects and classes of objects in the universe. In this view, Levi's 12 semantic functions are neither necessary nor sufficient, and the Clarks' claim that "innovative" or "contextual" uses are interpreted by principles distinct from those used for regular uses is mistaken.

Metaphor

The most extreme case of so-called contextually determined meaning is figurative language, or metaphor (construed broadly enough to include metonymy and synecdoche). The interpretation of standard, cliched, or stored metaphors like those cited in (40) appears to depend on principles not significantly different from those that define Nunberg's fifth stage of conventionalization of referring functions.

40a.   Hedley is a *pig*.
40b.   That's a *half-baked* idea.
40c.   x *shot down/shot holes in/poked holes in* y's argument
40d.   x *stabbed* y *in the back* in his review of her book
40e.   The Mets *jumped on/rocked* the Cards for 11 hits.
40f.   They have given this program a real[27] *shot in the arm*.

These principles, described in chapter 3, Sec. 4, characterize cases where the speaker believes that given some fairly standard use R' of an expression e, there are beliefs which would license use R, though the speaker might not know who might hold those beliefs. The difference is that the beliefs licensing metaphorical uses such as those in (40) are recognized to be fanciful, nonrational beliefs; the speaker does not assume that (anyone assumes that) anyone actually believes them. That is, no one has to believe that anyone believes that ideas are explored and developed by baking them, or that arguments have mass and can be physically damaged, to expect success in communicating with expressions like (40b) or (40c). Rather, it is assumed that there are beliefs that the development of an idea is *like* the cooking of a cake (or in other metaphors, like the cultivation of a crop) or that the construction or structure[28] of an argument is like a structure or organism that will collapse if its vital parts are damaged. Thus the referring

---

[27]I.e., metaphorical—cf. G. Lakoff, 1972.

[28]It is probably impossible to talk about abstract ideas without expressions that are (at least ultimately) metaphorical.

functions inferred in the interpretation of metaphors involve the referring function 'like x' (cf. Miller, 1979).

Indeed, Nunberg defined metaphor (1978, pp. 150–151) as cases where a speaker (a) uses an expression e to refer to A in context C even though there is another expression (e') which the speaker expects the addressee is more likely to be successful in interpreting as referring to A; and (b) realizes that the use of e to refer to A is not rational, and expects the addressee to recognize that the speaker realizes this, and so on, and despite this; (c) is acting in accord with the Cooperative Principle, and expects to be understood as so acting. Nunberg argued (1978, p. 152) that there is no need to make the rhetorician's distinctions between metaphor, metonymy, synecdoche, and the like, because they are simply reflections of the use of different referring functions (viz., 'similar to,' 'entity with,' 'part of') in the same general process. Nunberg analyzed (1978, pp. 153–163) in some detail the beliefs that license an expectation of interpretability for Byron's metaphorical use of *frown* in the lines "The castled crag of Drachenfels/ frowns o'er the wide and winding Rhine." These involve beliefs that (a) the crag has a face (i.e., a front side, as when we speak of the face of a clock, or a building facing a street); (b) the face faces the Rhine; (c) the face has a brow; and (d) the face expresses an attitude. Belief (a) involves a metaphor (and a referring function) so common that we hardly notice it; belief (b) is what the sentence asserts; belief (c) involves a straightforward similarity function; belief (d) is the irrational belief that licenses the metaphor which, I take it, is supposed to convey that the crag does not merely overlook the Rhine, but has a somewhat threatening appearance[29]. This is not really an unusual irrational belief; Nunberg cited cliched expressions as *raging stream, threatening clouds, oppressive heat.*

Although I have suggested that metaphors are understood by means of strategies that involve the same mechanisms as are used for understanding implicatures (i.e., indirect speech), and more particularly, the same mechanisms as are used for so-called literal uses of language, indicating just how all (or most) meaning is metaphorical,[30] it would be misleading to imply that there are no differences between indirect speech, poetic metaphor, and ordinary mechanisms of reference. There are at least two dimensions on which the use of metaphor differs from the use of more standard referring expressions, and from the use of indirect speech (implicature). For one, as mentioned, the beliefs that license a clearly metaphorical use are not rational beliefs. Consequently, the referring function ultimately derived will

---

[29]Or, as Nunberg pointed out (1978, p. 155), a bemused or worried appearance, though this seems less likely in this context.

[30]Cf. Lakoff and Johnson (1980) for evidence of the pervasiveness of such metaphor in ordinary language.

not be the "best" referring function for that referent, compared to other referring functions for other expressions to indicate the same referent, but it will be the best one for that expression for that referent. With a novel metaphor like the ones in (41), the hearer will have to do some work to infer the intended referent.

41a.   Sheathe thine impatience.
41b.   Eks's mind is a meadow in winter.

If the metaphor is a good one, he will be rewarded with a rich set of consistent associations and the security of having made a (most likely) correct inference. Thus, (41a) implies that (in the context) impatience is dangerous, like a sword or dagger, and (41b) implies that Eks's mind is either barren, or dormant and awaiting a (metaphorically) environmental event to awaken it to (metaphorical) growth, blossoming, and fruition. The speaker is aware of all this, and thus aware that the hearer must pay a price in mental effort for the speaker's economy of words in conveying all that she chooses to convey with her metaphor.

Second, and this is not unrelated, metaphor as ordinarily understood is an art form. Part of a speaker's motivation in choosing to use metaphor over more literal language is to display his talent or virtuousity with words, a sort of verbal athleticism. But Nunberg pointed out (1978, pp. 163–171) that the expressions that constitute slang frequently involve metaphors as recherché as those of poets, and the purpose of being potentially obscure in using slang may be not so much pure aesthetics as it is a desire to display membership in an exclusive subculture. Like a secret handshake, it identifies the speaker to other members, and can be used as a filter to exclude nonmembers.

Metaphors differ from hints conveyed by conversational implicature in another way as well. At a superficial level, a metaphor often involves a proposition that is intended to be recognized as literally false. At the level of what is intended to be conveyed, however, it presumably represents a proposition that is intended to be taken as uttered in conformance with the maxim of quality. (Both metaphors and hints may, however, appear to violate the maxim of relevance at the superficial level, while conforming to it at the level of what is intended to be conveyed.)

Sadock (1979, pp. 61–62) suggested that conventionalization or not of the means and strategies that Morgan (1978) described could be used to define four categories of linguistic convention. Elaborating on this idea, it may be helpful to look at conventionalization of the analogic means and directness of the communicative strategy (cf. Morgan, 1979) as situating referring expressions of the sorts we have considered in a somewhat richer constellation, perhaps as in Fig. 5.1. The vertical axis in Fig. 5.1 represents the conventionality of the metaphor (i.e., of the analogy), while the horizontal

STRATEGY: DIRECT ←   → INDIRECT

MEANS:

Conventional

SO-CALLED LITERAL MEANINGS AND GENUINE IDIOMS	SHORT-CIRCUITED IMPLICATURES	CONVERSATIONAL IMPLICATURE
a. Fido is a *dog* b. Eks *gave* Hou *the cold shoulder.*	c. *Can you pass the salad.*	d. *Is the Pope Catholic?* e. *Do you know the time?* f. *when hell freezes over* PROVERBS [cf. Green 1975b] g. *Birds of a feather flock together.*
FROZEN METAPHORS AND CLICHES h. Eks is a *pig*, 'selfish'; 'slovenly' i. *half-baked* idea 'poorly thought-out' j. *stab* someone *in the back* 'betray' k. references to facts/ arguments as *swords, daggers, bullets; shooting* or *poking holes in* an argument l. *cruel frost, oppressive heat* m. He has been *cool/warm* 'unfriendly/friendly' n. *Mickey-Mouse* 'non-serious' o. *Familiarity breeds contempt.* p. *Beauty is in the eye of the beholder.*		r. [Q: How can I make John feel at home?. A: *Buy him some Purina Hog Chow.* [Morgan 1979: 139]
EXTENSIONS OF FROZEN METAPHORS q. He suspected that most of his listeners were sympathetic to the position that selection restrictions were totally inadequate. But he attacked the sputtering tyrant once again, if only to place his *little penknife* alongside the daggers of his companions. [Reddy 1969: 242]		
NOVEL METAPHORS s. Her souffle is *death,* 'awful' t. *Sheathe* twine impatience! u. Eks' mind is a *meadow in winter.* [Morgan 1979: 140] v. *plastic, Wonder Bread* 'non-genuine' w. The castled crag ... *frowns* ... UNCONVENTIONAL	**INDIRECT REFERENCE TO NOVEL METAPHOR** x. On arriving home, I found I had been *sentenced* by She Who Must Be Obeyed to the eggplant souffle promoted in last month's "Gourmet Anglais", for what *capital crime,* I never knew.	**IMPLICATURE OF NOVEL METAPHOR** y. [Q: How do you like the souffle?] A: *On the whole, I'd rather be in Philadelphia.* [Morgan, 1979: 145]

FIGURE 5.1

dimension refers to the transparency of the connection between what is said and what is intended to be conveyed.

Cutting across the "categories" defined by these orthogonal parameters[31] are motives for being indirect; one might indulge in indirectness because one enjoys word play, or as a sign of subgroup membership (cf. Chap. 7), or to be diplomatic, avoiding confrontation, or to be politic, and intentionally vague or ambiguous, or for any of a number of other reasons.

Examples (h & r), (s, x, & y), and (k & q) illustrate how metaphors may be recycled into more indirect or less conventional forms. A final example illustrates how a sentential cliche may be reinterpreted as containing an independent metaphor. The football player Richard Dent was interviewed after his team defeated the New England Patriots in the Superbowl. Alluding to the sportscasters' cliche "It isn't over until you hear the fat lady sing" (itself an allusion to the belief that in the 1940s and 1950s, the end of many events broadcast by American radio and television was marked by the late Kate Smith singing "God Bless America"), and probably equating that cliche with related ones, "It isn't over until the final gun" and "It isn't over until it's over," Dent referred to the Patriots trailing 23-3 at halftime, saying:

> It was over at the half. When you're going in with those points, and you're facing such a great defense—you know, *the fat lady began to sing.*

making *the fat lady begin to sing* into a metaphor for 'the game be over'.[32]

Multiple Explanations: Killing One Bird With Two Stones

Sadock's (1970) syntactic analysis of indirect requests like *Can you pass the salad,* referred to previously, is partially redundant in the face of an independently motivated pragmatic analysis. Some of the phenomena discussed in the previous section may be equally susceptible to more than one analysis. It is important to understand that in general, the fact that an

---

[31]I have not taken a position on whether these parameters are discrete or continuous, although I suspect the latter is the case.

[32]Similarly, *hear the fat lady sing* is taken as a metaphorical reference to the fisherman's battle with flies, or as an idiom for 'win' in this jingle for fly repellent:

Didn't have the strength to cope
And ward off a nasty sting
Until he bought Irving's Fly Dope
And heard the fat lady sing.
[*Yankee* May 1986: 16]

explanation provided by analysis is redundant is not a reason to reject that analysis out of hand. There is reason to believe that it is natural for linguistic systems to tolerate a certain amount of redundancy. Hankamer (1977), Sadock (1983), and Green (1985a) argued that in many cases, linguistic principles overlap to provide two different but non-contradictory explanations for a single phenomenon (e.g., number agreement between subject and verb), and are both necessary; overlapping may be avoidable only at the cost of arbitrariness. Furthermore, it seems clear that a system which offers more than one principle to motivate the use of a linguistic expression, expression type, or construction type would be easier to learn than one which doesn't, since one kind of support for an analysis might be easily inferred in a particular situation when the other kind would not. Consequently, it should not bother us too much if we can motivate an analysis as governed both by convention and by very general rules and principles of cooperative communication, as long as we can account for the regularity of form-use correspondences. Where the correspondence is partially irregular, only one of the analyses may be adequate. This is the case, for example, with the imperative syntax of *Can you please pass the salt,*[33] and for Gordon and Lakoff (1975), the unpredicted indirectness of *Are you able to pass the salt* and the ungrammaticality of ??*Are you able to please pass the salt.* But where either makes correct predictions, the question of which one a flesh-and-blood language user actually employs (or employs on a given occasion) will be a very subtle, and often inconsequential one.

---

[33]Bach and Harnish's reaction to this form is to call it ungrammatical but acceptable to speakers anyway (Bach & Harnish 1979, p. 199). For commentary on this strategy, see Green (1983).

6 Pragmatics and Syntax

In chapter 5, we discussed how what people said reflected, and was more or less consciously intended to reflect, their intentions and beliefs, especially beliefs about their interlocutors' beliefs. The focus of this chapter is how the way in which something is said reflects speakers' attitudes toward and beliefs about the topics and referents of an ongoing discourse. The aspect of what is said that we focus on is the choice of a syntactic construction from among the many which the grammar of the language makes available for the proposition to be expressed, although intonational choices (Cutler, 1977; Olsen, 1986; Schmerling, 1976; Ward & Hirschberg, 1985) and phonological choices (Cutler, 1974, p. 117; Zwicky & Sadock, 1975, pp. 26–27) have also been discussed, as well as the choice of which language to use (Gumperz, 1976). The first section treats syntactic devices that reflect the speaker's assumptions about the structure of the discourse. The second section examines some constructions which differ from their truth-conditionally equivalent counterparts in various other ways. Some differ in rhetorical function (i.e., in what gets asserted and what is presupposed), but most reflect different beliefs about or attitudes toward referents of linguistic expressions constituting the utterance. The third section deals with syntactic constructions which enable a speaker to compensate for (perceived) difficulties in producing or parsing a complex utterance. Many of the constructions have more than one use or function, and appear in more than one category.

1. REFLECTIONS OF DISCOURSE STRUCTURE

Language scholars have recognized for some time that there are correlations between the order of syntactic constituents in a sentence and the discourse role of the information which a particular constituent represents (Firbas, 1964; Halliday, 1967; Kuno, 1972; Mathesius, 1928).[1] In general, and all other things being equal, the first phrase in a sentence tends to be intended to denote familiar (or TOPICAL, or GIVEN, or OLD, or presupposed, or predictable, or THEMATIC) material, while phrases toward the end of the sentence tend to denote NEW (or asserted, or RHEMATIC) material. Other things are not always equal, however. Sentence stress or intonational accent (higher pitch which falls off rapidly and is perceived as louder) also correlates with information being treated as new (Schmerling, 1976), and new information may be expressed in phrases that occur toward or at the beginning of a sentence if they bear the main sentence stress, as in (1) (Olsen, 1986).

1.   *John* ate the cookies.

Furthermore, as Prince (1981b) demonstrated, *familiar, predictable, given, old, theme,* and *sentence topic* do not denote interchangeable notions, and different writers have used the same term to refer to rather different categories. Yet, the various writers seem to have been trying to get at the same point, summarized by Horn's observation that the initial slot in a sentence tends to be reserved for material taken to refer to the theme or sentence topic (i.e., what the sentence is about). Typically, this is material that the speaker (reflexively) assumes to be familiar to the addressee, and preferentially, it is material which is either salient (assumed by the speaker to be in the addressee's consciousness) or presupposed (taken as non-controversial) (Horn, 1986, p. 171). It is not surprising, then, that syntactic rules of the language provide for numerous alternative constructions which differ in the order of phrases while preserving truth-conditional semantics and illocutionary force. This is true even in a "fixed word order" language like English,[2] as illustrated by the incomplete list of options for English declarative sentences given in (2–5).

2a.   Eks delivered a rug to Aitchberg.
2b.   A rug was delivered to Aitchberg by Eks. [PASSIVE][3]

---

[1]For more recent treatments, see Prince (1981b), Zaenen (1982), Van Oosten (1986), Horn (1986).

[2]The writers have generally not claimed that the Old Information First principle is a universal principle, although it may be. Most of the illustrations have come from Czech, English, French, and Japanese.

2c.   There was a rug delivered (to Aitchberg) (by Eks). [THERE-INSERTION]
2d.   A rug, Eks delivered to Aitchberg. [TOPICALIZATION]
2e.   It was a rug that Eks delivered to Aitchberg. [CLEFT]
2f.   What Eks delivered to Aitchberg was a rug. [PSEUDO-CLEFT]
2g.   . . . and deliver a rug to Aitchberg, Eks did. [VERB PHRASE PREPOSING]

3a.   Finding typographical errors is never simple.
3b.   It is never simple to find typographical errors. [EXTRAPOSITION]
3c.   Typographical errors are never simple to find. [TOUGH-MOVEMENT]
3d.   Simple to find, typographical errors are not. [ADJECTIVE PHRASE PREPOSING]

4a.   Eks met a woman who said she was the Princess Anastasia's governess at Treno's.
4b.   At Treno's, Eks met a woman who said she was the Princess Anastasia's governess. [ADVERB PREPOSING]
4c.   Eks met at Treno's a woman who said she was the Princess Anastasia's governess. [HEAVY NP SHIFT]
4d.   Eks met her at Treno's, a woman who said she was the Princess Anastasia's governess. [RIGHT DISLOCATION]
4e.   A woman who said she was the Princess Anastasia's governess, Eks met her at Treno's. [LEFT DISLOCATION].

5a.   The little bunny scampered into its hole.
5b.   Into its hole, the little bunny scampered. [LOCATIVE PREPOSING]
5c.   Into its hole scampered the little bunny. [INVERSION]

Of course, old information does not tend to go first just because it is old, or become old just because it is first. Sometimes none of the material in a sentence represents "old information," and as noted above, new information sometimes goes first; generally, speakers have more particular reasons (not necessarily conscious reasons) for making a particular constituent first or last in a sentence (cf. Green, 1982a). Such functions of word order have been explored in some detail for a number of constructions. We look at two examples here.

---

[3]The construction names given here are those familiar in modern generative grammar. See Green and Morgan (in preparation) for further references.

Preposing

Ward's (1985) analysis of preposings like (2d), (2g), (3d), and (5b) indicated that although they may serve a variety of discourse functions, which he described in detail, they have two properties in common. In Ward's terminology, they first of all mark the preposed element as referring to an entity which is related in a certain way[4] (as a BACKWARD LOOKING CENTER) to entities previously evoked in the discourse (the set of FORWARD LOOKING CENTERS). Second, they mark the unstressed, presupposed part of the sentence (its OPEN PROPOSITION) as salient in the discourse. Viewed from a different perspective, these properties represent conditions that must be fulfilled for the utterance of a sentence with a preposed phrase to be acceptable in its context. Thus, a sentence like (2d) might be used in a context like (6a), where the referent of *one of these rugs* is very obviously in a subset relation to the previously mentioned set {rugs to be given as rewards} and the open proposition is 'Eks deliver a rug to someone.' It might also be used in a context like (6b), where *one of these rugs* is a member of the set {rugs containing cocaine}, and the open proposition 'Eks delivered something to Aitchberg' is salient in the discourse. But a sentence like (2d) could not be used in a context like (6c), where neither of these conditions holds.

6a.   An Eastern bloc embassy official gave Eks six full-size oriental rugs, and directed him to give them to the senators who had been most cooperative. One of these rugs Eks delivered to Sen. Aitchberg.[5]

6b.   FBI agents suspected both Eks and Aitchberg of trafficking in cocaine, and had been tailing them for months. In March, they learned from an informant that six oriental rgus containing 20 pounds of cocaine each had come through JFK airport, and as Exhibit B indicates, one of these rugs Eks delivered to Aitchberg.

6c.   Eks and Aitchberg played golf together regularly.
     ??An oriental rug Eks delivered to Aitchberg one day.

---

[4]Specifically, the backward-looking center must stand in a salient scalar relation to the partially ordered set constituting the forward-looking centers. Following Hirschberg (1985), Ward defined a partially ordered set as a set whose members are all related by some ordering relation that is transitive, and either reflexive and antisymmetric, like 'is as tall as or taller than', or irreflexive and asymmetric, like 'is taller than' (Ward, 1985, p. 64).

[5]The example is adapted from a passage in Nixon's *Six Crises* cited by Ward (1985, p. 71).

Inversion

English is graced with a number of inversion constructions which, like (5c) allow the subject noun phrase to appear after the main verb instead of before it (Green, 1980, 1982b, 1985b). The inversions are introduced by a preposed adjective phrase, participial phrase, or locative or directional adverbial phrase. Because of this, they can be called into service to perform any of a number of functions which exploit this phrase order (Green, 1980). For example, a writer may use an inversion with a preposed phrase which refers to a previously established or implied referent to describe how information following it relates to previous discourse, as in the examples in (7), where the initial phrase is explicitly ((7a), (7b)) or implicitly ((7c)) anaphoric to something preceding in the discourse.

7a. Attached to it, as always, is an application blank for next year's license.

7b. Jerome and Rita Arkoff and Tom and Fanny Irwin were in the front row. . . . Back of the Arkoffs and Irwins were William Lesser and Patrick Degan, and between them and slightly to the rear was Saul Panzer.
[Rex Stout, *Might as Well Be Dead,* p. 180. (New York: Viking Books, 1956]

7c. At issue is Section 1401(a) of the Controlled Substances Act.

In other instances, what is exploited is the fact that the inversion construction puts a subject noun phrase in the sentence-final position, which is typically reserved for focussed, new information. This enables a writer[6] to introduce a new disourse element (e.g., an important character or object or an element of the setting) in a focused position, as in (8).[7] Travelogue-style descriptions exploit this extensively, as in (8c).

---

[6]Or speaker, but these inversions are more typical of writing than of colloquial speech. Cf. Green, 1982b.

[7]This common function of inversions may be what has misled some writers (e.g., Longuet-Higgins, 1976) into thinking that inversions after directional phrases must describe a character coming into (the narrator's) view. Inversions have other uses, and we do find such inversions as (i–iii).

i. Then off marched the little tailor, cocky as could be, with his thumbs thrust through his boasting belt.

ii. Into the forest ran the four, and soon they could be seen no more.

iii. Off across the grass ran the three little girls.

Examples (i) and (iii) are from children's books whose exact titles I cannot locate.

8a.   In a little white house lived two rabbits.
       [Dick Bruna, *Miffy*. (New York: Two Continents (1975)]

8b.   Competing with the screamers for popularity are the phone-in
       programs, an adaptation of two rural American pastimes —
       listening in on the party-line and speaking at the town meeting.
       [Robert Dye, "The Death of Silence." *Journal of Broadcasting*
       12, 3 (1968). Reprinted in *Subject and Strategy,* ed by Paul
       Escholz and Alfred Rosa, 169–72, p. 170. (New York: St.
       Martins, 1978)]

8c.   The grounds were lavishly furnished with ceramic, stone, and
       wrought-metal sculpture. There were an enormous stainless steel
       frog and two tiny elves in the foyer of the guest house, and
       outside stood a little angel.

A related use of inversions is to describe an event or locative relationship
which resolves some puzzle in a narrative as it has been established up to
that point. It might be the whereabouts of an important character as in the
second inversion in (9a) or the identity of the previously unknown agent of
some significant action, as in (9b), or an event significant in the protagonist's execution of his plans, as in the second inversion in (9c) (the first
introduces a new discourse element).

9a.   Then at the darkest hour dawned deliverance. *Through the
       revolving doors swept Tom Pulsifer.*
       [S. J. Perelman, "The Customer is Always Wrong". *The Most of
       S. J. Perelman,* p. 227. (New York: Simon & Schuster, 1958)]

9b.   One night there was a tap on the window. Mrs. Rabbit peeped
       through the window. *Outside stood a little angel.*
       [Bruna]

9c.   . . . Dumble vanished and in his place rose a dark, angry cloud
       of bees. They flew straight at the soldiers' faces, and *from the
       soldiers came yells of anguish, of sorrow, and of despair.*
       [Jay Williams, *The King with Six Friends.* (New York: Parents'
       Magazine Press, 1968)]

The particular discourse values of several other of the constructions in
(2–5) have been explored in some detail (cf. for example, Prince, 1981c,
1984 — Topicalization and Left Dislocation; Prince, 1978 — Cleft and Pseudo-
cleft; Milsark, 1977; Napoli & Rando, 1978; Aissen, 1975 — There-
insertion).

2. REFLECTION OF BELIEFS AND ATTITUDES ABOUT CONTENT

Another kind of "stylistic variant" exhibiting a difference in rhetorical value involves constructions with sentential complements as in (10) and (11) or adjuncts as in (12). The (a) sentences in these examples differ from the (b) sentences in that the italicized subordinate clause represents a presupposed or otherwise subordinate proposition in the (a) sentences, but has its own illocutionary force in the (b) sentences.

10a. I bet *it'll float if you throw it in the lake.*
10b. It'll float if you throw it in the lake, I bet. [SLIFTING]
11a. That *Sandy thought it was Tuesday* is obvious/clear.
11b. It's obvious/clear that Sandy thought it was Tuesday. [EXTRAPOSITION]

12a. Someone *who said the girls were supposed to bring two quarts of potato salad* called.
12b. Someone called who said the girls were supposed to bring two quarts of potato salad. [RELATIVE CLAUSE EXTRAPOSITION]

Thus, depending on the sense intended for *bet* in (10a), (10a) is either a bet or a speculation, but (10b) can only be a speculation — *bet* does not have a performative interpretation in that construction (Horn, 1986; Ross, 1975). And while both (11a) and (11b) could be used to assert something about the claim that Sandy had some belief about the identity of a day, only (11b) could be used to make the claim that Sandy had that belief (Horn, 1986; Morgan, 1975b). In the case of (12), the (a) sentence reports who called, whereas the (b) sentence reports what someone said the girls were supposed to bring (Ziv, 1976).

Other constructions reflect particular kinds of beliefs speakers have about the objects of their discourse. For example, use of the INTERNAL DATIVE construction (Green, 1974) in (13b) implies that the speaker believes that the referents of the subject and indirect object noun phrases were alive at the same time.

13a. Win this one for the Gipper/me.
13b. Win me/!the Gipper this one.

Wierzbicka (1986) argued, more generally, that use of the internal dative construction reflects the speaker's greater interest in the referent of the indirect object noun phrase. The RAISED SUBJECT construction in (14b,

14d–14f) (Borkin, 1974; Postal, 1974; Schmerling, 1978; Steever, 1977) reflects the speaker's assumption that the (implied) experiencer (MacArthur in (14b), or agent (Eks in (14d–f)) interacted with the referent of the raised subject (Caesar, Sandy, Dale).

14a. It seemed to MacArthur that Patton/Julius Caesar was the greatest general in history.
14b. Patton/!Julius Caesar seemed to MacArthur to be the greatest general in history.
14c. Eks asked that Sandy leave.
14d. Eks asked Sandy to leave.
14e. Eks allowed Dale to examine Dana.
14f. Eks allowed Dale to be examined by Dana.

A slightly different case involves the use of the present tense to refer to future time in sentences like (15) (G. Lakoff, 1971).

15a. The Celtics are going to play the Bucks tomorrow.
15b. The Celtics play the Bucks tomorrow.

If the event is not (reflexively) understood to be prearranged or scheduled, simple present tense cannot be used for future time. Thus, the use of (16) would imply that the speaker (and the addressee, in the speaker's estimate) either (a) knew that the game was fixed, or (b) were staunch believers in predestination, and believed that the speaker had an inside line on the Omnipotent's plans for basketball games.

16.   The Celtics win tomorrow.

R. Lakoff (1969a) and Horn (1971, 1978b) have described the NEGATIVE TRANSPORTATION construction illustrated in (17a), where with a certain class of verbs and adjectives, a negative occurs one or more clauses away from the clause it conversationally negates. Thus (17a) would communicate the same as (17b), and (18a) would be conversationally ambiguous between a report that Dana lacks the desire to wash dishes, and a report like (18b) that Dana desires not to wash dishes.

17a. I don't think Sandy will arrive until Monday.
17b. I think Sandy won't arrive until Monday.
18a. Dana doesn't want to wash dishes.
18b. Dana wants to not wash dishes.

The difference between the (a) sentences and the (b) sentences in (17–18) is that the (a) sentences, with transported negatives, are hedged — they represent weaker claims, apparently by implicating rather than asserting the relevant negative proposition (cf. Horn, 1978b, pp. 131–136, 177–216 for discussion). A similar phenomenon is evident in the fact that the morphologically incorporated negative in (19b) is stronger than the unincorporated negative in (19a) (Sheintuch & Wise, 1976).

19a. I didn't see anyone there.
19b. I saw no one there.

The use of *some* or *any* described by R. Lakoff (1969b) provides a very clear reflection of speakers' attitudes. As Lakoff showed, although *some* and *any* have the same truth conditions, the use of *some* in conditional and hypothetical constructions indicates a positive attitude toward the situation described by the proposition it refers to, whereas *any* reflects a neutral or negative attitude. Thus, *if there are some apples on the table* is satisfied by the same states of affairs as *if there are any apples on the table,* but implies a different attitude towards the likelihood or desirability of that state of affairs, and the question in (20a) reflects the hope that Bill wants spinach, whereas (20b) may reflect the hope that he does not.

20a. Does Bill want some spinach?
20b. Does Bill want any spinach?

And (21a) could be a bribe, intended to get the addressee to eat bread (treating 'cooking hamburgers all week' as a reward), while (21b) would be a threat, intended to keep the addressee from eating bread (and treating 'cooking hamburgers all week' as an undesirable event).

21a. If you eat some bread, I'll cook hamburgers all week.
21b. If you eat any bread, I'll cook hamburgers all week.

Other NEGATIVE POLARITY ITEMS (cf. Baker, 1970; Horn, 1971; Schmerling, 1971), as in (22) reflect attitudes similar to those which *any* reflects:

22.   Do you think Sandy has ⎰ a red cent? ⎱
                               ⎰ eaten a bite? ⎱
                               ⎰ bothered to RSVP? ⎱

Similarly, both the inversion of subject and auxiliary verb in embedded questions and truncation of embedded questions (SLUICING) imply that the individual to whom the answer is implied or assumed to be relevant is in fact ignorant of the answer. Thus, the (a) sentences in (23) and (24) are more acceptable than the (b) sentences, which have contradictory implications which their acceptable, and uninverted or unreduced (c) counterparts lack. This property of sluicing and subject-auxiliary inversion explains why the (d) sentences induce the implicature that the speaker does not know the answer to the question.

23a.   She wants to know who did I appoint.
23b.   !She already knows who did I appoint.
23c.   She already knows who I appointed.
23d.   It never never occurred to me to wonder who did she appoint.

24a.   John broke something, but he won't say what.
24b.   !John broke something, and he said what.
24c.   John broke something, and he said what he broke.
24d.   John went somewhere with my car, and you know where.

Many languages have special particle words or morphemes whose use indicates an attitude toward the content or referent of some adjacent sentence constituent, or toward the addressee. For example, Japanese and Korean have a variety of honorific morphemes which indicate the degree of respect the speaker has for the addressee or some entity referred to in the sentence (Harada, 1976; Kuno, 1973; Levinson, 1979). Some languages have particles that indicate the speaker's degree of certainty about the utterance (Corum, 1975; Kendall, 1985; Matthews, 1965; Whorf, 1950). Even familiar languages like English have eloquent little particles. The use of *ah!* for instance, indicates (James, 1972, 1973) that the following material represents information that is news to the speaker, as in (25).

25a.   Ah, it says in the paper that Kissinger is a vegetarian.[8]
25b.   Mr. Eks will arrive at, ah, 3:35.

James also describes the use of *oh*—with high, level intonation as indicating that the following material represents a deliberate choice, with the knowledge that at least one other choice would have been equally correct or cooperative, as illustrated in (26).

---

[8]Sentence (25a) is conversationally ambiguous between an understanding that Kissinger's eating habits are news, and an understanding that their being reported in the paper is news. The first interpretation involves a very ordinary implicature from the second, whereby the subordinate clause is what is most relevant to the goals of the discourse, and a "prefix" like *It says in the paper* or *My father says* or *Dr. Kramer thinks* indicates the basis for the speaker's giving credence to the proposition expressed in the subordinate clause. In this way, the speaker can make a relevant contribution without violating the maxim of quality even when he has no direct evidence for the truth of the relevant proposition.

26a.   A: What'll we do when our cousins get here?
       B: Oh—we'll have a picnic. Or maybe we'll go to the movies.
26b: A: When are we going to get to Chicago?
       B: Be ready to leave at, oh—2:00, and we'll be there by 6:00.

Similarly, use of the particle *well* (R. Lakoff, 1973a; Schourup, 1982) indicates that a following answer is incomplete, while *why* reflects the speaker's opinion that the question need not have been asked. Thus, B's response in (27b) implies that B is not certain of her watch's accuracy; B's response in (27c) is odd unless B has reason to believe that the answer "2:30" would be misleading, as it would if B thought A really wanted to know what time it was in a nearby city which, unbeknownst to A, was in a different time zone, or if B thought that A really wanted to know if some TV program had started yet, and assumed that A didn't know it had been postponed.

27a.   A: What time is it?
27b.   B: Well, my watch says 2:30.
27c.   B: Well, 2:30.

B's response in (28b) implies that A ought to have known the answer, while her response in (28c) indicates that she may believe someone besides Grant is buried in Grant's tomb.

28a.   A: Who is buried in Grant's tomb?
28b.   B: Why, General Grant is.
28c.   B: Well, General Grant is.

3. REFLECTIONS OF PERCEIVED DIFFICULTY

Finally, speakers may take advantage of constructions like Extraposition (29b) and Heavy NP Shift (30b) which allow a constituent to appear at the end of the sentence to put the longest or most conversationally significant constituent last. It is not clear whether this serves to make the sentence easier to articulate (cf. Olsen, 1986) or simply easier to keep track of, or whether the motivation is altruistic—accommodating the addressee's likely strategies or difficulties in parsing, or some combination of these.

29a.   Whether Kim will visit museums in France and Dana will go to concerts in Vienna, or Dana will visit museums in France and Kim will go to concerts in Vienna is unclear.

29b. It is unclear whether Kim will visit museums in France and Dana will go to concerts in Vienna, or . . .

30a. Dana attributed a poem in which intuitions were compared to anemones and academic theories were described as battlements to Coleridge.

30b. Dana attributed to Coleridge a poem in which intuitions were compared to anemones and academic theories were described as battlements.

Length and discourse significance seem to be at least partially independent factors. Longer postposed noun phrases tend to sound better, as in (31a), even if they have no more semantic content, as in (31b), but of two noun phrases of equal length the more significant-sounding sounds better, as (31c) shows.

31a. But they attributed to Blake *?Typee/The Rise and Fall of the Roman Empire.*

31b. The district attorney considers indictable ?Rose Budd/ Montgomery J. Jingleheimer-Smith III.

31c. The committee has attributed to Margaret Thatcher ?the 27-line poem/an extraordinary poem.

4. SOME OTHER CASES

This chapter has only sketched some of the kinds of pragmatic factors which may be reflected in the speaker's choice of syntactic construction. It did not examine all of the factors which might enter into the choice to use a passive construction, for example. These include ensuring that the phrase describing the agent is at the end rather than the beginning of the sentence (32a), and, where there is no agent phrase, accommodating the fact that the agent is not known (32b) or suppressing the fact that the agent is known (32c). The use of a passive also commonly implies that the event described had a particular effect on the speaker or some other explicitly mentioned affected person (Davison, 1980; Fukada, 1986; Lakoff, 1971).

32a. The car was stolen by two young men wearing designer jogging suits.

32b. My bike was taken between 3:00 and 5:30 on Monday.

32c. This idea has been attacked as being simplistic and naive.

In fact, there are truth-conditionally equivalent alternatives to practically every describable construction,[9] and to the extent that this is true, the alternatives will tend to have different pragmatic values.[10] It would not be too surprising to discover that even constructions as similar as the (a) and (b) examples in (33) and (34) (cf. Bolinger 1972) really differed systematically in their use, reflecting different assumptions of the speakers, for example, that the (b) examples imply a stronger conviction on the part of the subject.

33a.   He expects that he will win.
33b.   He expects to win.

34a.   I know that it's raining.
34b.   I know it's raining.

In this chapter we have diverged from the pervasive emphasis on the hearer's need to make on-line inferences (to what was intended to be conveyed) from what the speaker has said and the way it was said. This chapter draws attention to a variety of cases where potential inferences from the way something is said have been grammaticized. In these cases, the connection between the way something is said and what is intended to be conveyed is automatic, a function of knowledge concerning the use of the language, if not knowledge of it. Some of these cases may involve fossilized implicatures, but in general, the meanings taken to be intended cannot be denied as they can with genuine implicature. Since implicatures exploit (assumed) literal meanings, it is often reasonable to deny that an implicature was intended, as in (35).

35.   The committee money disappeared from the safe that day, and Lee came home with a new jacket that night, but I don't believe or intend to imply that the two events have anything to do with each other.

But in the cases considered here, use conditions which refer to beliefs or attitudes of the speaker are so strongly linked to the syntactic construction that it sounds irrational to use such constructions and then deny that the conditions are in effect, as in (36).

---

[9]In English, anyway, and probably in other languages.

[10]Even verb agreement (Morgan, 1972a, 1972b) as in (i) and (ii) induces inferences from the fact that one choice was made rather than another, in fact, inferences that affect the truth conditions, not just "mere" pragmatic differences. Thus, (i) would be used to extol the virtues of two foods, while (ii) is about a single somewhat bizarre dish.

i. Pickles and ice cream taste good.
ii. Pickles and ice cream tastes good.

36.   !The Celtics win tomorrow, but it's not preordained or fixed;
       there's an off chance the Pistons might beat them.

In the following chapter, we diverge from our previous approach in a
different direction, and look at ways in which speakers manipulate what
they say in order to manage conversation and maintain and change social
relations.

7

Conversational Interaction

In chapter 1, the point was made that a speaker performs a particular communicative act to further plans for specific, possibly nested, goals. Most of the goals we have assumed in subsequent discussions have involved getting the addressee to have a certain belief or attitude (including a desire to do something) about events or entities in the real world. In a simple case, A says "X" to B in order to tell B 'Y,' with the purpose of getting B to believe 'Y,' and therefore, to want to do Z by doing W. In this chapter, we focus on how language is used to further other sorts of goals. The first section deals with politeness phenomena: strategies for maintaining or changing interpersonal relations. Such goals are sometimes an end in themselves, as in purely social conversation ("small talk"); other times they are a link in a chain of goals whose ultimate end is to influence someone's behavior or attitude. In the most direct cases, it is the addressee's attitude or behavior which is the target, but it could be the attitude or behavior of an individual linked to the addressee in a series or hierarchy of interacting plans. In the second section, we look briefly at strategies for managing the mechanics of conversation — the lowest level of goals: getting to speak, and getting the addressee to respond. The final section provides a cross-sectional view of the functions of one sentence type: the sorts of goals a speaker might use a question to accomplish.

1. POLITENESS

R. Lakoff (1972) asked why it is that it is considered polite for an English-speaking hostess to offer a guest something to eat with (1a), that if she used

(1b) it would be accounted familiar, and that use of (1c) for the same purpose would be considered downright rude.

1a.   You must have some of this fruitcake.
1b.   You should have some of this fruitcake.
1c.   You may have some of this fruitcake.

After all, on the face of it, (1a) would appear to be more overbearing, and (1c) less imposing. Why isn't (1c) the more polite offer? In this section, we examine a couple of approaches to the question of what makes one utterance act more polite than another, and how to explain the phenomena of (1).

Participants in a conversation can choose to be polite, they can choose to avoid being rude, or they can choose to do as they please conversationally with utter disregard for others' feelings and wishes. They can even exploit their knowledge of the principles of politeness to be intentionally rude. Lakoff (1973b) has described three different rules[1] a speaker might follow in choosing to be polite.

The most formal politeness rule, Lakoff's Rule 1: Don't Impose, is appropriate to situations in which there is an acknowledged difference in power and status between the participants, such as between a student and a dean, or between a factory worker and the vice-president in charge of personnel. Imposing on A means impeding A's desires to act as he or she pleases; refraining from imposing on A means not impeding these desires. A speaker (S) who is being polite according to this rule will avoid, mitigate, or ask permission or apologize for making the addressee (A) do anything which A does not want to do. This includes acts which distract A from whatever A may be doing or thinking about when S addresses him or her.

Formal politeness is impersonal; S will also choose his acts so as to minimize the extent to which he imposes on A by forcing A to acknowledge that he and A are human beings with human foibles and shared experiences, and therefore (presumably) should not be dealt with as if they were objects and had no feelings. Consequently, not imposing means not giving or seeking personal opinions, avoiding personal reference, avoiding reference to family, personal problems, habits, and the like — in short, upholding a pretense that participants have no personhood or shared experience. More particularly, this means avoiding earthy, slangy, and even merely emotional language, and also whatever topics of conversation are taboo because they are considered too personal to discuss in public: love, sex, politics, religion,

---

[1]These are descriptive rules (principles), of course, not injunctions. Although behavior appears to conform to them, people are generally not consciously aware of them, any more than they are of rules of grammar.

economic difficulties, the human body, and the like. In most English-speaking cultures, avoiding personal reference means using titles (e.g., *Mr., Dr., Professor, Captain*). In some cultures (e.g., Japan, Korea), both participants may use special words or particles which honor the addressee, either directly, or by humbling themselves.

A more informal politeness rule, Lakoff's Rule 2: Offer Options, is appropriate to situations in which the participants have approximately equal status and power, but are not socially close, for example, the relationship between a businessperson and a new client in a business, or the relationship between two strangers sharing a semiprivate room in a hospital. Offering options means expressing oneself in such a way that one's opinion or request can be ignored without being contradicted or rejected, for example: saying "I wonder if it would help to get a perm" or "Maybe you should get a perm," instead of "You should get a perm." Generally, if S wishes to persuade A of some view or course of action, S will phrase his speech so that A does not have to acknowledge S's intent; statements and requests will be hedged or implicated as in (2) and (3).

2a.　It *looks like* you and I got into the wrong line.

2b.　This style comes in a size 14 also. [implicates: The size you're trying on is too small (or too large) for you]

3a.　Could you *perhaps* let me see that newspaper *for a few seconds*?

3b.　Are you done reading that newspaper? [implicates: Please let me have that newspaper, if you're finished with it]

Utterances that (the speaker recognizes) might be interpreted as imposing the speaker's will or opinion (and thereby not offering the addressee any options for their interpretation) are likely to be phrased in a pragmatically ambiguous way so as to give A a graceful out if she prefers not to agree, comply, or answer, as in (4).

4a.　Some people think buying a Japanese car is an insult to all the unemployed American autoworkers. [indirect assertion about buying Japanese cars]

4b.　I was wondering if it would inconvenience you if I asked to use your telephone. [indirect request to use a telephone]

4c.　I don't suppose the number 2 bus stops here. [indirect question about the bus]

Lakoff's Rule 3 for friendly or intimate politeness: Encourage Feelings of Camaraderie, is appropriate to intimates or close friends. Even lovers have to abide by certain "politeness" norms with each other, or their relationship will come unstuck, as evidenced by the fact that if a spouse or lover or best friend chose to display formal politeness behavior, the significant other would interpret it as being given the cold shoulder, and wonder what had caused the relationship to change. In intimate politeness, almost any topic of conversation is fair game, assuming that with a close friend, one should be able to discuss anything, although there may still be some propositions that "even your best friend won't tell you,"[2] and which will have to be broached with all of the informal politeness devices a soul can muster.

Generally, however, participants are expected not to mince words; to speak indirectly implies that participants do not know each other well enough to forego offering options for how utterances are to be interpreted (by implicating that what one did not say is significant — namely, that intimate politeness tactics are inappropriate because participants do not have a close relationship). In contrast to informal politeness, the governing principle here is not only to show an active interest in the other, by asking personal questions and making personal remarks, but also to show regard and trust by being open about the details of one's own life, experiences, feelings, and the like. Participants use intimate forms of address, including nicknames and in some contexts, abusive epithets.

Brown and Levinson (1978) provide a slightly different perspective on politeness phenomena. In their highly detailed and profusely exemplified analysis, politeness is seen as trade in a commodity they call face. FACE is defined as consisting of the freedom to act unimpeded (negative face) and the satisfaction of having one's values approved of (positive face) (Brown & Levinson, 1978, p. 67). To engage in normal interaction is to risk losing face, for example, being asked to do something or to change your opinion of something. Maintaining face requires the cooperation of others, since it is defined in terms of others' actions and value systems, so interactants trade in face, paying face whenever they must perform a face-threatening act in the course of accomplishing their goals. According to Brown and Levinson, when S contemplates an act which he believes may threaten A's face, S is confronted with calculating how much he is risking in performing the face-threatening act. According to Brown and Levinson, the factors that enter into this calculation are S's estimates of the social distance assumed to separate S and A, the relative social power of S and A, and the extent to which the act contemplated is considered to be an imposition in the culture of which S and A are members. On the basis of this calculation, S determines whether he can (a) forego trading in face and perform the act without apology or mitigation ("baldly on record"), or whether he should (b) choose a POSITIVE POLITENESS strategy of making A feel good, and feel that her values are shared, or, in more extreme cases, (c) choose a

---

[2]This slogan was part of an advertising campaign in the 1950s for a product that purported to cure or prevent body odor, halitosis, dandruff, or some other social liability.

NEGATIVE POLITENESS strategy of hedging, apologizing, offering options, or asserting a desire to avoid interfering with A's freedom of action. In cases where the risk of face loss is greater still, S may decide to (d) perform the face-threatening act by implicature ("off record"), giving A the option of not acknowledging whatever face-threatening act is intended. S might even decide to (e) forego performing the face-threatening act altogether.

Although many people associate the notion of politeness exclusively with formal (Don't Impose) or informal (Offer Options) behavior, both Lakoff and Brown and Levinson take the ways in which intimates are expected to show their regard for each other as a natural extension of the formal and informal politeness principles that govern interpersonal interactions between non-intimates. I follow this usage in using *politeness* to refer to whatever means are employed to display consideration for one's addressee's feelings (or face), regardless of the social distance between the speaker and addressee.

In a very rough way, Brown and Levinson's strategy 1 (Bald on Record) corresponds to Lakoff's Rule 3 politeness (Promote Camaraderie): mincing no words implicates that S and A share so much that what might threaten an outsider's face is no threat to them. The correspondence between Lakoff's Rule 3 and Brown and Levinson's strategy 2 (positive politeness) is obvious. Strategies 3 (negative politeness) and 4 (implicating) correspond roughly to Rule 2 (Offer Options), since implicating and all of the various tactics for accomplishing negative politeness involve either offering A a range of interpretations for an utterance, or at least attempting to mitigate any impositions that are unavoidable from S's point of view. Brown and Levinson's strategy 5 (refraining from the act) corresponds to Lakoff's rule 1 (Don't Impose).

There are two main differences between the two approaches. First, Brown and Levinson attempt to characterize the factors which make one rule or strategy more appropriate than the others, allowing a large power, small distance relationship (e.g., parent–child) to count the same as medium power, medium distance (e.g., doctor–patient) in determining that the informal, negative politeness strategy of offering options is called for. Second, Brown and Levinson's scheme predicts that in situations where there is a large power differential between participants, they will use different politeness strategies (cf. Brown & Levinson, 1987, pp. 17–22) for discussion).

Obviously, cultures will differ in terms of what counts as conventionally polite in various stereotypical situations, but it is important to note that within a culture, individual speakers may also vary somewhat in employing conversational devices to execute politeness strategies. Speakers, even a particular speaker and addressee, may differ in their respective estimates of the social distance between them. In addition, speakers apply the various politeness strategies and tactics in different ways according to their desire to change that social distance, their beliefs about what kind of situation a certain behavior is appropriate to (i.e., the degree to which they evaluate a contemplated act as face-threatening), and finally, according to their personal style. For example, speakers differ on what kinds of facts are inviolably private, so that some people believe that asking personal questions like "What were you in the hospital for?" or "How much did your TV cost?" is a good way to show interest, and thus conform to the conventions for positive, intimate politeness, whereas their conversational partners may feel threatened by this opportunity to reveal personal weakness, or may feel that they do not know each other well enough for this sort of talk, and take such questions as implying a greater intimacy than exists or is desirable. Another example: as Tannen (1984) showed, some people believe that interrupting with relevant remarks shows interest in what the other person is talking about; other people feel that it shows utter disregard for the interrupted speaker.

It may be helpful here to offer a wider range of linguistic examples[3] of politeness choices than has been provided so far. For example, as Lakoff (1973b) pointed out, if it is necessary in a situation evaluated as a "don't impose" situation to discuss such face-threatening, "unmentionable" topics as sex, death, money, or body functions, technical terms such as *intercourse, coitus; expired; poverty, disadvantaged; defecation* will be preferred because as words belonging to a formal, technical, scientific or bureaucratic register, they treat the threatening topics impersonally, as subjects of disinterested, objective inquiry, not as personal matters that could pertain to the speaker or addressee. In a negative politeness, "offer options" situation, speakers will use euphemisms like *sleep with, do it; gone to a better place; in difficult circumstances; go to the bathroom,* expressions that are ambiguous or taken literally, very vague,[4] so that the addressee can choose whether or not to acknowledge that S is talking about an "unmen-

---

[3]That is, we do not touch, here, on the ways in which choice or change of conversational topic may exemplify a politeness strategy, although this is obviously an important component. For example, a speaker may be uncooperative and not maintain conversation on the addressee's topic of conversation if the speaker feels more threatened by that than by offending the addressee by changing the topic or remaining silent.

[4]A few euphemisms (e.g., *hard up*) are not ambiguous; their only conventional interpretation is the one the speaker uses them to avoid bluntly indicating. And the literally ambiguous ones may be in fact conversationally unambiguous in context. The point is that they function as euphemisms precisely because they do not refer clearly and unambiguously; as Lakoff (1973c) and no doubt others have pointed out, if a euphemism begins to refer clearly and unambiguously to its unmentionable referent (like *toilet*), it ceases to be a euphemism, and a new euphemism must be found to replace it.

tionable" topic. (As with many politeness techniques, the speaker is really only going through the motions of offering options or showing respect for the addressee's feelings. The offer may be a facade, the options nonviable, and the respect a sham. It is the fact that an effort was made to go through the motions at all that makes the act an act of politeness. In the case of euphemisms, the addressee has no difficulty recognizing what the speaker is referring to when a vague euphemism is chosen, but the fact that the reference is vague allows the addressee the option of declining to acknowledge the nature of the topic, and choosing for himself what terminology is to be used in continuing this discussion, or even of changing the topic, without implying that his interlocutor was gauche to bring it up.)

In a situation where discussion of such topics is not perceived as threatening, plain English is appropriate: *die; poor; pee,*[5]. Among some groups (especially groups of young males), using four-letter type expressions particularly offensive to "polite society" for these topics[6] counts as positive politeness in that it implies that speaker and addressee are so close that they do not have to worry about offending each other with mere words.

To take another example, Brown and Levinson (1978, p. 272) cite a number of cultures where phonetic properties of speech are apparently used as politeness tactics, for example, palatalization of consonants in intimate, low face-threat situations among the Basques (Corum, 1975) and the Japanese (O'Neill, 1966, p. 134; Sansom, 1928, p. 205), falsetto in high face-threat/Don't Impose situations among speakers of Tzeltal and Tamil. Brown and Levinson suggested that the use of falsetto in highly face-threatening situations is not arbitrary, but is natural in light of the fact that falsetto approximates the acoustic properties of the speech of a child, suggesting that the speaker has little power and is in no position to impose his will upon the addressee.

As is well known, many languages have special deferential forms, ranging from the special pronouns used for the addressee in such European languages as German and Spanish,[7] and for the speaker in Japanese, to deferential affixes on nouns and verbs typical of Japanese and Korean, to

---

[5]It is no doubt a measure of how taboo a topic sex is in English-speaking cultures that the only expression that strikes me as approaching plain English *(make love)* is patently a euphemism.

[6]E.g., *fuck, ball, screw, lay; bought it, croaked; piss, shit.* Apparently, poverty is not quite so taboo a topic as the others; the street slang terms *broke, busted, cleaned out* are not generally considered any more offensive or disrespectful to the addressee than other slang terms like *nuts* 'crazy' or *blotto* 'drunk.'

[7]The special use of the second person singular pronoun forms in French is a slightly different case, as they are used to indicate intimacy and/or inferiority of the addressee, not deference to the addressee. The second person plural is not so much a respect form as it is a neutral form.

the wholesale substitution of vocabulary items among the Dyirbal (Dixon, 1971, 1972, pp. 32–34, 292–293) in the face-threatening encounters when a taboo relative is within earshot.

By convention, the use of deferential forms indicates the speaker's respect for the addressee, referent, or bystander; it is customary to use them when addressing a person to whom one is expected to show deference, for example, teachers, parents, grandparents. Consequently, they are typically employed (a) to mitigate face threat in highly face-threatening situations, by feeding the addressee's ego, by explicitly acknowledging her superior status, or (b) to minimize face threat by implying that since the addressee is so superior in status and authority to the speaker, the speaker is not in a position to demand or force any action or reaction from the addressee. For example, in Japanese and Korean, special affixes are attached to verbs to indicate the speaker's respect for or humility towards a referent, and to nouns to indicate (a) the speaker's respect for the addressee or an individual identified as responsible for the noun's referent (e.g., the individual himself, a child's father, a book's author or owner), or (b) the speaker's low status and power or unworthiness if the speaker is responsible for the referent. All of this is illustrated in the examples in (5). (NOM, GEN, ACC, DAT refer to case markers; HON and HUM to respect and humility particles or meanings; REL refers to the relative clause marker.)

5a. cə-ʉy   atʉl-i   tangsin-ʉy   halabə-nim-kkesə   ssʉ-si-n
     I(HUM)-GEN son-NOM you -GEN   grandfather-title-NOM(HON) write-HON-REL

     chaek-ʉl   phyɵncipa-eke   ponae-ryɵko   hamnita
     book-ACC editor-DAT   send-in order to   do(FORMAL)

     'My son sent the editor the book that your grandfather wrote.'

5b. watashi-no gusoku-ga   anata-sama-ni   shachoo-no   go-shisoku-ni
     I -GEN   son(HUM)-NOM   you-HON-DAT   president-GEN HON-son-DAT

     o-kome-o   o-okuri-shite-itadaki-tai   to
     HON-rice-ACC HUM-send-HUM- have(HUM)-want   that

     mooshite   ori-mas-u
     say(HUM) PROGRESSIVE(HUM)-FORMAL-present

     'My son (says he) wants you to send some rice to the president's son.'

In (5a), choosing the form *hamnita* indicates the speaker's respect for the addressee, while the title *nim* and the special nominative case marker *kkesə* indicates the speaker's respect for the addressee's grandfather, and the humble form *cə* of the first person singular pronoun indicates respect for the addressee by debasing or depreciating the speaker's respect for himself.

In (5b), the prefix *go* on *shisoku* 'son' indicates respect for the referent of *shachoo,* the father of that son, while the *o* prefixed to 'rice,' and the formal verb suffix *mas* honor the addressee. The speaker also indicates respect for the addressee, as referent of *anata,* with the honorific suffix *sama.* In addition, the humiliative forms *mooshite, orimasu,* and the *o-...- shite* surrounding 'send' indicate respect for the addressee by indicating the speaker's lack of self-respect, as do the special lexical items for 'son'*(gusoku)* and 'have' *(itadaki).*

Naturally, speakers of Korean and Japanese exploit this rich system in sarcasm and in switching levels of honorification to indicate a belief that the relationship between the speaker and the addressee has changed, or a desire that it change to the relation implied by the honorific morphemes. Similarly, in English-speaking cultures, strangers who want to have the privileges of an intimate relationship (e.g., insurance and real-estate salesmen, telephone solicitors) often use positive politeness tactics to imply that that relation already exists, asking personal questions about the addressee's family and state of mind *(Good evening. How are you tonight? And how is Mr. Eks?).* Often telephone solicitors do not identify themselves at the beginning of the interaction, speaking as if you should know who they are and reciprocate with intimate, positive politeness behavior.

Among the Dyirbal, speakers must use a special language, Dyalŋuy (the "mother-in-law tongue"), in the presence of taboo relatives. Dyalŋuy has only about one quarter as many words as the regular Dyirbal language (Dixon, 1972, pp. 292–293), so, for example, while the regular Dyirbal language has five different words for distinct kinds of grubs, and no generic term for 'grub,' Dyalŋuy has only a single word meaning 'grub'; the regular language has distinct words nudin 'cut deeply, cut off' and gunban 'cut (into),' but Dyalŋuy has only a single word dʸalŋgan for 'cut.' Because the Dyalŋuy lexicon is so much smaller than the lexicon of the everyday language, expression in Dyalŋuy is necessarily more general and vague. This exemplifies, even ensures, an Avoid Imposing strategy for highly face-threatening situations.

In languages which, like English, lack special honorific affixes, existent words are frequently pressed into service to indicate the speaker's deference to the addressee, as R. Lakoff (1972) pointed out. The politeness contrasts described above in the use of *may, should,* and *must* to offer food to a guest are an example of this. Thus, because *should* conventionally indicates that the referent of its subject is obliged to perform the action described by the verb phrase, the utterer of (1b) (repeated below for reference) asserts that the addressee has an obligation to have some cake, and by asserting that, implies that the addressee did not realize this, and that the speaker has the superior knowledge and position which authorize her to presume to give advice. Speaking this way may be OK in an intimate situation, where such an act poses little or no face threat; elsewhere it is implicitly a boast, and therefore threatens the face (self-image) of the addressee. Similarly, to utter (1c) not only implies that the speaker is so far above the addressee in the social hierarchy that she has the authority to grant permission, but also threatens the addressee's face in implicitly referring to the addressee's wanting something which the speaker has. But when *must* refers to the requirement that an agent perform an action, as it does here, uttering (1a) implicates that the agent might not perform the action without prompting, and so implies that accepting some of the offered food is not something the addressee would be inclined to do, presumably because it is not appetizing.[8] Thus, in this context, the use of *must* functions like the humiliative affixes described above.

1a.   You must have some of this fruitcake.
1b.   You should have some of this fruitcake.
1c.   You may have some of this fruitcake.

Notice that (1a) is polite if the hostess utters it, since she is responsible for the food offered. However, a person hired to serve the food would commit a gross breach of etiquette in offering it with (1a), since it would imply that he or she was in a position to give orders; such a person is expected to use a negative politeness/Offer Options strategy, and say something like (6).

6.   Would you care for some fruitcake?[9]

Note that to the extent that (1a) involves a conventionalized politeness formula, the implicature will not necessarily be consciously intended or sincere, and the explanation will be historical, rather than an explication of actual inference in context. This is often the case with politeness forms (cf. Brown & Levinson, 1987, p. 23), including honorifics and particles like *please*.

2. TAKING TURNS

Perhaps the aspect of interactive conversation that most distinguishes it from other kinds of discourse production is the choreographing of the

---

[8]If the addressee is known to be self-conscious about being overweight, (1a) wil not be so polite, because the implied reluctance will not be so unambiguously attributable to the quality of the food offered.

[9]Note the choice of *care for* as opposed to *like*. A positive answer to (i) commits the speaker (i.e., the addressee of (i)) to a stronger desire than a positive answer to (6).

i.   Would you like some fruitcake?

Thus (i) poses more of a threat to the addressee's freedom than (6), and is therefore less polite.

switch in roles from addressee to speaker and vice versa. How does an addressee A get to take the floor and become a speaker? Does he just break in at the end of a sentence, hoping that the one speaking (X) is finished? If X is not finished, how do they know who gets the floor? Is it a matter of status and deference, or persistence and brute force? If there is more than one addressee, how do A, B, and C know which of them gets to speak next? Since we are not usually conscious of having to resolve these problems while we are carrying on a conversation (whether small talk, or executive boardroom discussions) the question arises: How come? Why does conversation seem to flow so smoothly? Only a very small portion of a participant's conversation overlaps another's, and gaps between different speakers' turns are generally measured in fractions of a second.

How participants manage this delicate task has been investigated by a group of sociologists known as ethnomethodologists. In work pioneering the microanalysis of turn-taking, Sacks, Schegloff, and Jefferson (1974) noted recurrent features of conversants' speech at points where the floor is yielded to another participant (Transition Relevance Places or TRPs). The rules themselves are very simple, and apply recursively at all TRPs, in order:

I   If the current speaker S selects the next speaker (N) in the current turn, S is expected to stop speaking, and N is expected to speak next.

II   If S's utterance or behavior does not select the next speaker, then any other participant may self-select. Whoever speaks first gets the floor.[10]

III If no speaker self-selects, S may continue.

Sacks, Schegloff, and Jefferson claimed that these rules predict that speakers are able to distinguish among (a) the brief GAPS that occur when the right to speak is transferred according to the first or second rule, (b) the longer gaps that occur when the third rule is invoked, (c) PAUSES that occur in a party's speech which are not at a TRP, and (d) attributable SILENCES that occur when a selected party fails to speak. Such a party might have nothing to say, or might be too embarrassed to speak, or might intend his silence to convey (implicate) an attitude such as disapproval, displeasure, or disassociation.

Thus, we would expect from the content of the conversations below that the gap between the (a) and (b) contributions in conversation (7) will be

---

[10]Sacks, Schegloff, and Jefferson do not mention that this speaker may defer to another whose speech overlaps his, and abandon his turn before he has a chance to contribute anything significant to the conversation. By the definition in their second rule, he is still, of course, the next speaker.

shorter than in conversation (8).[11] (The notation "(n.n)" indicates time in seconds between stretches of discourse flanking it.)

7a. Ann: Didn't you go to Haverford, Dan? (0.1)
7b. Dan: Yeah.

8a. Jo: Well, *I* think we should spend it all on the camping trip. (0.7)
8b. Jo: I mean, if we're gonna do something, we should do it right.

Furthermore, we interpret the period of silence in (8) as Jo waiting for another participant to comment, whereas in (9) we know that she is not done speaking.

9.   Jo: That class is really (0.5) *bor*ing.

Finally, we would tend to invest the pause between stretches of discourse by the same speaker in (10) with more significance than either that in (8) or that in (9).

10a. Jo: I want you to come straight home from school this after-noon and clean your room. (1.5)
10b. Jo: You got that?

Of course, speakers distinguish all of these periods of no speech from those that occur when the conversation has simply lapsed, as in (11).

11a. Mo: We'll go see *Blazing Saddles* then. (16.0)
11b. Mo: Did I tell you someone stole my bike last week?

Ethnomethodologists have extended the structural, context-independent, inductive techniques used in their analysis of turn-taking to more substantive aspects of conversation as well, identifying such ADJACENCY PAIRS as question-answer, greeting-greeting, offer-acceptance, summons-answer (e.g., Schegloff, 1979), and their PRE-SEQUENCES (e.g., Merritt, 1976), and discovering preferred and dispreferred second parts of such pairs. Often the results are consistent with analyses based on the inference of speakers' plans and intentions as described here in chapters 2–6. However, the two systems of analysis are incompatible since the ethnomethodologists reject as unverifiable and premature theorizing, all reference to participants'

---

[11]Ethnomethodologists would not approve of my using adapted and fabricated conversation here. I have chosen to do so to enable the reader to concentrate on the relevant properties of the conversations.

plans and intentions, as well as reference to inferences, and all of these have been central to the investigation of pragmatics in these chapters. A close reading of ethnomethodological analyses indicates, however, that it is equally based on hypotheses (i.e., theories) about behavior, although the constructs and assumptions underlying the hypotheses are rarely explicitly acknowledged.

It seems likely that further investigation will show that not only the ability to correctly interpret periods of no speech, but even the smooth and apparently effortless turn-taking that characterizes ordinary conversation involves inferring speakers' plans for the conversation, and their intent in uttering forms interpretable as selecting a next speaker.[12] For example, in a two-party conversation, a question will usually indicate that a TRP is at hand, and by default, the other party is selected to speak next, although, by definition, rhetorical questions so understood will not do this. When there are more than two participants, probably the most nearly foolproof tactic for selecting the next speaker is to name the selected party by directly addressing him, as in (7a). Even this may fail, though; if potential (but not actual) addressee B thinks S's turn is over before S utters A's name, B may self-select according to the second rule. To forestall this, S would have to order the vocative first, as in (12).

12.   Dan, didn't you go to Haverford?

Not surprisingly, (12) sounds like the speech of a schoolteacher who keeps very rigid control of the classroom. Part of the art of successfully managing smooth conversation must be in appearing not to manage it.

Accompanying a question or a pause at a TRP with a shift of eye gaze to the selected next speaker is an effective technique for speaker selection in face-to-face environments. Its utility and its ubiquity are demonstrated by the difficulty speakers have conversing the first time they participate in a multiparty telephone conference call where no one can see anyone else's face. Needless to say, the reason why eye-gaze and direct address are effective in selecting the next speaker is that conversants assume that when a speaker addresses or focuses his gaze on a participant at the end of an utterance, it is because the speaker wants and/or expects that participant to make the next contribution to the conversation.

Speakers who have self-selected regularly select the previous speaker as the next speaker (accounting for the A-B-A-B-A . . . character of conversation, even in groups larger than two participants), by the use of brief questions like *Where?* or *Who did?,* and repetitions intended to get the

---

[12]Ethnomethodologists would probably object vigorously to this claim, and to my assumption that inference of plans and interests is relevant or even possible.

previous speaker to elaborate on his contribution to the conversation (Sacks et al., 1974, p. 717). By the same token, speakers who are not ready to give up the floor, but who sense that a pause will be interpreted as indicating a TRP, may indicate that they are not done speaking by prefacing the pause with a conjunction (e.g., *And, But, Or, Yet*), which indicates that a sentence is in the process of being uttered, so that taking the floor will be have to be construed as an interruption. Or, the speaker may vocalize the pause (with *Uhhhhhhh*) while he collects his thoughts; as long as one is vocalizing, he has the floor, even if he is not saying anything.

3. FUNCTIONS OF QUESTIONS IN CONVERSATION

In chapter 4 we noted that, interpreted directly, the utterance of a question is a request for information. In chapter 5, it became evident that one could exploit this fact in a number of ways to implicate attitudes relating that information to the addressee's previous utterances or other behavior. In Section 1 of this chapter, it was pointed out that the subject matter of a question, the way it is asked, even the decision to ask a question at all, will be understood as reflecting the speaker's evaluation of the social relationship between himself and the addressee. In Section 2 above, it was seen that the basic speech act properties of questions are also exploited to manage the orderly transfer of speaking rights in conversation. In this section we examine some of the other functions of questions in discourse, as a way of illustrating the one-to-many nature of the form-function relation that is pervasive in language use.

In chapter 4, we discussed SINCERE questions which indicate that the speaker S wants some information which S believes the addressee A has, namely the information that provides a true answer to the question. Questions like those in (13) are likely to be sincere questions.

13a. When was Sandy Smith's application for admission received?
13b. Is your brown suit at the cleaners?

RHETORICAL questions, like those discussed in chapter 5, include questions like those in (14), which S assumes not only that A knows the answer to, but also that A knows that S and everyone else know the answer to.

14a. Who understands Piaget?
14b. Is the Pope Catholic?

There are also rhetorical questions such as those in (15), where the speaker assumes not only that the addressee does not know the answer, but that in fact no one does.

15a. What makes people do a thing like that?
15b. Why is the sky blue?

As discussed in section 2 of chapter 5, both types function in conversation to implicate assertions (e.g., No one understands Piaget; The answer to that implied question is obviously "Yes"; What makes people do that is a mystery; The question your utterance asks or implies cannot be answered directly), rather than to request information. Consequently, the speaker does not expect an answer, and often will not bother to make even a pro forma pause for one. The addressee who provides an answer risks being evaluated as dim or hostile.

In between there are types of questions where the speaker's and the addressee's knowledge of the answer is a matter of degree rather than an absolute. Asking a CLARIFICATION question indicates that the speaker knows that he has been spoken to, but isn't sure exactly what was said or meant (cf. Ochs, 1984). Examples range from very general questions like (16a) and (16b) to more specific "echo" questions like (16c) and (16d), and metaconversational questions like (16e) and (16f).

16a. Huh?
16b. What?
16c. He did what?
16d. Eks said *whose* job would be on the line?
16e. A hundred fans to move air, or a hundred admirers?
16f. Did you mean that literally or as a figure of speech?

The speaker's utterance of a CONFIRMATORY question indicates that S has a hunch or assumption about what the correct answer is, but is not sure, and believes that the addressee does know for sure. In asking the question, the speaker is seeking confirmation of the expected answer. Confirmatory questions range from tagged assertions like (17a) and (17b), to general requests for confirmation of a previous utterance by the addressee, as in (17c).

17a. University Avenue is south of Church St., right?
17b. You did put the mayonnaise back, didn't you?
17c. Really?

Sometimes a speaker S will ask a nonrhetorical question to which he knows the answer, and knows that the addressee A knows that S knows the answer, as in (18).

18a. Boy, we really beat them good, didn't we?

18b. Remember when we played baseball on the Midway without a ball or bat?

In contrast to the rhetorical questions just discussed, where the purpose was to implicate an assertion about the discourse or its topic, with these questions the normal use is as a Friendly/Positive politeness technique; to display, or evoke in the addressee a feeling of agreement and solidarity. Sometimes the purpose of questions like (18) is to allocate the right to speak, and so facilitate the smooth flow of conversation. In the same vein, sometimes people use questions like those in (19) to encourage the addressee to keep talking and say more about the subject of the conversation.

19a. Is that so?

19b. Yeah?

19c. He did?

Sometimes this is a Friendly/Positive politeness tactic, indicating interest in the addressee. Other times, the speaker has ulterior motives as well—trying to keep the addressee talking in hopes he will let slip some piece of information that the speaker cannot, for some reason, ask for directly—or maybe just because the speaker does not want to get seriously involved in the conversation.

In general, however, there is not even any one-to-one correspondance between particular question types and politeness, nor, as should be clear, between question forms and question functions. Depending on the topic, the presuppositions, and the relationship between the speaker and the addressee, asking a sincere question could be an act of Friendly/Positive politeness, an act conforming to the Offer Options strategy of negative politeness, or it could be a gross violation of the injunction against imposing on the addressee. Similarly, some rhetorical questions (e.g., (14b)) will be rude if it would be rude to assert what the rhetorical question implicates, while with others (e.g., (15b)), the fact that they broach the topic indirectly allows their use as a Don't Impose/Off Record politeness technique. Clarification questions are polite to the extent that they indicate the speaker's interest in the addressee's topic, but not so polite to the extent that they indicate that the speaker has not been paying close attention. As noted, confirmatory questions may be used as a positive politeness/ solidarity device, but they can also be used to pressure the addressee into admitting or agreeing to a proposition the speaker is putting forth, by speakers with little thought of genuine politeness, as in (20).

20a. And then you told Officer Bradley you'd never seen the .45 with your fingerprints on it, didn't you?

20b. And the verb has to agree with the subject, doesn't it?

20c. Don't you think that's a naive attitude?

Depending on where the speaker stands in a power relationship with the addressee, questions can be used to effect suggestions, requests, or even demands for action, as in (21a), (21b), and (21c–21d) respectively.

21a. Do you want to put some salt in there?

21b. Do you think you could hand me that wrench?

21c. Why are your crayons still all over the floor?

21d. Don't you think you had better pick them up?

Readers wishing to explore these relationships in more detail are referred to Goody (1978), where many insightful observations on the uses of questions and their relation to status and deference are discussed. In any case, it should be clear that the illocutionary and perlocutionary uses of question forms, and by extrapolation, of other syntactic types, are probably limited only by speakers' imagination and ingenuity in exploiting the fact that questions demand answers (and the fact that particular kinds of questions demand particular kinds of answers) in order to further their private agendas.

8 Perspective

This book is about the factors that influence a speaker's choice to say something the way she does, and a hearer's interpretation of what has been said, and what was meant by it. In chapter 2 it was shown that speakers must depend on estimates of their addressee's beliefs in order to make rational choices involving even aspects of linguistic structure assumed to be simple and straightforward, such as which pronoun or pronominal adverbial or tense to use.

In chapter 3 (and later in chapter 5) we examined the matter of what is involved in using descriptions and predicating expressions to say what you mean. We saw that choice of descriptive or predicative expression to indicate a referent not only depends on what the speaker believes, or believes the addressee believes, but on what the speaker believes the addressee believes (the speaker believes) others believe.

Chapter 4 described the phenomena of illocutionary force and presupposition, many of which, it was suggested in chapter 5, may be ultimately reducible to matters of implicature: by the act of saying something, a speaker conveys or implies something else in addition or instead. Much of the value of implicature in conversation lies in its indirectness, in the fact that it allows the speaker to avoid saying exactly what she means to convey, and so (as elaborated in chapter 7) to temper any social repercussions that may arise from going "on record" with beliefs or desires that may be contrary to the addressee's.

In chapter 6, we looked at syntactic structures which reflect the speaker's plans for the discourse, interpretation of the discourse, or evaluation of language processing requirements. Chapter 7 treated the interaction of linguistic devices and mechanisms with the social goals of participants in conversation: maintaining, improving, and exploiting social relationships.

The recurring theme of these chapters has been the extent to which language interpretation and production depends on language users' reflexive assumptions and inferences about each other, varying particular aspects of the world, and even about the language they share. Elucidation of the relevant assumptions and the logic of the inferences is the domain of pragmatics. It is obviously relevant to undertakings in all of the disciplines that comprise cognitive science. Much of the impetus for the exploration of the domain of pragmatics came from issues raised in philosophical arenas, logic in particular (e.g., the distinction between sense and reference, the nature of reference, presupposition, illocutionary force, implicature, etc.), and natural language research in these areas continues to be relevant to the resolution of these issues. It goes without saying that insofar as work in artificial intelligence purports to simulate natural language processing, natural language understanding systems will need to reflect the extent to which a speaker's (reflexive) model of her addressee's belief system affects what is said, how it is said, and how it is interpreted. The cultural (and subcultural) assumptions that are so essential in making correct inferences (and thus essential in the inference of reference, illocutionary force, politeness moves, and implicature of all sorts) are elucidated through anthropological studies. Studies in experimental cognitive psychology both inform and are informed by studies in linguistic pragmatics of the sorts that have been discussed in these chapters. This includes the interpretation of utterances and discourses or texts, and thus encompasses, among other things, presupposition, illocutionary force, implicature, reference, metaphor, and the management of interpersonal relations.

To conclude this brief review of the significant issues in the study of pragmatics as outlined in these chapters, a metaphor that summarizes the negotiation of interpretations and roles that characterizes pragmatics: It takes two to tango.

References

Aissen, J. (1975). Presentational there-insertion: A cyclic root transformation. In R. Grossman, J. San, & T. J. Vance (Eds.), *Papers from the 11th Regional Meeting of the Chicago Linguistic Society* (pp. 1–14). Chicago: Chicago Linguistic Society.

Allen, J. F. (1983). Recognizing intentions from natural language utterances. In M. Brady & R. C. Berwick (Eds.), *Computational models of discourse* (pp. 107–166). Cambridge, MA: MIT Press.

Allen, J. F., & Perrault, C. R. (1980). Analyzing intention in utterances. *Artificial Intelligence* 15, 143–178.

Anderson, S. (1971). *On the linguistic status of the performative/constative distinction.* Bloomington, IN: Indiana University Linguistics Club.

Åqvist, L. (1965). *A new approach to the logical theory of interrogatives.* Uppsala: University of Sweden.

Åqvist, L. (1971). Revised foundations for imperative-epistemic and interrogative logic. *Theoria 37,* 33–73.

Austin, J. (1962). *How to do things with words.* Cambridge, MA: Harvard University Press.

Bach, E., & Partee, B. (1980). *Anaphora and semantic structure.* In Kreiman & Ojeda, 1–28.

Bach, K., & Harnish, R. M. (1979). *Linguistic communication and speech acts.* Cambridge, MA: MIT Press.

Baker, C. L. (1970). Double negatives. *Linguistic Inquiry, 1,* 169–186.

Bar-Hillel, Y. (1954). Indexical expressions. *Mind, 63,* 359–379.

Bechtel, W. (1988). *The philosophy of mind.* Hillsdale, NJ: Lawrence Erlbaum Associates.

Boer, S., & Lycan, W. (1976). *The myth of semantic presupposition.* Bloomington, IN: Indiana University Linguistics Club.

Bolinger, D. (1972). *That's that.* The Hague: Mouton.

Borkin, A. (1972). Coreference and beheaded NPs. *Papers in Linguistics* 5: 28–45.

Borkin, A. (1974). *Raising to object position.* Unpublished doctoral dissertation, University of Michigan, Ann Arbor, MI.

Bransford, J., & Johnson, M. K. (1973). Consideration of some problems in comprehension. In W. G. Chase (Ed.), *Visual information processing.* New York: Academic Press.

Brown, P., & Levinson, S. (1978). Universals in language usage: Politeness phenomena. In E. Goody (Ed.), *Questions and politeness: Strategies in social interaction* (pp. 56–311). Cambridge, England: Cambridge University Press.

Brown, P., & Levinson, S. (1987). *Politeness.* Cambridge, England: Cambridge University Press.

Bruce, B. C. (1980). Plans and social actions. In R. Spiro, B. C. Bruce, & W. Brewer (Eds.), *Theoretical issues in reading comprehension* (pp. 367–384). Hillsdale, NJ: Lawrence Erlbaum Associates.

Carlson, G. N. (1978). *Reference to kinds in English.* Unpublished doctoral dissertation, University of Massachusetts, Amherst, MA.

Carnap, R. (1947). *Meaning and necessity.* Chicago: University of Chicago Press.

Chomsky, N. (1965). *Aspects of the theory of syntax.* Cambridge, MA: MIT Press.

Chomsky, N. (1968). *Language and mind.* New York: Pantheon.

Chomsky, N. (1980). *Rules and representations.* New York: Columbia University Press.

Clark, E., & Clark, H. (1979). When nouns surface as verbs. *Language, 55,* 767–811.

Clark, H. H. (1979). Responding to indirect speech acts. *Cognitive Psychology, 11,* 430–477.

Clark, H. H., & Carlson, T. B. (1982). Hearers and speech acts. *Language, 58,* 332–373.

Clark, H. H., & Haviland, S. E. (1977). Comprehension and the given-new contract. In R. O. Freedle (Ed.), *Discourse production and comprehension* (pp. 1–40). Norwood, NJ: Ablex.

Cohen, P. & Levesque, H. (1987). Rational interaction as the basis for communication. *Symposium on Intentions and Plans in Communication and Discourse.*

Cole, P. (Ed.). (1978a). *Syntax and semantics, Vol. 9: Pragmatics.* New York: Academic Press.

Cole, P. (1978b). On the origins of referential opacity. In P. Cole (Ed.), *Syntax and semantics, Vol. 9: Pragmatics* (pp. 1–22). New York: Academic Press.

Collins, A. M., & Loftus, E. (1975). A spreading-activation theory of semantic processing. *Psychological Review, 82,* 407–428.

Collins, A. M., & Quillian, M. R. (1972). How to make a language user. In E. Tulving & W. Donaldson (Eds.), *Organization of memory.* New York: Academic Press.

Conklin, H. (1972). Folk classification: *A topically arranged bibliography of contemporary and background references through 1971.* New Haven: Yale University Press.

Copi, I., & Gould, J. (1967). *Contemporary readings in logical theory.* New York: Macmillan.

Corum, C. (1975). Basques, particles, and babytalk: A case for pragmatics. In C. Cogen, H. Thompson, G. Thurgood, K. Whistler, J. Wright (Eds.), *Proceedings of the First Annual Meeting of the Berkeley Linguistics Society* (pp. 90–99). Berkeley, CA: Berkeley Linguistics Society.

Cutler, A. (1974). On saying what you mean without meaning what you say. In M. LaGaly, R. A. Fox, & A. Bruck (Eds.), *Papers from the 10th Regional Meeting of the Chicago Linguistic Society* (pp. 117–127). Chicago: Chicago Linguistic Society.

Cutler, A. (1977). The context dependence of 'intonational meanings'. In W. Beach, S. Fox, & S. Philosoph (Eds.), *Papers from the 13th Regional Meeting of the Chicago Linguistic Society* (pp. 104–115). Chicago: Chicago Linguistic Society.

Davison, A. (1970). Causal adverbs and performative verbs. In *Papers from the Sixth Regional Meeting of the Chicago Linguistic Society* (pp. 190–201). Chicago: Chicago Linguistic Society.

Davison, A. (1978). Peculiar passives. *Language, 55,* 42–66.

Dinsmore, J. (1981). *The inheritance of presupposition.* Amsterdam: John Benjamins.

Dixon, R. M. W. (1971). A method of semantic description. In Danny D. Steinberg & Leon A. Jakobovits (Eds.), *Semantics, an interdisciplinary reader* (pp. 436–471). Cambridge, England: Cambridge University Press.

Dixon, R. M. W. (1972). *The Dyirbal of North Queensland.* Cambridge, England: Cambridge University Press.

Donnellan, K. (1966). Reference and definite descriptions. *Philosophical Review, 75,* 281–304.

Downing, P. (1977). On the creation and use of English compound nouns. *Language, 53,* 810–842.

Dowty, D. (1979). *Word meaning and Montague grammar.* Dordrecht: Reidel.

Dowty, D., Wall, R., & Peters, S. (1981). *Introduction to Montague semantics.* Dordrecht: Reidel.

Fauconnier, G. (1985). *Mental spaces.* Cambridge, MA: MIT Press.

Fillmore, C. (1971a). Verbs of judging: An exercise in semantic description. In C. J. Fillmore & D. T. Langendoen (Eds.), *Studies in linguistic semantics* (pp. 272–289). New York: Holt, Rinehart, Winston.

Fillmore, C. (1971b). Types of lexical information. In D. D. Steinberg & L. A. Jakobovits (Eds.), *Semantics: An interdisciplinary reader* (pp. 370–392). Cambridge, England: Cambridge University Press.

Firbas, J. (1964). On defining the theme in functional sentence perspective. *Travaux linguistiques de Prague, 1,* 267–280.

Fraser, B. (1971). *An examination of the performative analysis.* Bloomington, IN: Indiana University Linguistics Club.

Fraser, B. (1973). A partial analysis of vernacular performative verbs. In R. Shuy & C-J. N. Bailey (Eds.), *Towards tomorrow's linguistics.* Washington, DC: Georgetown University Press.

Fraser, B. (1974). An examination of the performative analysis. [A revised and expanded version of Fraser 1971] *Papers in Linguistics, 7,* 1–40.

Frege, G. (1952). On sense and reference. In P. T. Geach & M. Black (Eds.), *Translations from the philosophical writings of Gottlob Frege* (pp. 56–78). Oxford: Basil Blackwell.

Fukada, A. (1986). *Pragmatics and grammatical description.* Unpublished doctoral dissertation, University of Illinois, Urbana.

Gallagher, M. (1970). Does meaning grow on trees? In J. Sadock & A. Vanek (Eds.), *Studies presented to Robert B. Lees by his students* (pp. 79–93). Edmonton, Alberta: Linguistic Research Inc.

Gazdar, G. (1979). *Pragmatics, implicature, presupposition, and logical form.* New York: Academic Press.

Gazdar, G. (1980). Pragmatics and logical form. *Journal of Pragmatics, 4,* 1–13.

Goodwin, C. (1981). *Conversational organization: Interaction between speakers and hearers.* New York: Academic Press.

Goody, E. N. (1978). Towards a theory of questions. In E. N. Goody (Ed.), *Questions and politeness: Strategies in social interaction* (pp. 17–43). Cambridge, England: Cambridge University Press.

Gordon, D., & Lakoff, G. (1975). Conversational postulates. In P. Cole & J. Morgan (Eds.), *Syntax and semantics, vol. 3: Speech acts* (pp. 83–106). New York: Academic Press.

Green, G. M. (1973). The lexical expression of emphatic conjunction. *Foundations of Language, 10,* 197–248.

Green, G. M. (1974). *Semantics and syntactic regularity.* Bloomington, IN: Indiana University Press.

Green, G. M. (1975a). How to get people to do things with words: The whimperative question. In P. Cole & J. Morgan (Eds.), *Syntax and semantics, vol. 3: Speech acts* (pp. 107–142). New York: Academic Press.

Green, G. M. (1975b). Nonsense and reference; or, the conversational use of proverbs. In T. J. San, L. J. Vance, & R. E. Grossman (Eds.), *Papers from the 11th regional meeting of the Chicago Linguistic Society* (pp. 226–239). Chicago: Chicago Linguistic Society.

Green, G. M. (1979). Organization, goals, & comprehensibility in narratives; Newswriting, a case study. Technical Report 132, Center for the Study of Reading. University of Illinois, Champaign.

Green, G. M. (1980). Some wherefores of English inversion. *Language, 56,* 582–601.

Green, G. M. (1981). Pragmatics and syntactic description. In *Studies in the Linguistic Sciences, 11*(1), 27–38. Urbana, IL: Department of Linguistics, University of Illinois.

Green, G. M. (1982a). Linguistics and the pragmatics of language use. *Poetics, 11,* 45–76.

Green, G. M. (1982b). Colloquial and literary uses of inversions. In D. Tannen (Ed.), *Spoken and written language* (pp. 119–153). Norwood, NJ: Ablex.

Green, G. M. (1983). Review of Linguistic communication and speech acts, by K. Bach and R. Harnish. *Language, 59,* 627–635.

Green, G. M. (1984). *Some remarks on how words mean.* Bloomington, IN: Indiana University Linguistics Club.

Green, G. M. (1985a). Subcategorization and the account of inversions. *Proceedings of the first Eastern States Conference on Linguistics* (pp. 214–221). Columbus, OH: Ohio State University.

Green, G. M. (1985b). The description of inversions in generalized phrase structure grammar. In M. Niepokuj, M. VanClay, V. Nikiforidou, D. Feder, with C. Brugman, M. Macaulay, N. Beery, M. Emanatian (Eds.), *Proceedings of the 11th annual meeting of the Berkeley Linguistics Society* (pp. 117–145). Berkeley, CA: Berkeley Linguistics Society.

Green, G. M., & Morgan, J. L. (1976). Notes toward an understanding of rule government. In *Studies in the Linguistic Sciences, 6*(1), 152–169. Urbana, IL: Department of Linguistics, University of Illinois.

Green, G. M., & Morgan, J. L. (1980). Pragmatics and reading comprehension. In R. Spiro, B. C. Bruce, & W. Brewer (Eds.), *Theoretical issues in reading comprehension* (pp. 113–140). Hillsdale, NJ: Lawrence Erlbaum Associates.

Green, G. M., & Morgan, J. L. (in preparation) *Guide to the study of syntax.*

Grice, H. P. (1957). Meaning. *Philosophical Review, 66,* 377–388.

Grice, H. P. (1975). Logic and conversation. In P. Cole & J. Morgan (Eds.), *Syntax and semantics, vol. 3: Speech acts* (pp. 41–58). New York: Academic Press.

Grice, H. P. (1978). Further notes on logic and conversation. In P. Cole (Ed.), *Syntax and semantics, vol. 9: Pragmatics* (pp. 113–127). New York: Academic Press.

Gumperz, J. (1976). *Code switching in conversation.* Pragmatics microfiche 1.4 A2–D4.

Gundel, J. (1985). Shared knowledge and topicality. *Journal of Pragmatics, 9,* 83–107.

Halliday, M. A. K. (1967). Transitivity and theme, part 2. *Journal of Linguistics, 3,* 199–244.

Hankamer, J. (1977). Multiple analyses. In C. Li (Ed.), *Mechanisms of syntactic change* (pp. 583–607). Austin: University of Texas Press.

Hankamer, J., & Sag, I. (1976). Deep and surface anaphora. *Linguistic Inquiry, 7,* 391–426.

Harada, S. I. (1976). Honorifics. In M. Shibatani (Ed.), *Syntax and semantics, vol. 5: Japanese generative grammar* (pp. 499–561). New York: Academic Press.

Harrah, D. (1961). A logic of questions and answers. *Philosophy of Science, 28,* 40–46.

Hawkins, J. (1976). On explaining some ungrammatical sequences of Article + Modifier in English. In S. Mufwene, C. Walker, & S. Steever (Eds.), *Papers from the 12th Regional Meeting Chicago Linguistic Society* (pp. 287–301). Chicago: Chicago Linguistics Society.

Heim, I. (1982). The semantics of definite and indefinite noun phrases. Amherst: University of Massachusetts Graduate Linguistics Student Association.

Heringer, J. (1972). Some grammatical correlations of felicity conditions and presuppositions. In *Working Papers in Linguistics, 11,* iv–110. Columbus, OH: Department of Linguistics.

Hinrichs, E. (1986). Temporal anaphora in discourses of English. *Linguistics and Philosophy, 9,* 63–82.

Hintikka, J. (1974). Questions about questions. In M. Munitz & P. Unger (Eds.), *Semantics and philosophy* (pp. 103–159). New York: New York University Press.

Hirschberg, J. (1985). *A theory of scalar implication.* Unpublished doctoral dissertation, University of Pennsylvania, Philadelphia.

Horn, L. (1971). Negative transportation: unsafe at any speed? In *Papers from the Seventh*

Regional Meeting Chicago Linguistic Society (pp. 120–133). Chicago: Chicago Linguistic Society.

Horn, L. (1972). On the semantic properties of logical operators in English. Unpublished doctoral dissertation, UCLA, Los Angeles, CA.

Horn, L. (1973). Greek Grice. In C. Corum, T. C. Smith-Stark, & A. Weiser (Eds.), *Papers from the Ninth Regional Meeting of the Chicago Linguistic Society* (pp. 205–214). Chicago: Chicago Linguistic Society.

Horn, L. (1978a). Lexical incorporation, implicature and the least effort hypothesis. In D. Farkas, W. Jacobsen, & K. Todrys (Eds.), *Papers from the parasession on the lexicon* (pp. 196–209). Chicago: Chicago Linguistic Society.

Horn, L. (1978b). Remarks on neg-raising. In P. Cole (Ed.), *Syntax and semantics, vol. 9: Pragmatics* (pp. 129–220). New York: Academic Press.

Horn, L. (1984a). Toward a new taxonomy for pragmatic inference: Q-based and R-based implicature. In D. Schiffrin (Ed.), *Georgetown University Round Table on Language and Linguistics 1984: Meaning, form, and use in context: Linguistic applications* (11–42). Washington, DC: Georgetown University Press.

Horn, L. (1984b). Ambiguity, negation, and the London School of Parsimony. In C. Jones & P. Sells (Eds.), *Proceedings of the 14th annual meeting of the Northeast Linguistics Society,* (pp. 108–131). Amherst, MA: Graduate Linguistics Student Association.

Horn, L. (1985). Metalinguistic negation and pragmatic ambiguity. *Language, 61,* 121–174.

Horn, L. (1986). Presupposition, theme and variations. In A. M. Farley, P. T. Farley, & K.-E. McCullough (Eds.), *Papers from the 22nd Regional Meeting of the Chicago Linguistic Society.* Chicago: Chicago Linguistic Society.

Horn, L., & Bayer, S. (1984). Short-circuited implicature: A negative contribution. *Linguistics and Philosophy, 7,* 397–414.

James, D. (1972). Some aspects of the syntax and semantics of interjections. In P. M. Peranteau, J. N. Levi, & G. C. Phares (Eds.), *Papers from the Eighth Regional Meeting of the Chicago Linguistic Society* (pp. 162–172). Chicago: Chicago Linguistic Society.

James, D. (1973). *Some aspects of the syntax and semantics of interjections in English.* Unpublished doctoral dissertation, University of Michigan, Ann Arbor, MI.

Kamp, H. (1981). A theory of truth and semantic representation. In J. A. G. Groenendijk, T. M. V. Janssen, & M. B. J. Stokhof (Eds.), *Formal methods in the study of language,* 1. Amsterdam: Mathematisch Centrum.

Kantor, R. N. (1977). *The management and comprehension of discourse connection by pronouns in English.* Unpublished doctoral dissertation, Ohio State University.

Kantor, R. N., Bruce, B. C., Green, G. M., Morgan, J. L., Stein, N. L., & Webber, B. L. (1982). Many problems and some techniques of text analysis. *Poetics, 11,* 237–264.

Kaplan, D. (1978). DTHAT. In P. Cole (Ed.), *Syntax and semantics, vol. 9: Pragmatics* (pp. 221–243). New York: Academic Press.

Kaplan, D. (1977). Demonstratives "Draft #2". Unpublished manuscript, UCLA, Los Angeles, CA.

Karttunen, L. (1971). Implicative verbs. *Language, 47,* 340–358.

Karttunen, L. (1973). Presuppositions of compound sentences. *Linguistic Inquiry, 4,* 169–193.

Karttunen, L. (1977). The syntax and semantics of questions. *Linguistics and Philosophy, 1,* 3–44.

Karttunen, L., & Peters, S. (1979). Conventional implicature. In C. K. Oh & D.A. Dineen (Eds.), *Syntax and semantics, vol. 11: Presupposition* (pp. 1–56). New York: Academic Press.

Katz, J. J., & Langendoen, D. T. (1976). Pragmatics and presupposition. *Language, 52,* 1–17.

Keenan, E. (1971). Two kinds of presupposition in natural language. In C. Fillmore & D. T. Langendoen (Eds.), *Studies in linguistic semantics* (pp. 45–52). New York: Holt, Rinehart & Winston.

Keenan, E. (1972). On a semantically-based grammar. *Linguistic Inquiry, 3,* 413–462.

Keenan, E. O. (1976). The universality of conversational implicature. *Language in Society, 5,* 67–80.

Kempson, R. (1975). *Presupposition and the delimitation of semantics.* Cambridge, England: Cambridge University Press.

Kendall, S. A. (1985). Japanese sentence-final particles as committment markers. In M. Niepokuj, Mary VanClay, Vassiliki Nikiforidou, Deborah Feder, with Claudia Brugman, Monica Macaulay, Natasha Beery, Michele Emanatian (Eds.), *Proceedings of the 11th Annual Meeting of the Berkeley Linguistics Society* (pp. 164–174). Berkeley, CA: Berkeley Linguistics Society, University of California.

Kiparsky, P. (1968). Tense and mood in Indo-European syntax. *Foundations of Language, 4,* 30–57.

Kiparsky, P., & Kiparsky, C. (1971). Fact. In D. Steinberg & L. Jakobovits (Eds.), *Semantics, an interdisciplinary reader* (pp. 345–369). Cambridge, England: Cambridge University Press.

Kreiman, J., & Ojeda, A. (1980). *Papers from the parasession on pronouns and anaphora.* Chicago: Chicago Linguistic Society.

Kripke, S. (1959). A completeness theorem in modal logic. *Journal of Symbolic Logic, 24,* 1–14.

Kripke, S. (1972). Naming and necessity. In D. Davidson & G. Harman (Eds.), *Semantics of natural language* (pp. 253–355). Dordrecht: D. Reidel.

Kuno, S. (1972). Functional sentence perspective: A case study from Japanese and English. *Linguistic Inquiry, 3,* 269–320.

Kuno, S. (1973). *The structure of the Japanese language.* Cambridge, MA: Harvard University Press.

Kuno, S. (1975). Three perspectives in the functional approach to syntax. In R. Grossman, L. J. San, & T. J. Vance (Eds.), *Papers from the parasession on functionalism* (pp. 276–336). Chicago: Chicago Linguistic Society.

Lakoff, G. (1968). *Counterparts; or, the problem of reference in transformational grammar.* Paper presented at the July 1968 Linguistic Society of America meeting. Urbana, Illinois.

Lakoff, G. (1971). Presuppositions and relative well-formedness. In D. Steinberg & L. Jakobovits (Eds.), *Semantics, an interdisciplinary reader* (pp. 329–340). Cambridge, England: Cambridge University Press.

Lakoff, G. (1972). Hedges: A study in meaning criteria and the logic of fuzzy concepts. In P. M. Peranteau, J. L. Levi, & G. C. Phares (Eds.), *Papers from the eighth regional meeting of the Chicago Linguistic Society* (pp. 183–228). Chicago: Chicago Linguistic Society.

Lakoff, G. (1976). Pronouns and reference. In J. D. McCawley (Ed.), *Syntax and semantics, vol. 7: Notes from the linguistic underground* (pp. 275–336). New York: Academic Press.

Lakoff, G., & Johnson, M. (1980). *Metaphors we live by.* Chicago: University of Chicago Press.

Lakoff, R. (1968). *Abstract syntax and Latin complementation.* Cambridge, MA: MIT Press.

Lakoff, R.(1969a). A syntactic argument for negative transportation. In R. J. Binnick, A. L. Davison, G. M. Green, J. L. Morgan (Eds.), *Papers from the Fifth Regional Meeting of the Chicago Linguistic Society* (pp. 140–147). Chicago: Department of Linguistics, University of Chicago.

Lakoff, R. (1969b). Some reasons why there can't be any *some-any* rule. *Language, 45,* 608–615.

Lakoff, R. (1971). Passive resistance. In *Papers from the Seventh Regional Meeting of the Chicago Linguistic Society* (pp. 141–162). Chicago: Chicago Linguistic Society.

Lakoff, R. (1972). Language in context. *Language, 48,* 907–927.

Lakoff, R. (1973a). Questionable answers and answerable questions. In B. B. Kachru, R. B. Lees, Y. Malkiel, A. Pietrangeli, S. Saporta (Eds.), *Issues in linguistics: Papers in honor of Henry and Renee Kahane* (pp. 453–567). Urbana: University of Illinois Press.

Lakoff, R. (1973b). The logic of politeness: Or Minding your P's and Q's. In C. Corum, T. C. Smith-Stark, & A. Weiser (Eds.), *Papers from the Ninth Regional Meeting of the Chicago Linguistic Society* (pp. 292–305). Chicago: Chicago Linguistic Society.

Lakoff, R. (1973c). Language and women's place. *Language in Society, 2,* 45–80.

Lakoff, R. (1974). Remarks on *this* and *that*. In M. Lagaly, R. Fox, & A. Bruck (Eds.), *Papers from the 10th Regional Meeting of the Chicago Linguistic Society* (pp. 345–356). Chicago: Chicago Linguistic Society.

Langacker, R. (1966). Pronominalization and the chain of command. In D. Reibel & S. Schane (Eds.), *Modern studies in English* (pp. 160–186). Englewood Cliffs, NJ: Prentice-Hall.

Larkin, D., & O'Malley, M. H. (1973). Declarative sentences and the rule-of-conversation hypothesis. In C. Corum, T. C. Smith-Stark, & A. Weiser (Eds.), *Papers from the Ninth Regional Meeting of the Chicago Linguistic Society* (pp. 306–319). Chicago: Chicago Linguistic Society.

Lemmon, E. (1965). Deontic logic and the logic of imperatives. *Logique et analyse, 29.*

Levi, J. N. (1978). *The syntax and semantics of complex nominals.* New York: Academic Press.

Levinson, S. (1979). Pragmatics and social deixis. In *Proceedings of the Fifth Annual Meeting of the Berkeley Linguistic Society* (pp. 206–223). Berkeley, CA: Berkeley Linguistic Society.

Levinson, S. (1983). Pragmatics. Cambridge University Press.

Lewis, D. (1968). Counterpart theory and quantified modal logic. *Journal of Philosophy, 65,* 113–126.

Linsky, L. (1966). Reference and referents. In C. Caton (Ed.), *Philosophy and ordinary language* (pp. 74–89). Urbana: University of Illinois Press.

Longuet-Higgins, C. (1976). . . . And out walked the cat. Pragmatics microfiche 1.7: G10-G14.

Mathesius, V. (1928). On linguistic characterology with illustrations from modern English (Reprinted 1967 in A Prague school reader in linguistics, compiled by Josef Vachek, pp. 59–67). Bloomington, IN: Indiana University Press.

Matthews, G. H. (1965). *Hidatsa syntax.* The Hague: Mouton.

McCawley, J. D. (1968). The role of semantics in grammar. In E. Bach & R. Harms (Eds.), *Universals in linguistic theory* (pp. 124–169). New York: Holt, Rinehart & Winston.

McCawley, J. D. (1971a). Tense and time reference in English. In C. Fillmore & D. T. Langendoen (Eds.), *Studies in linguistic semantics* (pp. 97–113). New York: Holt, Rinehart, & Winston.

McCawley, J. D. (1971b). Where do noun phrases come from? In D. A. Steinberg & L. Jakobovits (Eds.), *Semantics, an interdisciplinary reader* (pp. 217–231). Cambridge, England: Cambridge University Press.

McCawley, J. D. (1975a). Review of N. Chomsky: Studies on semantics in generative grammar. *Studies in English Linguistics, 3,* 209–311.

McCawley, J. D. (1975b). Verbs of bitching. In D. Hockney (Ed.), *Contemporary research in philosophical logic and linguistic semantics* (pp. 313–332). Dordrecht: Reidel.

McCawley, J. D. (1977). Remarks on the lexicography of performative verbs. In A. Rogers, R. Wall, & J. Murphy (Eds.), *Proceedings of the Texas Conference on Performatives, Implicature, and Presupposition* (pp. 13–25). Washington, DC: Center for Applied Linguistics.

McCawley, J. D. (1978a). Conversational implicature and the lexicon. In P. Cole (Ed.), *Syntax and semantics, vol. 9: Pragmatics* (pp. 245–259). New York: Academic Press.

McCawley, J. D. (1978b). Notes on Japanese clothing verbs. In J. Hinds & I. Howard (Eds.), *Problems in Japanese syntax and semantics* (pp. 68–78). Tokyo: Kaitakusha.

McCawley, J. D. (1978c). World-creating predicates. VS 19/20. Bompiani.

McCawley, J. D. (1979). Presupposition and discourse structure. In C. K. Oh & D. Dineen (Eds.), *Syntax and semantics, vol. 11: Presupposition* (pp. 225–234). New York: Academic Press.

McCawley, J. D. (1981). *Everything that linguists have always wanted to know about logic* *but were ashamed to ask.* Chicago: University of Chicago Press.

McKinley, R. (1981). *The door in the hedge.* New York: Greenwillow.

Merritt, M. (1976). On questions following questions (in service encounters). *Language in Society, 5,* 315–357.

Meyer, D. E. (1970). On the representation and retrieval of stored semantic information. *Cognitive Psychology, 1,* 242–300.

Mill, J. S. (1843). *A system of logic.* London: Longmans.

Miller, G. A. (1979). Images and models, similes and metaphors. In A. Ortony (Ed.), *Metaphor and thought* (pp. 202–250). Cambridge, England: Cambridge University Press.

Milsark, G. (1977). Toward an explanation of certain peculiarities of the existential construction. *Language Analysis, 3,* 1–30.

Montague, R. (1970). Universal grammar. *Theoria, 36,* 373–398.

Montague, R. (1973). The proper theory of quantification. In J. Hintikka, J. Moravcsik, & P. Suppes (Eds.), *Approaches to natural language.* Dordrecht: Reidel.

Montague, R. (1974). Formal philosophy: Selected papers of Richard Montague. New Haven: Yale University Press.

Morgan, J. L. (1969). On the treatment of presupposition in transformational grammar. In R. I. Binnick, A. L. Davison, G. M. Green, J. L. Morgan (Eds.), *Papers from the fifth regional meeting Chicago Linguistic Society* (pp. 167–178). Chicago: Chicago Linguistic Society.

Morgan, J. L. (1970). On the criterion of identity for noun phrase deletion. *Papers from the Sixth Regional Meeting of the Chicago Linguistic Society* (pp. 380–389). Chicago: Chicago Linguistic Society.

Morgan, J. L. (1972a). Verb agreement as a rule of English. In P. M. Peranteau, J. N. Levi, & G. C. Phares (Eds.), *Papers from the Eighth Regional Meeting of the Chicago Linguistic Society* (pp. 278–286). Chicago: Chicago Linguistic Society.

Morgan, J. L. (1972b). Some problems of verb agreement. In *Studies in the linguistic sciences, 2*(1), 84–90. Urbana: Department of Linguistics, University of Illinois.

Morgan, J. L. (1973a). How can you be in two places at once when you're not anywhere at all? In C. Corum, J. C. Smith-Stark, & A. Weiser (Eds.), *Papers from the Ninth Regional Meeting of the Chicago Linguistic Society* (p. 410–417). Chicago: Chicago Linguistic Society.

Morgan, J. L. (1973b). *Presupposition and the representation of meaning: Prolegomena.* Unpublished doctoral dissertation, University of Chicago, Chicago, IL.

Morgan, J. L. (1973c). Sentence fragments and the notion 'sentence'. In B. B. Kachru, R. B. Lees, Y. Malkiel, A. Pietrangeli, & S. Saporta (Eds.), *Issues in linguistics: Papers in honor of Henry and Renee Kahane* (pp. 719–751). Urbana: University of Illinois Press.

Morgan, J. L. (1975a). On the nature of sentences. In R. Grossman, L. J. San, & T. J. Vance (Eds.), *Papers from the parasession on functionalism* (pp. 433–449). Chicago: Chicago Linguistic Society.

Morgan, J. L. (1975b). Some interactions of syntax and pragmatics. In P. Cole & J. Morgan (Eds.), *Syntax and semantics, vol. 3: Speech acts* (pp. 289–304). New York: Academic Press.

Morgan, J. L. (1976). *Pragmatics, common sense, and the performative analysis.* Paper presented at the 12th regional meeting of the Chicago Linguistic Society, Chicago. April 1976.

Morgan, J. L. (1977). Conversational postulates revisited. *Language, 53,* 277–284.

Morgan, J. L. (1978). Two types of convention in indirect speech acts. In P. Cole (Ed.), *Syntax and semantics, vol. 9: Pragmatics* (pp. 261–280). New York: Academic Press.

Morgan, J. L. (1979). Observations on the pragmatics of metaphor. In A. Ortony (Ed.), *Metaphor and thought* (pp. 136–147). Cambridge, England: Cambridge University Press.

Morgan, J. L. (1981). Discourse theory and the independence of sentence grammar. In D.

Tannen (Ed.), *Georgetown University Roundtable on Languages and Linguistics 1981: Analyzing discourse: Text and talk* (pp. 176-204). Washington: DC: Georgetown University Press.

Morgan, J. L., & Sellner, M. (1980). Discourse and linguistic theory. In R. Spiro, B. C. Bruce, & W. Breuer (Eds.), *Theoretical issues in reading comprehension* (pp. 165-200). Hillsdale, NJ: Lawrence Erlbaum Associates.

Myers, F. (1984). *The language of political elites*. Paper presented at the LSA/AAAL winter meeting, Linguistic Society of America/American Association of Applied Linguistics. December, 1984.

Napoli, D. J., & Rando, E. (1978). Definites in *there*-sentences. *Language, 54,* 300-313.

Norton, M. (1952). *The borrowers*. New York: Harcourt, Brace & World.

Nunberg, G. (1978). *The pragmatics of reference*. Bloomington, IN: Indiana University Linguistics Club.

Nunberg, G., & Pan, C. (1975). Inferring quantification in generic sentences. In R. Grossman, L. J. San, & T. J. Vance (Eds.), *Papers from the 11th Regional Meeting of the Chicago Linguistic Society* (pp. 412-422). Chicago: Chicago Linguistic Society.

Ochs, E. (1984). Clarification and culture. In D. Schiffrin (Ed.), *Georgetown University Round Table on Languages and Linguistics 1984: Meaning, form, and use in context* (pp. 325-341). Washington, DC: Georgetown University Press.

Olsen, M. (1986). *Some problematic issues in the study of intonation and sentence stress*. Unpublished doctoral dissertation, University of Illinois, Urbana.

O'Neill, P. G. (1966). *A programmed guide to respect language in modern Japanese*. London.

Over, D. E. (1985). Constructivity and the referential/attributive distinction. *Linguistics and Philosophy, 8,* 415-430.

Partee, B. (1973). Some structural analogues between tenses and pronouns in English. *Journal of Philosophy, 70,* 601-609.

Peterson, T. (1969). A case for the declarative performative verb; dependent and independent conjunction in Moore and English. In R. I. Binnick, A. L. Davison, G. M. Green, J. L. Morgan (Eds.), *Papers from the Fifth Regional Meeting of the Chicago Linguistic Society* (pp. 421-428). Chicago: Department of Linguistics, University of Chicago.

Philbrick, F. (1949). *Language and the law*. New York: MacMillan.

Pollack, M. E. (1986). *Inferring domain plans in question answering*. Unpublished doctoral thesis, University of Pennsylvania, Philadelphia.

Postal, P. M. (1970). On coreferential complement subject deletion. *Linguistic Inquiry, 1,* 439-500.

Postal, P. M. (1974). *On raising*. Cambridge, MA: MIT Press.

Prince, E. (1978). A comparison of WH-clefts and pseudo-clefts in discourse. *Language, 54,* 883-906.

Prince, E. (1981a). On the inferencing of indefinite *this* NPs. In A. K. Joshi, B. L. Webber, & I. A. Sag (Eds.), *Elements of discourse understanding* (pp. 231-250). Cambridge: Cambridge University Press.

Prince, E. (1981b). Toward a taxonomy of given-new information. In P. Cole (Ed.), *Radical pragmatics* (pp. 223-256). New York: Academic Press.

Prince, E. (1981c). Topicalization,-focus movement, and Yiddish-movement; a pragmatic differentiation. In D. K. Alford, K. A. Hunold, M. A. Macaulay, J. Walter, and C. Brugman, P. Chertok, I. Civkulis, and M. Tobey (Eds.), *Proceedings of the seventh annual meeting. Berkeley Linguistics Society* (pp. 249-264). Berkeley: Berkeley Linguistics Society.

Prince, E. (1982). *Grice and universality: A reappraisal*. Unpublished manuscript.

Prince, E. (1984). Topicalization and left-dislocation: a functional anaysis. In S. J. White & V. Teller (Eds.), Discourses in reading and linguistics. *Annals of the New York Academy of Sciences, 433,* 213-225. New York: New York Academy of Sciences.

Prince, G. (1973). *A grammar of stories*. The Hague: Mouton.

Putnam, H. (1962). The analytic and the synthetic. In *Mind, language and reality: Philosoph-*

ical papers (Vol. 2, pp. 33–69). Cambridge, England: Cambridge University Press.

Putnam, H. (1965). How not to talk about meaning. Reprinted in *Mind, language and reality: Philosophical papers,* vol. 2, 117–131. Cambridge University Press.

Putnam, H. (1970). Is semantics possible? Reprinted in *Mind, language and reality: Philosophical papers,* vol. 2, 139–152. Cambridge University Press.

Putnam, H. (1973). Explanation and reference. Reprinted in *Mind, language and reality: Philosophical papers,* vol. 2, 196–214. Cambridge University Press.

Putnam, H. (1975a). The meaning of 'meaning'. Reprinted in *Mind, language and reality: Philosophical papers,* vol. 2, 215–271. Cambridge University Press.

Putnam, H. (1975b). Language and reality. Reprinted in *Mind, language and reality: Philosophical papers,* vol. 2, 272–290. Cambridge University Press.

Quine, W. V. O. (1953). *Reference and modality. From a logical point of view.* New York: Harper & Row.

Quine, W. V. O. (1956). Quantifiers and propositional attitudes. *Journal of Philosophy, 53,* 177–187.

Quine, W. V. O. (1960). *Word and object.* Cambridge, MA: MIT Press.

Reddy, M. J. (1969). A semantic approach to metaphor. In R. I. Binnick, A. L. Davison, G. M. Green, J. L. Morgan (Eds.), *Papers from the fifth regional meeting of the Chicago Linguistic Society* (pp. 240–241). Chicago: Department of Linguistics, University of Chicago.

Reddy, M. J. (1979). The conduit metaphor—a case of frame conflict in our language about language. In A. Ortony (Ed.), *Metaphor and thought* (pp. 284–324). Cambridge, England: Cambridge University Press.

Reinhart, T. (1983). *Anaphora and semantic interpretation.* Chicago: University of Chicago Press.

Rescher, N. (1966). *The logic of commands.* New York: Dover.

Rescher, N. (Ed.). (1967). *The logic of decision and action.* Pittsburgh, PA: Pittsburgh University Press.

Riddle, E. (1975). Some pragmatic conditions on complementizer choice. In R. Grossman, L. J. San, & T. J. Vance (Eds.), *Papers from the 11th regional meeting of the Chicago Linguistic Society* (pp. 467–474). Chicago: Chicago Linguistic Society.

Riddle, E. (1978). *Sequence of tenses in English.* Unpublished doctoral dissertation, University of Illinois, Urbana.

Rosch, E., & Mervis, C. (1975). Family resemblances: Studies in the internal structure of categories. *Cognitive Psychology, 7,* 573–605.

Ross, J. R. (1967). Constraints on variables in syntax. MIT dissertation. (Published 1983 as Infinite syntax, Norwood, NJ: Ablex).

Ross, J. R. (1969). The cyclic nature of English pronominalization. In D. Reibel & S. Schane (Eds.), *Modern studies in English* (pp. 187–200). Englewood Cliffs, NJ: Prentice-Hall.

Ross, J. R. (1970). On declarative sentences. In R. Jacobs & P. S. Rosenbaum (Eds.), *Readings in English transformational grammar* (pp. 222–272). Waltham, MA: Ginn.

Ross, J. R. (1975). Where to do things with words. In P. Cole & J. Morgan (Eds.), *Syntax and semantics, vol. 3: Speech acts* (pp. 233–256). New York: Academic Press.

Rumelhart, D. (1975). Notes on a schema for stories. In D. Bobrow & A. Collins (Eds.), *Representation and understanding* (pp. 211–236). New York: Academic Press.

Rumelhart, D. (1979). Some problems with the notion of literal meanings. In A. Ortony (Ed.), *Metaphor and thought* (pp. 78–90). Cambridge, England: Cambridge University Press.

Russell, B. (1905). On denoting. *Mind, 14,* 479–493.

Sacks, H., Schegloff, E. A., & Jefferson, G. (1974). A simplest systematics for the organization of turn-taking in conversation. *Language, 50,* 676–735.

Sadock, J. M. (1970). Whimperatives. In J. Sadock & A. Vanek (Eds.), *Studies presented to Robert B. Lees by his students* (pp. 223–238). Edmonton, Alberta: Linguistic Research, Inc.

Sadock, J. M. (1972). Speech act idioms. In P. M. Peranteau, J. N. Levi, & G. C. Phares (Eds.), *Papers from the Eighth Regional Meeting of the Chicago Linguistic Society* (pp. 329–339). Chicago: Chicago Linguistic Society.

Sadock, J. M. (1974). *Toward a linguistic theory of speech acts.* New York: Academic Press.

Sadock, J. M. (1978). On testing for conversational implicature. In P. Cole (Ed.), *Syntax and semantics, vol. 9: Pragmatics* (pp. 281–298). New York: Academic Press.

Sadock, J. M. (1979). Figurative speech and linguistics. In A. Ortony (Ed.), *Metaphor and thought* (pp. 46–63). Cambridge, England: Cambridge University Press.

Sadock, J. M. (1983). The necessary overlapping of grammatical components. In J. F. Richardson, M. Marks, & A. Chukerman (Eds.), *Papers from the parasession on the interplay of phonology, morphology, and syntax* (pp. 198–221). Chicago: Chicago Linguistic Society.

Sansom, G. B. (1928). *An historical grammar of Japanese.* Oxford, England: Oxford University Press.

Schegloff, E. A. (1979). Identification and recognition in telephone conversation openings. In G. Psathas (Ed.), *Everyday language: Studies in ethnomethodology* (pp. 23–78). New York: Irvington.

Schmerling, S. F. (1971). A note on negative polarity. *Papers in linguistics, 4*(1), 200–206.

Schmerling, S. F. (1973). Subjectless sentences and the notion of surface structure. In C. Corum, T. C. Smith-Stark, & A. Weiser (Eds.), *Papers from the 9th regional meeting, Chicago Linguistic Society* (pp. 577–586). Chicago: Chicago Linguistic Society.

Schmerling, S. F. (1976). *Aspects of English sentence stress.* Austin: University of Texas Press.

Schmerling, S. F. (1978). Synonymy judgements as syntactic evidence. In P. Cole (Ed.), *Syntax and semantics, vol. 9: Pragmatics* (pp. 299–314). New York: Academic Press.

Schourup, L. (1982). *Common discourse particles in English conversation.* Doctoral dissertation, Ohio State University, Columbus, OH. Published 1985 by Garland Publishing, Inc. New York.

Scott, D. (1970). Advice on modal logic. In K. Lambert (Ed.), *Philosophical problems in logic* (pp. 143–174). Dordrecht: D. Reidel.

Searle, J. (1969). *Speech acts.* Cambridge, England: Cambridge University Press.

Searle, J. (1975a). A taxonomy of speech acts. In K. Gunderson (Ed.), *Language, mind, and knowledge* (pp. 344–369). Minnesota Studies in the philosophy of science, 7. Minneapolis: University of Minnesota Press.

Searle, J. (1975b). Indirect speech acts. In P. Cole & J. Morgan (Eds.), *Syntax and semantics, vol. 3: Speech acts* (pp. 59–82). New York: Academic Press.

Searle, J. (1976a). A classification of illocutionary acts. *Language in Society, 5,* 1–23.

Searle, J. (1976b). Review of Toward a linguistic theory of speech acts, by Jerrold Sadock. *Language, 52,* 966–971.

Searle, J., Kiefer, F., & Bierwisch, M. (1980). *Speech act theory and pragmatics.* Dordrecht: Reidel.

Sheintuch, G., & Wise, K. (1976). On the pragmatic unity of the rules of Neg-raising and Neg-attraction. In S. Mufwene, C. Walker, & S. Steever (Eds.), *Papers from the 12th Regional Meeting of the Chicago Linguistic Society* (pp. 548–557). Chicago: Chicago Linguistic Society.

Smith, E., & Medin, D. (1981). *Categories and concepts.* Cambridge, MA: Harvard University Press.

Smith, E., Shoben, E. J., & Rips, L. (1974). Structure and process in semantic memory: A featural model for semantic decisions. *Psychological Review, 81,* 214–241.

Sperber, D., & Wilson, D. (1981). Irony and the use-mention distinction. In P. Cole (Ed.), *Radical pragmatics* (pp. 295–318). New York: Academic Press.

Sperber, D., & Wilson, D. (1982). Mutual knowledge and relevance in the theory of comprehension. In N. V. Smith (Ed.), *Mutual knowledge* (pp. 61–131). London: Academic Press.

Sperber, D., & Wilson, D. (1986). *Relevance: Foundations of pragmatic theory.* Cambridge, MA: Harvard University Press.

Stalnaker, R. (1974). Pragmatic presuppositions. In M. K. Munitz & P. K. Unger (Eds.), *Semantics and philosophy* (pp. 197–214). New York: New York University Press.

Stalnaker, R. (1978). Assertion. In P. Cole (Ed.), *Syntax and semantics, vol. 9: Pragmatics* (pp. 315–332). New York: Academic Press.

Stampe, D. (1975). Meaning and truth in the theory of speech acts. In P. Cole & J. L. Morgan (Eds.), *Syntax and semantics, vol. 3: Speech acts* (pp. 1–40). New York: Academic Press.

Steever, S. (1977). Raising, meaning, and conversational implicature. In S. Mufwene, C. Walker, & S. Steever (Eds.), *Papers from the 12th Regional Meeting of the Chicago Linguistic Society* (pp. 590–602). Chicago: Chicago Linguistic Society.

Strawson, P. F. (1950). On referring. *Mind, 59,* 320–344.

Strunk, W. Jr., & White, E. B. (1979). *The elements of style* (3rd ed.). New York: Macmillan.

Tannen, D. (1984). *Conversational style: Analyzing talk among friends.* Norwood, N.J.: Ablex.

Tuchman, B. (1978). *A distant mirror.* New York: Alfred A. Knopf.

Tulving, E. (1972). Episodic and semantic memory. In E. Tulving & W. Donaldson (Eds.), *Organization of memory.* New York: Academic Press.

Uyeno, T. Y. (1971). *A study of Japanese modality: A performative analysis of sentence particles.* Unpublished doctoral dissertation, University of Michigan.

van Dijk, T. (1972). *Some aspects of text grammars.* The Hague: Mouton.

van Dijk, T. (1977). *Text and context: Explorations in the semantics and pragmatics of discourse.* London: Longmans.

Van Oosten, J. (1986). *The nature of subjects, topics, and agents.* Bloomington, IN: Indiana University Linguistic Club.

Verschueren, J. (1976). *Speech act theory: A provisional bibliography with a terminological guide.* Bloomington, IN: Indiana University Linguistics Club.

Voigt, C. (1983). *Dicey's song.* New York: Atheneum.

Von Wright, G. (1963). *Norm and action: A logical inquiry.* London: Routledge & Kegan Paul.

Ward, G. (1985). *The semantics and pragmatics of preposing.* Unpublished doctoral dissertation, University of Pennsylvania.

Ward, G., & Hirschberg, J. (1985). Implicating uncertainty: The pragmatics of fall-rise intonation. *Language, 61,* 747–776.

Weiser, A. (1974). Deliberate ambiguity. In M. LaGaly, R. Fox, & A. Bruck (Eds.), *Papers from the 10th Regional Meeting, Chicago Linguistic Society* (pp. 732–741). Chicago: Chicago Linguistic Society.

Whorf, B. L. (1950). An American Indian model of the universe. *International Journal of American Linguistics, 16,* Reprinted in Language, thought, and reality: Selected writings of Benjamin Lee Whorf, ed. by J. B. Carroll, 57–64. New York: Wiley.

Wierzbicka, A. (1986). The semantics of 'internal dative' in English. *Quaderni di semantica, 7,* 121–135.

Wilson, D. (1975). *Presupposition and non-truth-conditional semantics.* New York: Academic Press.

Wilson, D., & Sperber, D. (1979). Ordered entailments: an alternative to presuppositional theories. In C. K. Oh & D. Dineen (Eds.), *Syntax and semantics, vol. 11: Presupposition* (pp. 299–323). New York: Academic Press.

Yanofsky, N. (1978). NP utterances. In D. Farkas, W. Jacobsen, & K. Todrys (Eds.), *Papers from the 14th regional meeting Chicago Linguistic Society* (pp. 491–502). Chicago: Chicago Linguistic Society.

Yanofsky, N. (1980). *The semantics of NP utterances.* Unpublished doctoral dissertation, Georgetown University, Washington, DC.

Zaenen, A. (1982). *Subjects and other subjects.* Bloomington, IN: Indiana University Linguistics Club.

Ziv, Y. (1976). *On the communicative effect of relative clause extraposition in English.* Unpublished doctoral dissertation, University of Illinois, Urbana.

Zwicky, A., & Sadock, J. M. (1975). Ambiguity tests and how to fail them. In J. Kimball (Ed.), *Syntax and semantics, vol. 4,* (pp. 1–36). New York: Academic Press.

Author Index

Subject Index

G

Goals 4f, 14, 110, 141ff, 157

H

Hearer 1n
Hedges 134f, 143, 145
Hints 108, 122
Historical chain 39
Homonymy 48ff
Honorifics; *See* Deference

I

I 19f
Idioms 60, 119
Illocutionary act 65; *see also* Speech acts
Illocutionary force 2, 8, 64–71, 106–112,
    133
  declarative 66, 68
  imperative 107f, 111f
  interrogative 75, 78, 154–157
Implicative verbs 72
Implicature 64, 80, 91–125, 135, 136, 139f,
    143, 144, 145
  cancellability 94
  conversational 91–125
    generalized 94f
  conventional 94; *see also* Presupposition
  short-circuited 108f
  universality 95–97
Indeterminacy, *see Vagueness*
Indexical 2, 17ff, 38f; *see also* Pronoun
  adverbs 22f
  connectives 30ff, 94n
  personal pronouns 19ff, 28, 52
  predicates 29f, 34
  tenses 20f, 22n
Inference 5, 9, 11, 14ff, 43f, 104
Information, relative order of old and new
    128–132
Interjections 136f
Interpretation 4, 10ff, 14ff, 17, 24, 29,
    115–118, 119–120

K

Kinds 43f, 45
  natural 43f
  non-natural 44

M

Maxims, convertsational 88–101
  exploitation 93
  manner 89, 90, 93, 99f
  quality 89, 90, 91, 93, 96, 98, 115–118
  quantity 88f, 91, 93, 96, 98f, 113,
    116–118
  relation 89, 90, 91, 92, 93, 97f, 115–118
Meaning 6, 11
  truth-conditional 6ff, 20
  natural 7
  non-natural 7
Metalinguistic discourse 83, 113
Metaphor 115, 120–124
  conduit 10f
  toolmakers' 11

N

Negation
  metalinguistic 113

P

Parsing 118, 127, 137–138
Performative expression 66–71, 109, 110,
    133
Performative hypothesis 67–71, 106–112
Plans 4–5, 13ff, 103f, 110, 112
Politeness 141–150, 154, 156
Polysemy 48–62
Possible worlds 40ff
Presupposition 64, 71–86, 112–114, 128
  counterfactual 73
  existential 45f, 71, 81, 113
  factive 71, 113
    epistemic 71
    emotive 71
    inchoative 72, 79
  negation/question "test" 75, 78
  pragmatic 75–82
  projection 76, 79–82
  semantic 75–82
  suspension 76, 83f
Pronouns 9, 83f; *see also* Reference
Pronominalization, backward 27
Pro-predicate 29, 34
Pro-propposition 34
Psenses 51f, 59